Practical Classroom English

Glyn Hughes
Josephine Moate

with Tiina Raatikainen

OXFORD
UNIVERSITY PRESS

OXFORD
UNIVERSITY PRESS

Great Clarendon Street, Oxford OX2 6DP

Oxford University Press is a department of the University of Oxford.
It furthers the University's objective of excellence in research, scholarship,
and education by publishing worldwide in

Oxford New York

Auckland Cape Town Dar es Salaam Hong Kong Karachi
Kuala Lumpur Madrid Melbourne Mexico City Nairobi
New Delhi Shanghai Taipei Toronto

With offices in

Argentina Austria Brazil Chile Czech Republic France Greece
Guatemala Hungary Italy Japan Poland Portugal Singapore
South Korea Switzerland Thailand Turkey Ukraine Vietnam

OXFORD and OXFORD ENGLISH are registered trade marks of
Oxford University Press in the UK and in certain other countries

ISBN: 978 0 19 442211 6   Book
ISBN: 978 0 19 442278 9   CD
ISBN: 978 0 19 442279 6   Pack

Printed in China

Acknowledgements

Practical Classroom English (PCE) has a long history. It began life in 1975 as a four-page handout called *Some Useful Classroom English Phrases*. Trainee English teachers in Finland were given a copy as part of their teaching practice. By 1978 it had expanded into a textbook called *Teacher-Talk*, which was then republished by OUP in 1981 as *A Handbook of Classroom English*. After twenty years the original book was beginning to show its age and needed serious updating. In 2004 a new Finnish version, called *ETC: English Teaching Companion*, was published by Tammi. PCE is a radically revised version of ETC.

Over the years, many people have contributed to PCE in one way or another. We would like to express our sincere thanks to all of them. Our special thanks go first and foremost to the generations of student teachers at the Department of Teacher Education of Jyväskylä University, Finland, for their ideas, insights and enthusiasm. Similarly, we are indebted to the many other teachers and students elsewhere who have taken part in classroom English training courses and given us invaluable feedback.

We are extremely grateful to the teachers and students in the following classes and schools for allowing us to record their lessons and to use extracts from them.

María Lourdes Arnaiz and year 3 of IES Casas Nuevas, Telde, Gran Canaria, Spain.

Susanne Dielmann and class 10e3 of Johann-Gottfried-Herder-Oberschule, Berlin-Lichtenberg, Germany.

Mari Kalaja and classes 6B and 6C of Jyväskylä University Teacher Training School, Finland.

Keiko Mondo and students of the Nippon Institute of Technology, Japan.

Paul Pienaar and students of Tainan Municipal Jhongsiao Junior High School, Taiwan.

Eunice Ryu and students of Goyang Women's Community College in Ilsan, Seoul, South Korea.

Jesús Lesmes Suárez and year 4 of IES José Arencibia Gil, Telde, Gran Canaria, Spain.

Frieda Van der Mast and classes 5WKD, 5LMT and 6LMT of H. Pius X- Instituut, Antwerp, Belgium.

Gabriele Weigelhofer and Thomas Bauer, with class 3B of KMS Stromstrasse, Vienna, Austria.

Brian Young and Feng Ho Senior High School, Taiwan.

We would like to thank the following for help in obtaining recordings:

Maria Bosch, University of Las Palmas, Gran Canaria, Spain.
Brett Bowie, OUP Field Editor, Korea.
Harumi Ito, Naruto University, Japan.
Kaoru Ito, OUP Field Editor, Japan.
Kerry Nockolds, OUP Field Editor, Taiwan.

Wolfgang Zydatiss, Freie Universität, Berlin, Germany.
Renate Neuburg and Ilse Schindler, Pedagogical Academy of Vienna, Austria.
Dirk Van Hemeldonck, H. Pius X- Instituut, Antwerp, Belgium.

Our thanks go to the following for their invaluable help at various stages of the project:
Teija Lehmusvuori of Tammi Publishers

Loes Coleman and Hilary van der Starre-Phillips, University of Nijmegen, The Netherlands
Bernd Voss, Dresden Technical University, Germany
Colleagues at the Teacher Education Department, University of Jyväskylä, Finland, especially Marja-Kaisa Pihko.

We are deeply indebted to our editors and design team at OUP, not only for their professionalism, but above all for their encouragement and support. Thank you Julia, Merinda, Lucy, Donna, Mark, and Peter.

Last but not least, we would like to thank our respective families for their understanding and patience.

The authors and publisher are grateful to the following for permission to reprint copyright material:

Alex Bartel/Science Photo Library, p 49;
Daily Herald/Mirrorpix, for permission to reproduce a cartoon from the Daily Herald, 13 February 1945, p 158;
Richmond Publishing for permission to reproduce a page from Can Do (4° ESO). Address: 4 King Street Cloisters, Albion Place, London W6 0QT. Tel. +44 (0)208 748 7755, Fax: +44 (0) 208 741 8403, email: edit@richpub.co.uk;
Speakeasy Publications for permission to reproduce a page from the September 2005 edition of Speakeasy magazine, © Speakeasy Publications 2005.

Although we have tried to trace and contact copyright holders before publication, in some cases this has not been possible. If contacted we will be pleased to rectify any errors or omissions at the earliest opportunity.

Illustrations by: Kathy Baxendale pp 46, 126, 129.
Sophie Grillet pp 4, 6, 10, 29, 31, 33, 34, 37, 39, 53, 54, 59, 60, 63, 65, 80, 82, 85, 86, 87, 88, 91, 92, 108, 111, 113, 114, 119, 140, 144, 146, 147.
All illustrations are copyright of the artists

Contents

Introduction

Practical Classroom English (PCE): A coursebook and a handbook

— *What is it?*
PCE is basically a comprehensive list of classroom phrases that you will need when running a lesson in English. It also has extensive exercises and activities to help you practise and use the phrases.

— *Who is it for?*
PCE is intended for non-native teachers of English who work with teenagers and young adults in formal education; in other words, at secondary and post-secondary levels.

— *Who else can use it?*
Teachers at the late primary level. PCE is also suitable for content and language integrated learning (CLIL) teachers, i.e. teachers who are teaching other subjects through the medium of English.

— *How can I use it?*
Although PCE is primarily meant as a coursebook for use in pre-service and in-service teacher training, it also works well as a handbook or work of reference. You can, for example, refer to it when preparing lessons, or dip into it and take an in-depth look at a particular topic.

— *Can I use it on my own?*
The dual format of the book (coursebook and handbook) means that it can be used both by tutors running a course, and by individual students working alone or in a study group.

— *Is the material difficult?*
We hope that the contents of the book will appeal not only to teachers who are already confident and fluent classroom managers, but also to less experienced teachers, who may feel apprehensive about running their classes in English.

Encouragement and inspiration

Hopefully, you have identified yourself somewhere amongst the different possible user groups mentioned above. If so, you will need to know how we think you will benefit from using PCE. In other words, what the aims of PCE are. We think there are five key aims:

1 To encourage you to use more English in the day-to-day running of your English classes;
2 To extend the range of classroom situations and learning activities that you feel confident and competent to handle in English;
3 To make you think more deeply about the role of your English in the classroom;
4 To inspire you with ideas for making the classroom a more dynamic and authentic environment for your students to practise their English;
5 To develop your language skills in two important areas of teaching: instruction giving and question asking.

All in all, then, we believe that PCE will help you to develop some of the core linguistic skills that you will need to work effectively in the classroom. At the same time we hope that this development will carry over into more confident classroom management and enhanced pedagogical skills.

Real and realistic

PCE has been developed on the basis of more than thirty years' experience of running classroom English courses for student teachers. Another important source of material has been the observation reports on some 1,500 practice lessons given by trainee English teachers. In addition, during the winter of 2005–06 we collected and transcribed about thirty hours of classroom recordings from eight different countries: Austria, Belgium, Finland, Germany, Japan, Korea, Spain, and Taiwan. The recordings have given us an insight into the reality of English language teaching around the world: the regular, routine, ordinary English lessons that are given every day by hard-working and skilful teachers. PCE, then, is written with these daily realities of school life very much in mind. Although it encourages a communicative approach, it accepts that not everything that happens in the English classroom can be or needs to be 'authentic', 'activating' and 'creative'.

Comprehensive and flexible

PCE consists of six units. The units are not strictly graded and there is material at a variety of levels in each unit. In other words, you could choose to work through the book randomly. Nevertheless, the units do form a clear progression. Unit 1, for example, deals with the most basic and frequent situations in the classroom (greeting, sequencing activities, saying goodbye). In other words, if you are a teacher who wants to introduce English as the main language of classroom management, then the phrases in this unit form a natural starting point, both for yourself and for your students. Unit 2 looks at phrases that increase your students' involvement in classroom interaction, helping them to play a bigger part in what happens. Unit 3 deals with the actual classroom learning environment, its challenges and its opportunities. The focus in Unit 4 is very much on the textbook: dealing with a basic text and doing language exercises. Unit 5 examines the phrases connected with classroom technology, ranging from chalkboards to computers. The most demanding unit is Unit 6, which covers advanced written and spoken activities. It also attempts to take you—and your students—across the divide between basic interpersonal communicative skills and cognitive academic language proficiency. (In other words, an important divide that Jim Cummins calls the BICS (Basic Interpersonal Communicative Skills) and CALP (Cognitive Academic Language Proficiency) divide.) Critical thinking is also introduced as a way to encourage students to use their spoken and written skills for more academic purposes.

The structure of the book

Each of the six units of PCE is divided into three sections, A, B and C. After its **Introductory page**, each section deals with some five or six classroom situations, making a total of more than ninety situations. These classroom situations are, in turn, broken down into almost 400 key phrases. The key phrases are supplemented by phrase lists, followed by detailed footnotes and comments. Each of the six units ends with a section on **Classroom essentials** (practice with giving instructions and asking questions), some **Exercises and activities** (for individual and group practice), and **Audio practice** (pronunciation and listening), which is recorded on an accompanying CD. The book also has its own website (http://www.oup.com/elt/teacher/pce), which offers additional exercises and a multilingual reference list of key vocabulary related to school and teaching. In the following we shall look at each of these sections in detail.

The Introductory page

The Introductory page includes the following parts:

1 Introductory paragraph

Each section begins with a short introductory paragraph. This briefly outlines the contents of the section and orientates you to the material. In addition, and perhaps more importantly, it suggests ways in which you can help your students to accept and use English as the natural language of classroom management.

2 Overview

The overview lists the classroom situations and key phrases dealt with in the section. As such, it is useful for quickly finding a relevant phrase, and as a checklist to monitor your own progress.

3 Points to think and talk about

PCE is not a handbook of English language teaching methodology. Nevertheless, there are aspects of using English in the classroom that do have methodological implications. In this section we invite you to think and talk about these implications, to look at the routines of classroom teaching in a critical way, and to find your own viewpoint. Ideally, the questions should be discussed before you begin work on the key phrases, but you can also come back to them at any stage of your work on the section. Sharing your own personal experiences is an important part of the activity, so discussion in groups may be more productive. If you don't have enough time to discuss all of the points, concentrate on the ones that are most relevant to your teaching situation. Notice that we don't provide a list of answers because there are no simple answers to the questions we ask, at least no answers that apply to all contexts and situations.

4 Language to think about

This gets you thinking about the language in the section by checking what you already know. You may be asked to come up with a particular phrase, or to offer alternatives in a particular classroom situation, or even to correct typical classroom English mistakes. The answers to these questions can be found by studying the key phrases in the section that follows.

5 Classroom English vocabulary to collect

We think that English teachers should be able to talk about their own profession and work environment in English. In this section we invite you to start collecting vocabulary that is relevant to the activities covered in the section. Some of the vocabulary will be very concrete (for example, *extension lead*), some more abstract (for example, *Ministry of Education*). If you think this sounds useful, then we can suggest a number of ways of beginning your collection:

1 You can keep a notebook handy and jot down any useful words you come across, both in the unit material and elsewhere;
2 You can brainstorm the topic, either alone or in a group;
3 You could arrange to circulate your word lists via email;
4 You can refer to (and contribute to) PCE's own website (http://www.oup.com/elt/teacher/pce).

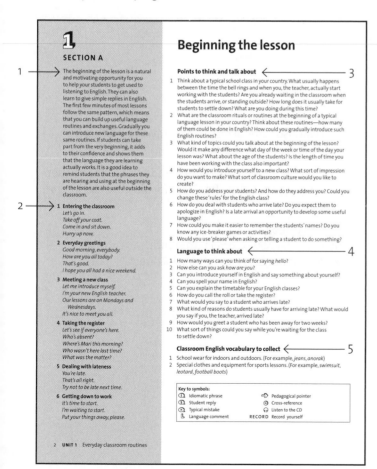

Key phrases and footnotes

The core of PCE is made up of the key phrases and accompanying footnotes. Later on we will suggest how you can make the most effective use of these sections.

1 Key phrases

Each classroom situation is identified by its section (A, B, C), a number (1, 2, 3, ...) and a heading (for example, *C6 Clearing the class*). The key phrases, which are numbered and listed under the classroom situation heading, should be seen as basic, straightforward expressions. Additional phrases are then presented under the key phrase. These may be simple alternatives, or they may be more complex in their structure or have a slightly different meaning. Notice that the alternative phrases are emboldened. For example, in the phrase *Let's **change/switch** (over) to English*, the use of bold shows that both words, *change* and *switch*, are interchangeable. The brackets show that the word *over* is optional, and can be used or left out. The numbering of the key phrases is important because the footnotes related to the phrase are identified by the same number.

Some of the phrases are straightforward and easy, whereas others are more complex. We have not even tried to classify the phrases according to their level of difficulty. Ultimately, it is your choice, and you will make this choice based on a number of factors: the students' age, the level of their language skills and your own, the formality of the classroom situation, your own familiarity with your students, and, of course, your own personal preferences. There is a whole range of teaching contexts where PCE will be useful, and we have tried to cover as many as possible. You will notice that occasionally there is some overlap between the different sections.

2 Footnotes

There are eight kinds of footnote in PCE, each identified by its own symbol:

- ℒ Language comment: additional phrases and comments on classroom language.
- ⓘ Idiomatic phrase: idioms for use mainly with advanced learners.
- ⇨ Pedagogical pointer: comments on classroom management and ideas for running your class in English.
- ⊗ Mistake: a typical classroom English error. The incorrect part of the phrase is crossed out. The correct version can be found in the list of phrases.
- ⓢ Student response: phrases that you can encourage your students to use.
- ⊘ Cross-reference: references to other units, exercise or sources.
- ⌒ Listen to the audio CD.

RECORD An opportunity to record and listen to yourself.

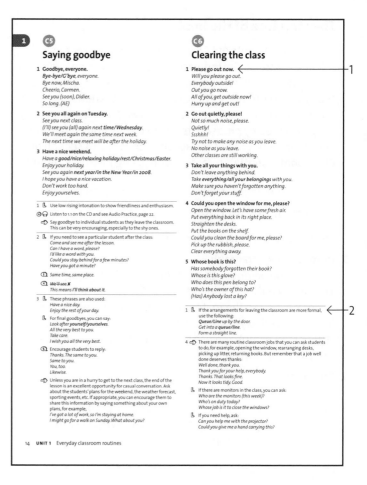

You will also come across the abbreviations BE (British English) and AE (American English).

The footnotes, then, not only give additional information on language, but also offer ideas for effective classroom management.

Other symbols:
- ✔ A tick denotes a correct utterance.
- ✗ A cross indicates something incorrect.

Additional practice

At the end of each unit there are three sections that offer additional practice with the material presented in the unit.

1 Classroom essentials

We think that this is an appropriate name since it deals with two areas of language use that are essential to your work as a teacher: giving instructions and asking questions. We look at the key structures and grammatical rules associated with each topic in three separate parts, spread over the entire book. The sample sentences have been chosen to reflect the contents of the rest of the unit. After the structural presentation there are exercises, both formal and more communicative. In some cases you are asked to make use of the accompanying CD and even to record yourself (see below).

2 Exercises and activities

The idea here is to activate and recycle the phrases presented in the unit. The more formal exercises (for example, prepositions and vocabulary) are accessible online through PCE's website. In the printed materials we try to offer a mixture of traditional and more creative activities, including games, role-plays, and actual teaching practice. The key symbol (🔑) next to an exercise tells you that there are answers at the back of the book. In this section, too, there are activities that require you to record yourself (marked **RECORD**). For this you will need a microphone and a cassette recorder, a minidisk player, or an MP3 recorder. Having recorded yourself, you should naturally also listen to yourself and even allow others to listen. Apart from developing your confidence and general classroom fluency, this exercise will help reinforce the unit phrases. You will also have a chance to think about your teaching style and the classroom language you use.

3 Audio practice

This section, which makes use of the accompanying CD, includes four types of activity. The first one, **Classroom intonation**, practises important patterns of English intonation relevant to the classroom, for example in asking questions and giving instructions. The second part is called **Key sounds** and focuses on some of the phonological difficulties of English (for example, the /θ/ and /ð/ sounds). As the name suggests, part three, **Word stress**, deals with some of the problems of English word stress. In the fourth part, **Live lessons**, you can listen to extracts of recordings made in actual classrooms. In some cases, where the recording quality was poor, the extracts have been re-recorded by actors. The extracts include classes with students aged 13–20, and a variety of levels. In all but one case, the teachers are non-native speakers of English. In some classes, the teacher is using a normal textbook; in others, a variety of materials. In one class the students are studying history through the medium of English.

Each extract is accompanied by a number of short listening tasks, encouraging you to listen to the extract several times. The aim of these is to improve your listening skills as well as to make you think about how effective teaching works.

Hopefully, the extracts will also stimulate some lively discussion. Notice that there is a full transcription of the classroom extracts at the end of the book. We suggest that you begin with the audio recording and only later look at the transcript. It is useful to compare the transcript with the actual live lesson extract, which is often full of hesitations, rephrasings, and interesting intonation.

The recordings are also a very useful starting point for discussion on aspects of classroom management. However, the most important role of the classroom extracts is to show you that teachers really do manage to run their classes in English—at all levels, with all types of students, in all sorts of classroom environments. Some teachers have a near-native command of the language, others stumble and hesitate, but they are all using English successfully in their classrooms.

Using the book for self-access

Ideally, students using PCE without a teacher should try to team up with fellow students to form small study groups of say two or three people. The motivational support of a partner or group is invaluable. If the members of such a study group can also observe each other teaching and give encouraging but realistic feedback to each other, the chances of completing the material and making real use of it in the classroom will increase.

There is no single, well-tried way of working through the material in PCE. If you want to be systematic, we suggest that you begin with the Introductory page of the section you have chosen. You can then move on to the classroom situations and key phrases. Experience has shown that the following method of working is quite successful.

— Read each phrase aloud in turn and make sure you understand it.
— Look up (or close your eyes) and imagine a classroom situation in which you would use that phrase.
— Imagine the student(s) you might address the phrase to.
— Say the phrase aloud again.
— After working through each group of phrases in this way, go back and pick out one or two phrases that you particularly like (for whatever reason) or which you think you would use.
— Underline or highlight them.
— It is important for you to use phrases that you feel comfortable with and that are appropriate for the class(es) you work with.

There are other effective ways to help you memorize the phrases. One such way is to use a small piece of card to cover up part of the phrases under each key phrase. You could, for example, leave the first three words of each phrase visible and then try to recall the rest of the phrase. After this, cover up all the phrases, leaving just the key phrase visible. How many can you remember? Another method involves working with a partner: one of you reads out the first few words of a phrase and the other one tries to complete it. Another form of practice that also works well in groups is for one student to give the L1 translation and the other to give the English equivalent.

We believe that the footnotes following each classroom situation are extremely useful and important. They are closely related to the key phrases and will give you a lot of practical ideas. We hope that you will be able to devote time to studying them. However, if you are working to a tight schedule, you should see the footnotes in the first instance as extra material that you can dip into, or simply leave for later.

Once you have familiarized yourself with the three sections and fifteen or so classroom situations in each unit, you can move on to the exercises and activities. As with all textbook exercises, these have the simple purpose of giving you additional opportunities to practise using the unit material. We hope that you find the activities in PCE interesting, varied and useful.

Notice that you can choose to study the materials in the **Classroom essentials** section at any time while you are working with a unit. Similarly, the **Audio practice** sections are not tied to a particular section or classroom situation. We realize that PCE covers a lot of ground, but if you do want to go further and look at a topic in more detail, then you should make use of the list of resources in **Useful reading and resources** and on the PCE website.

Using the book as part of a taught course

We estimate that a thorough treatment of the material in PCE would require 50–60 hours of work, including some 20 hours of classroom contact. On the other hand, we know that some teachers have covered the contents in less than 30 hours. The level of English of the course participants will clearly affect the time needed, as will the amount of material used, especially in the **Classroom essentials**, **Exercises and activities** and **Audio practice** sections. On an intensive revision course, for example, students could just work through the Exercises and activities section, looking at the lists of phrases in more detail whenever required. Similarly, the materials in the Classroom essentials sections together form a useful and meaningful whole. The pronunciation and listening activities in the Audio practice section would also work as a stand-alone course.

If time permits and you decide to study the phrases in detail, then the methods for practising and learning them need not differ from those outlined above. Naturally, pair and group work can play an even more central role in class sessions. An appropriate conclusion for each unit would be for students to micro-teach in the group, or to give an actual lesson in their own classroom. These could be recorded and followed by constructive feedback and discussion. Ideally, in addition to allowing students to practise their own English classroom management skills, tutors should give them opportunities to observe experienced teachers at work.

Tips on how to use PCE

If you are a teacher or a student teacher, we recommend that you make a conscious effort to include more classroom English phrases in your lessons. One concrete way of doing this is, for example, to write them into your lesson plans, or to jot them down at appropriate places in the textbook. You can then rehearse the phrases while preparing your lesson. This is one way to increase your confidence and expand your repertoire of classroom phrases.

You will also have to persuade your students to devote time and energy to following more and more of your instructions in English rather than in their L1. This is a matter of saying how you plan to work, explaining your reasons, being consistent, and perhaps offering incentives, such as reduced homework or a less formal activity. It is a good idea to keep a diary of your experiences and, of course, to check how your students are coping. Jot down your thoughts and questions, the things you feel you have mastered, and the areas that you still feel unsure of. Later on you will find the diary a useful resource. You can also use it to remind your students of how far *they* have progressed.

Later on, you can use PCE for reference purposes as part of your own professional self-development. You can, for example, use it to find alternative phrases, to check particular points (for example, to write *on* a handout), to help prepare a new kind of lesson (for example, using the Internet), or to get ideas for lesson activities.

PCE is based on a generalized picture of English language teaching practice. It cannot take into account all the trends and traditions of individual national school systems. When you work with the key phrases and footnotes, it is important to think about them in the light of your own school system and accepted methodological practices. You will have to select and modify the phrases to suit your local context and your own pedagogical style. We believe, however, that the phrases in PCE do provide a solid basis for any teacher who wants to use English to manage their classroom.

The goal may seem distant and the journey difficult, but as with all journeys it is the first step that launches you on your way.

*Onnea matkaan!

Glyn Hughes, Jyväskylä, Finland
Josephine Moate
Tiina Raatikainen

* Finnish: *Good luck on your journey.*

Everyday classroom routines 1

1

SECTION A

The beginning of the lesson is a natural and motivating opportunity for you to help your students to get used to listening to English. They can also learn to give simple replies in English. The first few minutes of most lessons follow the same pattern, which means that you can build up useful language routines and exchanges. Gradually you can introduce new language for these same routines. If students can take part from the very beginning, it adds to their confidence and shows them that the language they are learning actually works. It is a good idea to remind students that the phrases they are hearing and using at the beginning of the lesson are also useful outside the classroom.

1 Entering the classroom
Let's go in.
Take off your coat.
Come in and sit down.
Hurry up now.

2 Everyday greetings
Good morning, everybody.
How are you all today?
That's good.
I hope you all had a nice weekend.

3 Meeting a new class
Let me introduce myself.
I'm your new English teacher.
Our lessons are on Mondays and Wednesdays.
It's nice to meet you all.

4 Taking the register
Let's see if everyone's here.
Who's absent?
Where's Mari this morning?
Who wasn't here last time?
What was the matter?

5 Dealing with lateness
You're late.
That's all right.
Try not to be late next time.

6 Getting down to work
It's time to start.
I'm waiting to start.
Put your things away, please.

Beginning the lesson

Points to think and talk about

1   Think about a typical school class in your country. What usually happens between the time the bell rings and when you, the teacher, actually start working with the students? Are you already waiting in the classroom when the students arrive, or standing outside? How long does it usually take for students to settle down? What are you doing during this time?

2   What are the classroom rituals or routines at the beginning of a typical language lesson in your country? Think about these routines—how many of them could be done in English? How could you gradually introduce such English routines?

3   What kind of topics could you talk about at the beginning of the lesson? Would it make any difference what day of the week or time of the day your lesson was? What about the age of the students? Is the length of time you have been working with the class also important?

4   How would you introduce yourself to a new class? What sort of impression do you want to make? What sort of classroom culture would you like to create?

5   How do you address your students? And how do they address you? Could you change these 'rules' for the English class?

6   How do you deal with students who arrive late? Do you expect them to apologize in English? Is a late arrival an opportunity to develop some useful language?

7   How could you make it easier to remember the students' names? Do you know any ice-breaker games or activities?

8   Would you use 'please' when asking or telling a student to do something?

Language to think about

1   How many ways can you think of for saying *hello*?
2   How else can you ask *how are you*?
3   Can you introduce yourself in English and say something about yourself?
4   Can you spell your name in English?
5   Can you explain the timetable for your English classes?
6   How do you call the roll or take the register?
7   What would you say to a student who arrives late?
8   What kind of reasons do students usually have for arriving late? What would you say if you, the teacher, arrived late?
9   How would you greet a student who has been away for two weeks?
10 What sort of things could you say while you're waiting for the class to settle down?

Classroom English vocabulary to collect

1   School wear for indoors and outdoors. (For example, *jeans*, *anorak*)
2   Special clothes and equipment for sports lessons. (For example, *swimsuit*, *leotard*, *football boots*)

Key to symbols:

ℚ	Idiomatic phrase	⇨	Pedagogical pointer
ⓢ	Student reply	»	Cross-reference
ⓧ	Typical mistake	🎧	Listen to the CD
Ⅼ	Language comment	**RECORD**	Record yourself

A1
Entering the classroom

1 Let's go in.
Let's go inside.
Let's go into the classroom.
(You can) Go in.
Go on in.
Go in and sit down.
*I'll **open/unlock** the door and let you in.*

2 Take off your coat.
*You can leave your **outdoor/sports** clothes in the corridor.*
Put your sports shoes in your locker.
***Take/Leave** your bag outside, please.*
Hang it up.
Hang up your things.
Use the coat rack.

3 Come in and sit down.
Come in and take your seat.
*Come **on/along** in, Mr Ito.*
In you come (now), Marco.
(Come) this way, please.
Close the door (properly) behind you.
*Please don't **slam/bang** the door.*
You can leave the door open.

4 Hurry up now.
Hurry up so that I can start the lesson.
Try to hurry, please.

---

1 ⟫ See Unit 5, page 105 for more about using **let's** and other suggestions.

2 ⌊ Idiomatic word order:
Off with your coats!
Out with your books!
*Away with your **books/phones/MP3 players**!*

  ⓢ *I'm cold so can I keep my anorak on?*
  It's so hot. Can I take my jacket off?
  Can I leave my bag here?
  Will my briefcase be all right here?
  *Is it **OK/all right** if I keep my coat on?*

  ⌊ Prepositions:
  in the corridor, in the hallway, in the classroom
  ***on** a peg, **on** a hook; **in** a locker; **on** a coat rack; **on** a coat hanger;*
  * **over** the back of your seat*

3 ⇨ Use of the student's first or family name will depend on local classroom culture.

4 ⓘ *Step on it! Get a move on! Let's get going!*
See also Unit 3, A4.

A2
Everyday greetings

1 Good morning, everybody.
Good afternoon, everyone.
Good evening to you.
Hello, everybody.

2 How are you all today?
How are you getting on?
How are things?
How are we all doing this morning?
How's everyone feeling today?
How's it going?
How's life?

3 That's good.
*That's **good/nice** to hear.*
*I'm **glad/pleased/happy/sorry** to hear that.*

4 I hope you all had a nice weekend.
*I hope you all had a **good/enjoyable/relaxing holiday/break**.*
*I hope you're all feeling **well/fit**.*
*I hope **you've had/you're having** a **nice/good** day so far.*

---

1 ⌊ You can also address the class as *class, ladies and gentlemen,* and, depending on the age of your students, as *boys and girls, girls and boys* or *children*. Informally, and with older learners, you can also use *people, folks, guys* and *you guys* (AE).

  ⌊ In an informal classroom, you could use *Hi, Hi there* (especially in AE), *Howdy* (AE) and *Hiya* /ˈhaɪjə/.

  ⌊ 'Good day' is used in Australian and New Zealand English.

  ⌊ A low-rising intonation makes the greeting cheerful and friendly. See 🎧 1.1.

  ⌊ If it is the first time you are meeting the class, you could say:
  Welcome, everybody.
  Welcome to all of you.
  I'd like to welcome you all to this course.

  ⓢ *Good **morning/afternoon/evening**, Mr **Hughes/teacher**.*

  ⓢ Teach your students to use your English title **Dr/Mr/Mrs/Miss/Smith** or your title in your own language, if this is appropriate.

2 ⓢ Some suitable replies:
  (I'm) Very well, thank you.
  (I'm) Fine, thanks.
  *(I'm) Not **so/too** bad, thanks.*
  I'm feeling great.
  All right.
  I'm good. (AE)

  ⓢ Where appropriate, the students can reply:
  I'm not feeling very well.
  Not too well.
  I think I've caught a cold.
  I've got (a bit of) a temperature.

  ⇨ After a general greeting, remember to ask one or two individual students. See also 🎧 1.2.
  *And what about you, Maria? How are **you** today?*
  *Good morning, Luis. How are **you** feeling today?*

  ⓢ If appropriate, you can encourage your students to ask you a follow-up question:
  And how about you?
  *And how are you today, **Miss/Sir**?*

Meeting a new class

1 Let me introduce myself.
Allow me to introduce myself.
Perhaps you're wondering who I am.
Let me tell you something about myself.

2 My name is Mrs Hanson.
*I'm your new **English/Maths/History/**... teacher.*
*I'll be teaching you **English/Geography/Science/**... this year.*

3 Our lessons are on Monday mornings and Wednesday afternoons.
I'll be teaching you on Tuesdays and Fridays.
I've got three lessons a week with you.
We'll meet three times a week.
Our lessons start at 9.15 every Monday and Thursday.
*From your **timetable/schedule**, you can see we start at 11.15 on Friday.*

4 It's nice to meet you all.
*I'm very pleased to **meet/see** you all (again).*
I'm looking forward to working with you.
It'll be fun getting to know you all.

---

1 📘 In more advanced classes, you could go into more detail:
Let me tell you (something/a little bit) about myself.

➡ A natural continuation would be to ask the students to introduce themselves:
And what about you? Can you introduce yourselves to me?
Can you tell your neighbour something about yourself?

---

2 📘 If you are a substitute or trainee teacher, introduce yourself like this:
*My name is ... and I'm a **trainee/student** teacher.*
I'm the substitute /ˈsʌbstɪtjuːt/ for Mr Jones.
*My name is ... and I'm **substituting for/standing in for/replacing** Mrs Perez.*

📘 You may want to add:
... but you can call me Julia.
... but I'd like you to call me Julia.

📘 If appropriate, the following may be useful with a new class:
What's your name?
*How do you pronounce your **first name/surname**?*
How do you spell that?
Do you have a nickname?
What do your friends call you?
Remember in English to say your first name first.

➡ It is very important to learn the names of your students as soon as possible. Even with adults, using name cards and tags helps:
Put your name cards up, please.
Make sure you are wearing your name tags.

---

3 📘 With adult learners (for example, at college, or in evening classes), you can explain the course programme in more detail:
The spring term begins on January the 10th.
There are no classes next week.
The last class will be on December the 8th.

4 ➡ These comments, used appropriately, help create a good, motivating atmosphere:
I hope we're going to work very well together.
I'm sure we'll have some good lessons together.
I've heard some very good things about this class.

➡ A few introductory comments and questions will help your students get used to your English and feel relaxed, for example:
It's been a lovely day, hasn't it?
Too bad it started raining, isn't it?
Do you think it will clear up later?

Perhaps you're wondering who I am?

Taking the register

1 Let's see if everyone's here.
I'll just check who's here.
I have to take/check attendance. (AE)
I'll mark/take/check the register. /ˈredʒɪstə/
I'm going to call your names/the roll.
Raise your hand and say 'Here'/'Present'.

2 Who's absent?
Who's missing/away/not here today?
Are you all here?
Is the whole class here?
Any absences?
Is anybody absent/away/missing?
Anybody whose name I haven't called?
Did I miss anybody (out)?

3 Where's Mari this morning?
What's wrong/the matter with Mari?
Has anybody seen Mari today?
Does anybody know where Mari is?
Mari's away. Does anybody know why?
Is she absent or just late?
When will Mari be back?

4 Who wasn't here last time?
Was anybody away/absent/missing last time?
Who was absent last time?
Who missed last Wednesday's lesson?
Why weren't you here last time?
Make sure you bring an absence note.

5 What was the matter?
What was the problem?
Have you been ill?

---

1 ⌊ If the whole class is present, you can say:
Everybody's here.
Nice to see you all here.
Nobody's away today.
I'm glad you could all make it.

Otherwise:
So everybody is here except (for) Timo and Lasse.
So only two people away today.

Ⓢ Students can reply:
Here.
Present.
Yes.

---

2 ⊗ Who's ~~lacking~~? ✗

⌊ Your students may enjoy this humorous phrase:
Put your hand up if you are not here.

---

3 ⇨ Talking about absences is a good opportunity for conversation:
Alain is away. Does anybody know why?
Maybe he missed the bus. What do you think?

Ⓢ Students may want to apologize for other students.
Even if they cannot express these ideas in correct English,
encourage them to try (even in their L1) and then you can recast
their ideas in correct sentences.
She missed the bus.
He's on his way.
She's (just) coming.
She won't be long.
She'll be here in a moment.
I haven't seen her today.
He's away on holiday/a business trip.
He can't make it today.
She asked me to tell you she can't come today.
(Perhaps) she's ill/not well. She's got the flu/a cold/a temperature.
She wasn't feeling very well, so she went home.

Ⓢ Encourage students to use phrases like:
(I'm sorry) I don't know.
(I'm afraid) I've no idea.

⌊ If appropriate, you can react to news about a student's absence:
Oh dear. I'm sorry to hear that.
Oh dear. I hope she gets better soon.
I hope it's nothing serious.
When will she be back?

---

5 ⌊ To a returning student, you can say:
You're back. That's good/nice.
I'm glad you're back.
Welcome back! We missed you.
It's nice/good/lovely to see you again.

⌊ If the student has been ill, you can say:
Are you all right/OK/feeling better now?
I hope you're feeling better.
Are you feeling better today, Kai?
I hope you've recovered from your cold, Mia.
What happened to your leg?

⌊ To remind the absentee of what was practised in the previous
lesson, say:
Ask your friends to tell you what we've been doing.
Could someone explain to Beatriz what we have been working on?
You missed three lessons.
I hope you can catch up.
Stay behind/See me after the lesson.

⌊ If you yourself have been away or ill, you could ask:
How did you get on/manage with Mr Lopez?
What did you do with Miss Kim?
How far did you get with this unit/chapter?

A5

Dealing with lateness

1 You're late.
Where have you been?
We started ten minutes ago.
What have you been doing?
Why are you late?
What do you say when you're late?

2 That's all right. Sit down and we can start.
OK/I see. Well, sit down and let's get started.
Never mind. Let's go on with the lesson.
It doesn't matter. Let's get back to what we were doing.
Please hurry up and sit down. We've already started.
*Take **a/your** seat and we can get on.*

3 But try not to be late next time.
Try to be here on time next time.
Don't let it happen again.
Don't let it become a habit.
Let this be the last time.
That's the second time this week.
I'll have to report you if you're late again.

---

1 Ⳑ Notice also:
 You're just in time.
 You just made it (in time).
 You're early for a change.

 Ⳑ If appropriate, you could also ask some follow-up questions. Sometimes, though, it is not necessary to comment at all.
 Did you oversleep?
 Didn't your alarm clock go off?
 Did you miss your bus?
 What happened?

 ✇ *We started* ~~for~~ *ten minutes ago.* ✗
 We started ~~since~~ *ten minutes.* ✗

2 ⇨ Encourage your students to apologize when they enter the classroom:
 (I'm) sorry I'm late.
 I missed my bus. I'm sorry.

 Ⳑ Naturally you should also apologize if you arrive late. More formal phrases include:
 My apologies /əˈpɒlədʒiːz/ for arriving late.
 I apologize /əˈpɒlədʒaɪz/ for my late arrival.
 I'm sorry I've kept you waiting.
 I hope I haven't kept you waiting too long.

 ⟫ See Unit 2, B4 for other apologies.

3 ✇ *Don't let this* ~~to~~ *happen again.* ✗

A6

Getting down to work

1 All right. It's time to start our English lesson.
Let's start the lesson.
Let's get on with the lesson now.
I think we can start now.
I hope you're all ready for your English lesson.
Now we can get down to (some) work.

2 OK, everybody. I'm waiting to start.
Is everybody ready to start?
I'm waiting for you to be quiet.
We won't start until everybody is quiet.
Stop talking now so that we can start.
Settle down, everybody.

3 Put your things away and close your desk, please.
Close the lid of your desk.
Put your school bag under your desk.
Put your geography /dʒiˈɒɡrəfi/ book away.
This is an English lesson, not a biology /baɪˈɒlədʒi/ lesson.

---

2 ⇨ Very often there is an ideal moment to begin the lesson (for example, students stop talking). Some teachers signal that they are ready by standing up, removing their coat, rolling up their sleeves, clapping their hands, or standing in a certain place. What do you do?

 ⇨ Positive comments at the start of a lesson can help to contribute to a good classroom atmosphere from the very beginning of the class.
 Is everybody ready to do their best today?
 I'm looking forward to seeing what you can do this lesson.
 It's good to see you looking ready to work.
 I'm glad to see you are ready to work.
 Excellent! Everyone is here and ready with their books out.

 ⟫ See the next section and Unit 3, B2 for attention-catching phrases.

1
SECTION B

Lessons usually consist of a number of clearly marked stages. The short phrases that begin and end these stages are important because they give structure to the lesson and help students to follow what is going on. Students get used to these phrases quickly because they probably occur in every lesson. Because there are several alternatives, they will also hear a variety of forms. In this way their receptive vocabulary grows and they are encouraged to guess the meaning of unknown words from the context. It is often a good idea to accompany a particular instruction with a distinct gesture, at least at the beginning. This way you help your students to remember the instruction and it also allows you to introduce alternative forms.

1 Starting something new
Let's speak English.
Right everyone.
Let's move on.
Now we'll do another exercise.

2 Making things clear
You have five minutes.
Is everything clear?
OK. You can start.

3 Sequencing activities
First, have a look at the text.
Next, read through the new words.
Last, try to do exercise 3.

4 Checking progress
Any problems?
Where are you up to?
What's the matter?

5 Stopping
OK, everybody. Two more minutes.
Have you finished?
Right. That's enough.
All right. Stop now.
We'll have a break.

Running the lesson

Points to think and talk about

1 Changing from one language to another is a natural and routine part of an English lesson. How many times do you think you change languages in a normal class? Have you noticed when you use English and when you use the students' L1? What proportion of each do you think you use?
2 Do you think it is important to announce a change of language, or is it better to switch without any warning?
3 When you begin the lesson, why is it important to make a link with what happened in the previous lesson(s)? And with what will happen in the next lesson?
4 Do you think that you should spend time telling the students what the goals of each lesson are? How would you do this?
5 Some teachers show or present an outline of the lesson to their students at the beginning. If the outline is, for example, displayed on the overhead projector, it could be in their L1, but the accompanying explanation could be in English. What are the advantages of this kind of so-called pre-organizer? Are there any possible disadvantages?
6 Ideally, good language teaching will activate each student, especially in making them speak. How could you best persuade a shy student to speak English? Are there any situations or events in the class that you could use to encourage a shy student to say something?
7 How would you deal with a situation where you ask a student a question in English and the student wants to reply in his/her L1? Would you insist on English? How could you make effective use of the student's reply, even if it is not in English? Would your reaction depend on the age of the students and their level of English?
8 When you plan a lesson, is it useful to think about the classroom phrases you will need and to include them in your lesson plan?

Language to think about

1 Think of a typical lesson. Can you describe the structure of the lesson, announcing the different phases, the activities and the amount of time to be spent on each?
2 How many ways can you think of for telling the students to stop working?
3 What phrases can you think of for moving from one stage of the lesson to the next?
4 What would you say to check whether students have finished the work you have given them?
5 How many different phrases can you think of that mean the same as *first*, *next*, and *last*?

Classroom English vocabulary to collect

The personal things that students carry with them. (For example, *a comb*, *mobile phone/cellphone* (AE)).

Starting something new

1 Let's speak English.
*Let's **change/switch** (over) to English.*
Now we can use English again.
Let me tell you this in Japanese.
*Now I'll **change/switch** back to **Spanish/French/...** .*
*The next part of the lesson will be in **Spanish/French/...** .*
Now, it's English-only time.

2 Right everyone.
Good/Fine/OK/Right/Now/Now then.
***OK/All right**, everybody.*
Quiet now, please.
Stop working now, please, and pay attention.

3 Let's move on.
(Now) we'll/let's go on.
On we go.
*Let's **move/go** on to something **else/different**.*
Now, we're going to do something else.
*Let's turn to something a little **more/less** serious.*

4 Now we'll do another exercise.
Now we shall do some group work.
Now let's have a look at exercise 13 B.
Now I want you to turn to page 17.
Now we can relax.
Now I have some music for you.

---

1 ⇨ It is useful to inform the students about what language (English or L1) you are going to use. That way you can gradually get them used to longer stages of the lesson in English. The important thing is to be consistent, with a clear policy for when to use English and when to use the L1.

⇨ If you know the class is capable of using English, or if you are conducting CLIL classes, you may have to remind them:
In English, please.
Try to use English.
***Say/Try** it in English, could you?*
*Now **try/say** the same thing in English.*
Use English as much as you can.
*Try not to use **Spanish/French/...** .*

2 🔉 These words and phrases (so-called markers) are for catching attention and marking a transition: the end of one activity and the start of something new.

3 🔉 ***Moving on*** is often used on its own to mark a transition:
Moving on, let's have a look at the new vocabulary.
Moving (quickly) on, I'd like you to get into groups.

🔉 ***Now*** followed by a pause, often announces a new activity.
Now. What's next?
Now. Let's play a game.
Now. How about listening to a song?

4 ⊗ Now ~~we listen~~ to the dialogue. ✗
Now we'll listen to the dialogue. ✔
When you explain what is about to happen, use the future tense.

⊗ *Look at ~~the~~ exercise 13 B.* ✗
There is no definite article before page, exercise or question numbers.

Making things clear

1 You have five minutes.
You can spend ten minutes on this.
*I'll give you five minutes **on this/to do this**.*
*You'll have to stop in two **minutes/minutes' time**.*
*Don't spend more than a few minutes **on/doing** this exercise.*

2 Is everything clear?
Is that clear?
*Are you clear about **what to do/what I mean/how to do it**?*
Are there any questions (before we start)?
Any questions anybody?
(Has) Anybody got any questions about what they have to do?
Have you all understood?
(Did) Anybody not understand?
Who still doesn't understand what they've got to do?
Have you all got that?
Did you all follow that?
*Shall I go over **it/the instructions** again?*

3 Right. You can start.
***Away/Off** you go.*
***Begin/Start** working.*
Is everybody ready?
If you're ready, we'll start.
Let's get to work.
Get on with it.

---

2 🔉 Abbreviated questions (without a verb) are useful. Notice the high-rising intonation. For practice, see 🎧 2.3.

⇨ To check understanding, you can ask one of your students for a translation, or say:
*Tell me in **Spanish/German/...** what you have to do.*
Put your hand up if you don't understand.
Anybody still not sure what you have to do?

A sample task may help make things clear:
*Let's do one together so you **get the idea/see what I mean**.*

Or a demonstration:
Look, like this.
Do it this way.

Ⓢ *Can I ask a question?*
I didn't get the idea.
I'm still not clear what I'm supposed to do.
Can you explain again?

3 🔉 If you are playing a recording or showing a video, you might say:
Here goes.
Here it comes.
Off we go then.
*Let's **start/begin**.*

🔉 If a student asks ***Shall I start?*** you can say:
Yes, go ahead.
If you would, please.

ⓘ *Let's get **cracking/moving/going/cooking**!*

Sequencing activities

1 First, have a look at the text.
Firstly, let's run through your homework.
First of all, (today) we'll listen to the tape.
To begin with, (this time) we'll check your homework.
For the first thing, we'll listen to a song.

2 Next, read through the new words.
For the next thing I would like you to get into threes.
To continue/go on with, *could you take out your workbooks?*
And now, we'll try an exercise.
*And now for **some grammar/something different**.*

3 Last, try to do exercise 3.
Finally (today), I want you to copy something down.
Lastly (this time), I would like you to work in groups.
To finish (off) with, you can do some reading.
For the last thing (today), take out your notebooks.
Last but not least, how about a song?
*Just before **we finish/you go**, let's talk about your test next week.*

---

1 ⓘ *For starters, .../To kick off with, ...*

ᒪ If you want to use a text or exercise more than once, say:
The first time, you can try it with your books open.
The second time, I want you to try it on your own.

⊗ *At first* ✗   *First* ✔

2 ᒪ The following are also useful when giving a series of instructions:
First, ... and then we shall do it in pairs.
After that, you can change roles.
After each part, you can check the answers.
As soon as/After/When *you have done that, you can continue with number 3.*
*The same (thing) again, **but/only** this time I want you to ...*

⇨ It's often a good idea to outline the lesson at the start:
What I've planned for today is the following: ...
What I want to do today is ...
This is what we're going to do today.
*Today's lesson consists of three **parts/sections/activities**.*
Let me run through today's programme.

Ⓢ Your students may also ask:
What are we going to do today?
What have you got planned for today?

ᒪ For presenting the overall structure of a lesson, the following are useful:

Later (on)	*we can watch a video.*
*In **half an hour/ten minutes***	*we'll move on to your presentations.*
Half way through the lesson	*I'll ask you to form groups.*
***Towards/Near** the end of the lesson*	*we'll check the answers.*

ᒪ If you want to present your plans for a longer period of teaching:
*Over (the course of) the next few **lessons/weeks**, we're going to ...*

---

3 ᒪ Notice also: *firstly ..., secondly ..., thirdly ..., lastly ....*

⊗ *At last we have some grammar!* ✗
At last suggests longing and anticipation.

Checking progress

1 Any problems?
*Are you **OK/all right**?*
Is there anyone who needs help?
*Who can't manage (on **his/her/their** own)?*
Who is finding this difficult?
*(Is there) anybody having **trouble/difficulty** (with the exercise)?*

2 Where are you up to?
How far have you got?
Which question are you on?

3 What's the matter?
What's the problem?
Is there something wrong?
Is everything OK?
*Is there **something/anything** the matter?*

---

1 ᒪ Other useful phrases include:
*How are you getting **on/along**?*
Ask if you're not sure.
Put your hand up if you need help.
Let me know/Tell me *if you run into a problem.*
Are you stuck?
I'll help you if you get stuck.
*I'll **come round/circulate** and check.*

---

2 ᒪ Some general questions are:
*Have you all got enough to **do/be getting on with**?*
*Does everybody have enough to **occupy them/keep them busy**?*

---

3 ⇨ Be prepared to deal with some typical problems; for example, no paper, no book:
Borrow one from someone else.
Share with someone else.
*Ask someone to lend you **one/a sheet of paper**.*
Use my copy.
There's an extra copy on my desk.
Can someone come to the rescue?

Ⓢ Student apologies:
(I'm afraid) I left my book at home.
I didn't have time to do my homework.

Ⓢ Your students might also ask:
Can you help me?
I need some help.
What shall we do when we've finished?
*What do we have to do **now/next**?*

Stopping

1 OK, everybody. Two more minutes.
You will have to finish in a minute.
I'll have to stop you in two minutes.
*(Just) a couple **more minutes/of minutes more**.*
*Just one or two **more minutes/minutes more**.*
*One minute **left/remaining/to go**.*

2 Have you finished?
*Are you **done/through**? (AE)*
***Who's/Who has** finished?*
Who has done them all?
(Has) everybody finished?
Is there anybody who still hasn't finished?
Have you done exercise 7 (yet)?
Have you finished reading page 10?
*Have you **done/completed/managed** everything?*
That was quick!
You were fast.

3 Right. That's enough.
That's enough for now.
That's fine.
That will do, thank you.
You've done enough of that.
You've probably had enough of that.
We've spent long enough on this.
*It's time **for/you had** a change.*

4 All right. Stop now.
Stop what you're doing.
Everybody stop what they are doing.
*Stop **writing/working**.*
All right, you can stop now.
Your time is up now, I'm afraid.
Finish off now.
Finish up. (AE)
*Put your **pens/pencils** down.*

5 We'll have a break before going on.
*You can **have/take** a two-minute break.*
Relax for a moment before we go on to something else.
We can take our coffee break now.

---

1 ⇨ It is important to warn students how much time they have left to finish an activity.

---

2 ⊗ ~~Are you ready?~~ ✗

To check whether students have completed an exercise or task, use ***Have you finished?*** rather than ***Are you ready?*** Use ***Are you ready?*** before you begin a new activity to check the class is with you.

Ⅼ If you think you're behind schedule, say:
I'll have to hurry you.
Let's pick up the pace.

Ⅼ To slower students you could say:
What have you been doing?
You've hardly started!

Ⓢ *I've finished.*
I'm done. (AE)

---

3 Ⅼ Notice also:
One more go and then we'll move on.
Just one more turn and that's it.
We'll do another two questions and then stop.
***Complete/Finish** the sentence you're writing.*
*Just finish the **sentence/task** you're **(working) on/doing** now and then we can stop.*
*Finish the question you're **(working)** on at the moment, and do the rest at home.*

---

4 Ⅼ When you finish an activity, you can say:
*So much for **that/grammar practice**.*
That's that.

Ⅼ Other phrases:
OK. We'll stop here.
Let's stop here for a while.
*Right. I think **we'll/we can** stop **there/here/now**.*
I think we can leave it there for a while.
We can come back to this later.

⨀ Phrases for checking exercises are in Unit 4, C.

---

5 Ⅼ Start work again after a break with these phrases:
Let's get back to work.
It's time to get started again.
***On/Off** we go again!*

Perhaps we've spent long enough on this...

1

SECTION C

Most lessons probably end in the same way: you try to draw things to a close, set any homework, possibly review the lesson, and perhaps make a few announcements. This, then, is another situation where students can become familiar with a limited but recurring range of everyday phrases. Much of what is said at the end of the lesson is connected with what has happened in the previous forty minutes, so it has great personal relevance to the students, especially if you can exchange a few words with individual students as they are leaving the classroom. This regular interaction helps them to develop their listening skills and also to build up their confidence. You can use the end of the lesson to boost students' motivation and give them a positive sense that they have been active participants in the lesson and are making progress.

1 Checking the time
What time is it?
It isn't time to finish yet.
We have five more minutes.
Carry on with your work.

2 Setting homework
For your homework, please ...
Finish off exercise 26 C at home.
There will be a test on this.
Don't forget about your homework.

3 Stopping work
It's time to stop.
So, today we have practised ...
We'll finish this next time.
That's all for today.

4 Making announcements
Wait a moment, please!
I have something to tell you.
Next time we'll meet in room 23.
Don't forget the English Club meeting.

5 Saying goodbye
Goodbye, everyone.
See you all again on Tuesday.
Have a nice weekend.

6 Clearing the class
Out you go.
Please go out now.
Go out quietly.
Take all your things with you.
Open the window, please.
Whose book is this?

Ending the lesson

Points to think and talk about

1 What usually happens at the end of a lesson in your school? What are the things that you usually have to complete in time? How can you avoid a rush at the end of the lesson?
2 What sort of atmosphere and general feeling do you want to create at the end of the lesson? How can you help create this atmosphere and motivate the students for the next lesson?
3 Would you set the homework in English? What would be the advantages of doing this? Could there be problems? How could you overcome these problems?
4 Are your students used to doing a lot of homework? How long will they spend on it?
5 Sometimes you may have a few minutes in hand at the end of the lesson. What could you do to effectively fill that time?
6 Can you think of any short, easily arranged language games that would be suitable for the end of a lesson? Would it be useful to start making a collection of such games and activities?
7 What topics of conversation would be suitable for the end of a lesson?
8 People talk about classroom culture. In the classroom culture you are used to, what things could the teacher expect help with during the lesson? What responsibilities could be given to the students?
9 Do you think you can change the 'language culture' of your class so that you can use more English to run the class? How would you do this? Would the students accept this?
10 At the end of a class, do you think it is a good idea to briefly review what the students learned or practised during the lesson? Should you tell them about the next lesson?

Language to think about

1 Can you tell the time in English?
2 How would you set homework in English?
3 How many ways can you think of for saying goodbye?
4 What other phrases might be useful at the end of a lesson?
5 Can you think of some useful phrases for the end of a lesson if the students are: a) going home; b) having their lunch; c) having their next lesson in the same room?
6 How can you tell someone to help you with a classroom task; for example, picking up rubbish?
7 How can you do the same thing politely?
8 Can you announce timetable and room changes?

Classroom English vocabulary to collect

1 The names of the school subjects in English. (For example, *maths*, *geography*)
2 The names of the hobbies and interests that your students have. (For example, *athletics*, *ballet*)

C1

Checking the time

1 **What time is it?**
What's the time?
Do you have the right time?
Could you tell me the time, please?
What time do you make it?
What time do you have? (AE)

2 **It isn't time to finish yet.**
The bell hasn't gone yet.
There are still two minutes to go.
We still have a couple of minutes left.
***We've/We're** almost finished.*
We're not through yet. (AE)
We're almost done. (AE)

3 **We have five more minutes.**
We have five minutes over.
We have an extra five minutes.
*(It seems) we have two or three minutes **in hand/to spare**.*
We (seem to) have finished a few minutes early.

4 **Carry on with your work until the bell goes.**
Carry on with the exercise for the rest of the lesson.
Carry on with what you are doing (until the end of the lesson).
Just finish the sentence you're working on and then you can go.
Sit quietly until the bell goes.

---

1 Notice the different ways of telling the time:

It's	*exactly*	*half*	*past*	*nine.*
The time is	*precisely*	*(a) quarter*	*to*	*eleven.*
I make it	*almost*	*ten (minutes)*		
I make the time	*just gone*			

Notice that:
It's half ten. = It's 10.30.

The time is often given in timetable form:
I make it 9.45 (nine forty-five).

It's five **after/before** *nine. (AE)*

---

2 Student time may differ from yours:
I make it only quarter to. There's another five minutes yet.
*This lesson isn't **supposed/due** to finish until five past.*
Is your watch right?
*Your watch must be **fast/slow**.*

---

3 It is a good idea to build up a collection of short games, puzzles and activities that you can use to fill any time left over at the end of a lesson. See Useful reading and resources, page 171.

---

4 With older students, you can say:
You can leave when you're ready.

Notice the following:

It's not worth	*starting anything else.*
*There's no **point/use/sense** (in)*	*starting a new exercise.*
There's not much point (in)	*beginning anything else this time.*
There isn't any point (in)	*starting the new unit.*

C2

Setting homework

1 **For your homework, please do exercise 27 A.**
*This **chapter/lesson/page/exercise/dialogue** is your homework.*
*This is your homework for **tonight/today/next time/next lesson/Monday**.*
***As/For** (your) homework I want you to …*
Your homework for tonight is to prepare Chapter 17.
Before (the) next lesson I would like you to …

2 **I want you to finish off exercise 26 C at home.**
Finish this off at home.
Finish off the exercise at home.
Do the rest of the exercise as your homework for tonight.
Read the rest of the story at home.
Complete your story at home.
Go through this section again on your own at home.
*I'll go **through/over** it with you next time.*

3 **There will be a test on this next week.**
There will be a test on chapters 5 to 8 next time.
You can expect a test on this in the near future.
I'll test you on the new words some time next week.

4 **Don't forget about your homework.**
Remember your homework.
Do you remember what you have to do for your homework?
Are you all clear about your homework?

---

1 Some examples of more precise instructions:
*Prepare **as far as/down to/up to** page 175.*
*Go **through/over** what we've learnt today.*
At home practise the dialogue we had in today's class.
Tonight, or for next time, read the text on page 44.
Please re-read this chapter for Friday's lesson.
Revise what we did today and then try exercise 4.

You may also decide that no homework is needed:
There's no homework this time.
I'm not going to give you any homework today.

The two first lines. ✘

Word order:
*The **first/last/next/following** + number.*
The next two lines.

---

3 ***A quiz** = **a test**, **a pop quiz** = **a surprise test*** (AE)

---

4 *When is this due?*
When do we have to do this for?

Give precise instructions for when students should hand in a piece of work:
***Give/Hand** it in **tomorrow/by Friday**.*
(Make sure that you) hand it in to me next lesson.
Bring it to me no later than next Monday.
The deadline for this work is next Tuesday afternoon (at the (very) latest).
Don't forget to turn this in next time. (AE)

In some cases it is useful to remind students:
Please pick up a copy of the exercise as you leave.
*Remember to take a **handout/sheet/copy** as you go out.*
Don't forget to collect a copy of your homework from my desk.

Stopping work

1 It's time to stop.
*We('ll) have to **stop/finish** now.*
*I make it almost time. We'll have to **finish/stop here/there**.*
*There's the **bell/buzzer/gong**, so we must stop working now.*
We have no more time for anything else.
We don't have any more time.
It's (about) time (for us) to stop.
*It's (about) time **we/you** stopped.*

2 So, today we've practised asking the time.
This time you have learned how to write a letter.
In this lesson we've begun a new unit.
*Let me just **remind you/recap/go over** what we've done.*
Let's just review today's lesson.

3 We'll finish this next time.
*We'll **do/read/look at** the rest of the chapter on Thursday.*
We'll finish (off) this exercise in the next lesson.
*We'll **go/carry** on with this dialogue next time.*
We'll continue working on this chapter next time.
*We'll come back to this **another time/a bit later**.*
There'll be more on this next time.
Next time we're going to have a look at your projects.
Next lesson we'll listen to your presentations.

4 That's all for today.
That will do for today. You can go now.
That's about it for today.
That will be all.
*Right. You **may/can** go.*
You can put your things away and go.

---

1 ⓘ These phrases are also used:
We've run out of time.
Time's up, I'm afraid.

📖 Notice you use the future tense even in phrases like:
We'll stop now.
We'll finish for today.

📖 Notice the past tense after *It's time...* and *It's about time...*

📖 You may have to cut short the lesson:
I'm sorry, I have to dash off to a meeting.
I've got another class, so we'll have to finish ten minutes early.
I'm sorry, I don't feel well.
Some of you are going to the museum, so I'll let you go at half past.

⇨ If appropriate, remember to thank the students for their contribution:
You have worked very well today. Well done everybody.
You were really active today. Thank you.
I'm really pleased with the way you worked today.
Excellent job! Well done, people!
Excellent work from everybody today.
(I'd like to) thank you for your hard work.
*I'm very **pleased/impressed** with the way you've worked today.*
You concentrated all the way through the lesson. Well done.
Everyone participated in this lesson. Well done.
Give yourselves a pat on the back for having worked so well today.

Making announcements

1 Wait a moment, please!
*Just a **moment/minute/second**, please.*
*Hang on a **moment/second**.*
Just hold on a minute.
Stay where you are for a moment.
One more thing before you go.
Don't go rushing off.
Back to your places!

2 I have something to tell you.
I have something to say to you.
I have some announcements to make before you go.
Please listen.
Please pay attention.

3 Next time we'll meet in room 23.
Tomorrow we'll meet in room 14
There's been a change of room for next week.
We'll be meeting in room 19 instead.
*I'll see you in room 7 after the **break/recess**. (AE)*
The fourth period has been cancelled next Tuesday.
There won't be an English lesson on Friday.

4 Don't forget the English Club meeting this afternoon.
*Please **remember/don't forget** to bring your project folders next time.*
*If you have time, watch **Pride and Prejudice** on Channel 4 at nine o'clock.*
We'll meet outside the museum at 9.30. Don't be late.

---

1 ⓘ Useful idioms include:
Hold it!
Stay put!
Not so fast!
Hold your horses!
*Hang on a **sec/tick**.*
Freeze!

2 ⇨ This is also the time to remind students about important things that affect your teaching, for example:
Don't forget to bring your textbook next time.
Remember your essays are due next week.
Let me remind you about the newsletter to your parents.

⇨ It's sometimes useful to get some immediate feedback on your lesson:
Did you enjoy that?
What did you think of the game?
What did you like most?

3 📖 If you yourself are going to be absent, you can say:
I won't be here next week.
*Miss Jones will **take/be taking** you instead.*
*Mr Brown will be **my substitute/substituting for me**.*
*I'll leave her some work **for you/to give you**.*

📖 Student teachers who have completed their teaching practice in a class might say:
This was my last lesson with you. I enjoyed working with you.
I wish you every success with your English studies. Thank you for all your hard work.

C5

Saying goodbye

1 Goodbye, everyone.
Bye-bye/G'bye, everyone.
Bye now, Mischa.
Cheerio, Carmen.
See you (soon), Didier.
So long. (AE)

2 See you all again on Tuesday.
See you next class.
(I'll) see you (all) again next time/Wednesday.
We'll meet again the same time next week.
The next time we meet will be after the holiday.

3 Have a nice weekend.
Have a good/nice/relaxing holiday/rest/Christmas/Easter.
Enjoy your holiday.
See you again next year/in the New Year/in 2008.
I hope you have a nice vacation.
Don't work too hard.
Enjoy yourselves.

1 🔔 Use low rising intonation to show friendliness and enthusiasm.

⊗🎧 Listen to 1.1 on the CD and see Audio Practice, page 22.

⇨ Say goodbye to individual students as they leave the classroom. This can be very encouraging, especially to the shy ones.

2 🔔 If you need to see a particular student after the class:
Come and see me after the lesson.
Can I have a word, please?
I'd like a word with you.
Could you stay behind for a few minutes?
Have you got a minute?

ⓘ *Same time, same place.*

⊗ *We'll see.* ✗
This means I'll think about it.

3 🔔 These phrases are also used:
Have a nice day.
Enjoy the rest of your day.

🔔 For final goodbyes, you can say:
Look after yourself/yourselves.
All the very best to you.
Take care.
I wish you all the very best.

💲 Encourage students to reply:
Thanks. The same to you.
Same to you.
You, too.
Likewise.

⇨ Unless you are in a hurry to get to the next class, the end of the lesson is an excellent opportunity for casual conversation. Ask about the students' plans for the weekend, the weather forecast, sporting events, etc. If appropriate, you can encourage them to share this information by saying something about your own plans, for example,
I've got a lot of work, so I'm staying at home.
I might go for a walk on Sunday. What about you?

C6

Clearing the class

1 Please go out now.
Will you please go out.
Everybody outside!
Out you go now.
All of you, get outside now!
Hurry up and get out!

2 Go out quietly, please!
Not so much noise, please.
Quietly!
Ssshhh!
Try not to make any noise as you leave.
No noise as you leave.
Other classes are still working.

3 Take all your things with you.
Don't leave anything behind.
Take everything/all your belongings with you.
Make sure you haven't forgotten anything.
Don't forget your stuff.

4 Could you open the window for me, please?
Open the window. Let's have some fresh air.
Put everything back in its right place.
Straighten the desks.
Put the books on the shelf.
Could you clean the board for me, please?
Pick up the rubbish, please.
Clear everything away.

5 Whose book is this?
Has somebody forgotten their book?
Whose is this glove?
Who does this pen belong to?
Who's the owner of this hat?
(Has) Anybody lost a key?

1 🔔 If the arrangements for leaving the classroom are more formal, use the following:
Queue/Line up by the door.
Get into a queue/line.
Form a straight line.

4 ⇨ There are many routine classroom jobs that you can ask students to do, for example, opening the window, rearranging desks, picking up litter, returning books. But remember that a job well done deserves thanks:
Well done, thank you.
Thank you for your help, everybody.
Thanks. That looks fine.
Now it looks tidy. Good.

🔔 If there are monitors in the class, you can ask:
Who are the monitors (this week)?
Who's on duty today?
Whose job is it to close the windows?

🔔 If you need help, ask:
Can you help me with the projector?
Could you give me a hand carrying this?

Classroom essentials

GIVING INSTRUCTIONS (1)

Simple commands and requests

You can give instructions in three ways – by ordering or commanding *stand up*, by requesting or asking *please stand up*, and by suggesting *how about standing up?* This unit focuses on giving simple commands and basic requests.

Imperative

- The simplest command is the imperative form of the verb. In the negative, *do not* is stronger than *don't*.

  Open the window.   *Close your books.*
  Don't write this down.   *Don't look at the answers.*
  Do not write this down!   *Do not interrupt!*

- You can direct a command to a particular student or group:

  Anna, try number 2.   *You boys, listen now.*
  Answer it, somebody.   *Come on, everybody.*
  Don't help him, Marco.   *Don't talk, you two girls.*
  Nobody move.   *Don't anybody move.*

- Notice the use of *and* after *go* and *come*:

  Go and fetch your book.   *Come and sit here at the front.*

just

- Using the word *just* at the beginning suggests that:
  1 you are encouraging the student;
     Just try the next one.   *Just come and sit here.*
  2 the task is small;
     Just pass me that book, Maria. *Just turn the lights off.*
  3 you are annoyed;
     Just sit down and be quiet. *Just put that book away.*

do

- By adding *do*, you make the command sound stronger or more polite:

  Do listen.   *Do be quiet now.*
  Do try to hurry up.   *Do try not to write too much.*
  Do sit down.   *Do help yourself to paper.*

be + to

- Notice the use of *be + to* in these quite formal instructions:

  You are to work in groups of four.
  You are not to talk.
  You are to finish this off at home.

must

- Using *must*, *have to* or *should* also has the force of a command. You can make these commands more polite with *I'm afraid* or *I'm sorry*.

  You must have this finished by Monday
  You will have to write this out again.
  You should write your name at the top.
  You must use the past tense here, I'm afraid.
  I'm sorry, but you will have to do this again.

Requests

- You can change a command into a request by using a low rising intonation:

Command
Try it a↘gain.

Request
Try it a↗gain?

» See 🎧 1.4.

please

- Probably the most useful word for asking is *please*. Notice it can come either at the beginning or end of the request. At the end it will also usually have rising intonation:

Command
Put your pencils down↘.

Request
Please put your ↗pencils down.
Put your ↗pencils down, ↗please.

» See 🎧 1.4.

- If you also use the name of a student when making a request, the word order is quite flexible with *please*. Before the verb, however, *please* sounds more formal:

Maria, please come here.
Please, Maria, come here.
Please come here, Maria.

Maria, come here, please.
Come here, please, Maria.
Come here, Maria, please.

- *Please* is very useful for nominating students, for example when working with exercises:

Number 7. Yes, Henning, please.
Right, the next one. Er, Luigi, please.
OK, Jeanne. Number 6, please.
All right. Atsuko. The next one, please.

» See 🎧 1.5.

Practice

1 Practise giving instructions. Use the simple commands below and change them using the words given at the end.

EXAMPLE
Come here. **a** please **b** Yutaka **c** everybody.
Come here, please.
Come here, Yutaka.
Everybody come here.

1 Stand up. **a** everybody **b** please **c** nobody
2 Carry on with the exercise. **a** this group **b** should **c** please
3 Go out quietly. **a** please **b** everybody **c** you are to
4 Remember the meeting. **a** please **b** do **c** everybody
5 Rewrite the exercise.
   a you must **b** I'm afraid you must **c** I'm sorry but you have to
6 Move to one side. **a** Pilar **b** please **c** just
7 Hand in your essays by next Wednesday.
   a everybody **b** you are to **c** do
8 Try the next one. **a** someone **b** please **c** Paco

2 Go though the phrases in section 1–4 on page 14 (C6) and re-express them, using different commands and requests. If you are working in a group, direct them at your fellow students. Take it in turns to express different ways of giving the same instruction. Then imagine situations where you would give the instruction.

3 Try playing 'Simon Says' with new rules. You must only follow a command if it is expressed politely, or if it is addressed to everybody. If the command is a straight imperative, or addressed to a particular person, then you shouldn't follow it. If you react incorrectly to a command, then you are out.

RECORD 4 Record one of your lessons. Then listen to the recording and notice how you gave your instructions. Did you mainly use commands? Where could you have used more polite requests?

Exercises and activities

1 Prepositions and vocabulary

See the OUP website http://www.oup.com/elt/teacher/pce.

2 Classroom scenario

Passages A–D below describe different situations of an English lesson. At the places numbered, try to think what the teacher could say in the situation. You are free to invent the information where necessary. Remember to use different forms of command and request in your instructions.

A It's Monday morning and it's raining heavily. Your first lesson is about to begin. You are in the corridor outside your classroom. Most of the students are already inside. Simon arrives. You greet him (1). He is carrying his school bag and a tennis racket. Simon's locker is in the corridor, so you suggest that he doesn't take the tennis racket into the classroom (2). Maya arrives wearing a very wet anorak, which you don't want in your classroom (3). You notice two of your students who are still hanging about in the corridor (4).

B You go into the classroom. A moment later there is a knock at the door and Will appears. You invite him in (5). He leaves the door open (6). You greet the whole class (7). You hope everybody is well after the weekend (8). You then ask two of the shyer students, Sonya and Mike, how they are (9, 10). Even though you know some of the students in the class, you have never actually taught them English, so you introduce yourself (11), tell them about the timetable for English lessons (12) and say something encouraging (13).

C You are half-way through the term. You are taking the register (14). One of the students tells you that Lena is absent. You wonder if any of the others have seen her (15). You plan to start the lesson with a short review test, but to be fair you check who actually attended the previous lessons (16). Marie, who has been away for two weeks, is back in the class. You welcome her (17) and suggest how she can catch up (18).

D You want to start the lesson (19), but first you have to get their attention. Liv is chatting with Lisa (20); Maya's desk is open (21); and Joe is busy reading his chemistry textbooks (22). At that moment the door opens and Tom comes in. He's twenty minutes late. You ask for some explanation (23). Tom explains sleepily that he forgot to get off the bus. You just want to get on with the lesson (24), but you make it very clear that he mustn't be late again (25).

3 Role-play

Use the classroom scenario above as the basis for a role-play. Take it in turns to play the part of the teacher. Look through the lists of alternative phrases for each event and try to use them in your instructions and questions. The rest of the group can play the students' parts. To make things more interesting, change some of the details:
1 it is the first lesson after the summer holidays;
2 you are substituting for John Adams;
3 you arrive five minutes late;
4 you're recovering from a cold;
5 you get the students to introduce themselves;

6 you call the roll;
7 there is a new student in the class;
8 you comment on the weather;
9 one of the students has returned after being absent for two weeks;
10 a student arrives late. S/he has a bandaged arm.

4 Running the lesson

The different stages in a lesson can be thought of as a series of self-contained blocks. Each stage can be presented in table form as follows:

Action	Sample sentence
1 Changing languages	*Now I'll use English again.*
2 Getting the students' attention	*Right, everyone.*
3 Moving to a new activity	*Let's move on to something else.*
4 Describing the new activity	*Now we'll …*
5 Setting the time limits	*You have five minutes.*
6 Checking everything is clear	*Is that clear?*
7 Starting work	*OK. Away you go.*
8 Checking students' progress	*Are you all managing?*
9 Giving a time warning	*Just a couple more minutes.*
10 Checking progress	*Have you all finished?*
11 Stopping the activity	*OK. Could you stop now, please?*

Notice that stage 4 often involves giving several tasks; *First, … next, … last, …*

Using the table above and the phrases in section B3 of Unit 1, give a series of instructions for the following stages of a lesson:

1 You will return the students' tests. They should go through their answers with their neighbour and try to correct their mistakes together. They have got fifteen minutes.
2 The students should copy down the words of a song in their notebooks. They should ask if they don't understand any words. They have got no more than five minutes.
3 The students should read through the dialogue on page 19, and then, together with a partner, underline any verbs that are in the past tense. They have got 10 minutes.
4 The students should work in pairs and take it in turns to ask each other the questions at the bottom of page 36. Give them about five minutes.
5 The students should work in groups of three or four. They must write a short conversation based on Chapter 3. They can then act out their conversation for the rest of the students. Stop at ten past ten.
6 The students have 10 minutes to try to do questions 1–7. They can refer to page 125 in their textbook for ideas.

5 A lesson plan

RECORD Draw up a plan for a lesson or part of one. Think about how you will give your instructions in a clear and logical way and how you will move from one stage of the lesson to the next. If possible, teach your lesson to a group of students and record it. Then listen to the way you made transitions between the different parts of the lesson.

6 A board game

Use the table opposite to practise the phrases needed at the end of a lesson.

- You need a dice (AE: die) and a counter each.
- The aim of the game is to move from the left-hand column to the right-hand column, by using suitable phrases for each situation that you move to.
- In each column some basic information about the situation is given; time, homework, the next class and so on.
- In the Bell (🔔) square you must react to the sound of the bell ringing.
- In the Stop (✋) square you must tell the students to stop working.
- In the Bye (☺) square you say goodbye.
- Throw a dice and look at the situation in the square with your dice number, in the first left-hand column. Think of a suitable phrase for the situation described.
- If your fellow students accept your reply, you can move your counter on to the square.
- In the next round, after everybody has had a turn, you can once again throw the dice.
- Keep playing until you reach the right-hand column.
- If you need more rules, work them out with the other members of the group.
- You can also work across the board systematically, row by row, if you want.

time	reaction	bell	comment	homework	next class	stop	bye	extra
It's ten to ten. The lesson finishes at five to. **4**	You'll finish the exercise next time. **5**	🔔	Good work from everybody. **3**	No homework this time. **6**	Begins 5 minutes earlier.	✋	☺	There is a meeting of the English Drama Club at 17.30. **2**
There are three minutes left. **1**	They have some time to begin their homework. They have **3**	🔔	A difficult exercise. You'll come back to it next time. **6**	Exercise 9B, page 25	Will be in room 223. **1**	✋	☺	You need help collecting books.
The bell rings early. **6**	You'll come back to this in the next lesson. **4**	🔔	They learned a new verb form, the future. **1**	Finish off exercise 7D. **2**	The lesson on Tuesday is cancelled. **4**	✋	☺	You find a purse on the floor. **5**
Check what time the lesson due to finish. **3**	You have a few minutes in hand. **2**	🔔	They practised ordering food in a restaurant. **6**	Learn the new words. Pick up a task sheet from your desk. **4**	You will be away. Mr Jones will substitute for you. **3**	✋	☺	Some fresh air is needed. **2**
Students start packing their bags. **2**	It is not worth beginning anything else. **6**	🔔	The boys were not very active this time. **3**	Revise Unit 6. There will be a test next time. **6**	No lesson on Wednesday. **2**	✋	☺	It is your very last lesson with the class. **6**
Your watch is fast. **5**	They are still in the middle of an exercise. **1**	🔔	Thank the students for their good work. **2**	Read as far as page 31. All clear? **1**	You are away next week. **5**	✋	☺	It is the last day of school before the summer break. **4**
Ask a student the time **3**	All the work you planned is finished **5**	🔔	Everybody was very active. **5**	Voluntary homework: workbook page 78. **2**	A room change on Friday. Meet outside the library. **3**	✋	☺	The Christmas vacation starts tomorrow. **5**
Your watch is slow. **1**	There's time to talk about the students' weekend plans. **4**	🔔	Excellent work. **4**	Do the rest of exercise 21. You'll check it next time. **3**	Meet in the language studio, not this room. **4**	✋	☺	The deadline for the essay is next Tuesday. **1**

Audio practice

1 Classroom intonation

🎧 1.1 Try to say the following greetings and goodbyes in a friendly and motivating way. Use a low-rising intonation. Then listen and repeat.

1 Good morning, everyone.
2 See you tomorrow.
3 Goodbye, Maria.
4 Bye-bye, everyone.
5 Hello there, Miss Lopez!
6 Have a nice weekend, everybody.
7 Hello again, all of you.
8 Cheerio now.
9 Good afternoon to you.
10 Hi, everybody.

🎧 1.2 Read the following sentences aloud and underline the word (or syllable) that has the main sentence stress (= *the tonic syllable*). Then listen and repeat.

1 How are you today, Paolo?
2 Have you all understood?
3 Who hasn't finished?
4 Does anybody know where Mia is?
5 Who was away last Friday?
6 And how are you, Birgit?
7 And have you all understood the idea?
8 Who hasn't done number 3?
9 Does anybody know why Tim's late?
10 Who wasn't here last time?

🎧 1.3 Read the following sentences aloud. Then listen and repeat.

1 Have you all understood? Is there anybody who hasn't understood?
2 I suppose you finished off the exercise at home. Did anybody not finish it at home?
3 No, I'm not teaching you French. I'm your new English teacher.
4 No, Mrs Schmidt isn't going to teach you English. I'm your new English teacher.
5 No, not Thursday morning. The deadline for your essays is Wednesday morning.
6 There's no hurry with your diaries, but the deadline for your essays is tomorrow.
7 I'm glad to hear you're feeling better, Jean. And how are you feeling, Lisa?
8 You were away last Tuesday and Wednesday. So that's two lessons you've missed.
9 I don't think we'll manage the whole text this lesson, so we'll finish it off next time.
10 Sorry, I didn't hear that? Did you say a quarter to or a quarter past?

🎧 **1.4** Read out the following instructions. Then make them more polite by adding 'please' and using a low-rising intonation. Then listen and check.

1 Try to hurry.
2 Finish this off at home.
3 Carry on with what you're doing.
4 Go out quietly.
5 Don't leave anything behind.
6 Put your textbooks away.
7 Stop what you're doing.
8 Go back to your places.

🎧 **1.5** Listen to some of examples of how *please* can be used when allocating tasks and nominating students. Then make up some more examples of your own.

1 Atsuko, the next one, please.
2 Yes, question 6. Harumi, please.
3 OK. Toshie, please. Number 7.
4 All right. The last one, please. Tokiko.

Task	Student
Number 3	Tim
The last one	Sally
Question 5	Ben
The next one	Jamie

2 Key sounds

🎤 🎧 **1.6** Read the following sentences aloud and identify examples of the sounds /θ/ and /ð/. Then listen to the model version and repeat.

1 That's the third time this week.
2 That will do for this time, thank you.
3 I'll go through this with you next Thursday.
4 I think you need more than three minutes on this exercise.
5 Do you think there's something the matter with Kathy?

3 Word stress

🎤 🎧 **1.7** Say the following words aloud and mark the stressed syllable. There are three types:

1 words stressed on the first syllable, for example, '*schedule*;
2 words stressed on the second syllable, *re'lax*;
3 words stressed on the third syllable, *elec'tricity*.

Then listen and check your answers.

1 register
2 alarm
3 vocabulary
4 corridor
5 excellent
6 apologies
7 success
8 museum
9 trainee
10 dialogue
11 biology
12 difficulty
13 history
14 substitute
15 report
16 introduce
17 geography
18 apologize
19 project (noun)
20 oversleep

4 Live lessons

You will hear some short extracts from different classroom situations. Listen to each extract and then answer the questions. Live lesson transcripts can be found on page 166.

1.8 Starting a lesson
1 What is special about the timing of this class?
2 When did the teacher last see her students?
3 What two short words does the teacher frequently use to check that the class is with her?
4 Why do you think the teacher chooses to begin with an account of her holiday trip?

1.9 Getting down to work
1 Why does the teacher greet his students twice?
2 What does the teacher talk about before getting down to work?
3 Have the students studied page 11 earlier?
4 The teacher uses two useful structures with the word *let*. What are they?

1.10 Outlining the lesson
1 Why does the teacher wait for everyone to be quiet?
2 What two things are planned for the lesson?
3 How does the teacher check that the students have understood?
4 What phrase does the teacher use to hear the students' reaction to the plan?

1.11 Making announcements
1 What two subjects does this teacher teach through English?
2 What will happen when? Match the information:
   A Wednesday September 28th   1 History test
   B Thursday September 29th   2 Less serious lesson
   C Friday September 30th   3 Extra history lesson
3 Why does the teacher review the arrangements?
4 Fill in the missing words:

   You've got another lesson on Friday _____ the others don't and

   I want you to be _____ .

1.12 Starting an activity
1 What will happen at the end of the class? Why do you think the teacher makes this decision?
2 Do the students know the Spanish for *before*?
3 When else is Spanish used? How does the teacher react?
4 How does the teacher prompt her students into answering her questions about homework?
5 What phrase does the teacher use to stop Julia talking?

🎧 **1.13** Ending a lesson

1 The teacher gives a lot of information to her students at the end of this lesson. Arrange the following ideas to match the order in which the teacher mentions them (she may use different words).

a Goodbye.
b Return the dice.
c Stop playing.
d Well done!
e See me at the end.
f The homework is on the blackboard.
g Improve your concentration.
h Your homework is on page 50.
i We've finished for today.

Involving the learners 2

Getting students to join in

Students only need to say a single word or a short phrase, or sometimes simply to react with a gesture, to show they have understood the phrases in this section. You can make understanding even easier by developing and systematically using various signs and gestures to accompany what you say. In this way students get used to actively listening to English and the barrier to speaking is lowered. Remember, though, that language skills develop slowly, so patience is needed. Each successful interaction is a sign of progress and a stimulus to continue. It is important to use different group sizes for various activities. This will affect the way students work together. The classroom phrases connected with group work can have a positive influence on class solidarity and sense of community.

1 Taking part
Can you all hear?
I'll speak a bit louder.
Can you see all right?
Is that better?
Has everybody got a pencil?

2 Taking turns
In turns.
Your turn.
Who's going to start?
Who's next?
Who hasn't had a turn?
Not you again.
Let's give someone else a chance.

3 Student choices
Who would like to do this?
Are there any volunteers?
Which group do you want to join?
You can decide.

4 Working in groups
Work in groups.
Find yourself a partner.
Could you join this group?
Work on your own.
One of you ... , the other (one) ...

Points to think and talk about

1 Is it necessary to speak more slowly and more clearly if you are using English to run your class? Do you modify your English in any way when speaking to students?
2 What are the benefits of slowing down your speed of speech? Are there any possible long-term problems? How else can you help your students understand and adjust to more normal spoken language?
3 If you want to make sure that all the students have understood and can take part equally in the lesson (for example, seeing, or hearing properly), what kind of signs and gestures could you use to accompany your words?
4 Do you prefer to give turns randomly or in a particular order? What are the advantages and disadvantages of each way?
5 Think about a typical lesson. How many opportunities do the students have to make choices? What kinds of things can they choose?
6 Pair work and group work give students more time for communicating and exchanging information. Can you think of any other benefits?
7 Do you think pair work and group work is always more motivating? What have been your own experiences of group work, both as a teacher and as a student?
8 Imagine that you have asked the class to work in pairs. Unfortunately, as is so often the case, there is an odd number of students. Think of some solutions to the problem. How do these solutions affect your role as a teacher?
9 Groups work at different speeds and so complete their tasks at different times. How can you prepare for this situation?
10 One popular idea, especially with younger learners, has been for teachers to give their students an English name. What do you think about this idea? Could it work with older students, even going so far as to give them a new identity?

Language to think about

1 What would you say to check that all the students can hear and see what is going on?
2 How many ways can you think of for saying, *Read one after another*?
3 If you needed volunteers to help you, how would you ask?
4 What phrases would you use to break the class up into pairs and groups?
5 Are you clear about the use of *one of you ... and the other one ...* in English?
6 What would you say if you had to make sure all the groups had an equal number of students?
7 What would happen if you told your students to *pair off*?
8 Think of different ways of politely saying *No*.

Classroom English vocabulary to collect

1 Words connected with educational administration in your country, including the names of different types of school. (For example, *ministry of education, elementary, secondary*)
2 School Staff (For example, *librarian, school secretary, caretaker, cook, deputy head, technician*).

Key to symbols:		
ⓘ Idiomatic phrase	⇨	Pedagogical pointer
Ⓢ Student reply	»	Cross-reference
Ⓧ Typical mistake	⌒	Listen to the CD
Ⓛ Language comment	RECORD	Record yourself

Taking part

1 Can you all hear?
*Can you hear **all right/clearly/properly/OK**?*
*Can you hear **at the back/in the corner**?*
Am I speaking loud enough?
*If you can't hear, come a bit **nearer/closer**.*
Come and sit at the front if you can't hear.

2 I'll speak a bit louder.
I'll speak up (a bit).
*I'll try and speak more **clearly/slowly**.*

3 Can you see all right?
*Can you all see **properly/clearly/OK**?*
Can everybody see?
*Can you see the **picture/board/screen**?*

4 Is that better?
(Is that) any better?
*Is **this/that** more like it?*
***What/How** about now?*
Any improvement?

5 Has everybody got a pencil?
Have you all got a sheet of paper?
Has everybody got everything they need?
Is there anybody without a textbook?

---

1 » If you are playing a DVD, MP3 file, CD or cassette, you can also ask:
*Is it **clear/loud** enough?*
Is the sound clear enough?
*Is the volume **OK/all right/fine**?*
I'll turn up the volume.

⌊ See Unit 5, A3 for more phrases dealing with educational technology.

---

3 ⌊ When showing a DVD, or using a data projector or overhead transparency, you can ask:
*Is the picture **clear/sharp/in focus**?*
Can you all read the text?

ⓘ *Has everybody the possibility to see?* ✗

5 ⌊ For other phrases to do with practical classroom problems, see Unit 3, A.

If you can't hear, come a bit closer

Taking turns

1 In turns.
In turn, starting with Laura.
Take it in turns, starting here.
One after the other, please.
One at a time, please.
One by one.

2 Your turn.
It's your turn (to read), Tim.
Now you, Anna.
You next.
You're next.
Next (one), please.
Go ahead, Ibrahim.

3 Who's going to start?
Who's first?
*Who wants to **start/begin**?*

4 Who's next?
*Whose **turn/go** is it next?*
Who is the next one to try?
Who's next to go?

5 Who hasn't had a turn?
Anybody (still) not had a turn?
Anybody else?
Who else is there?
Who's left?
Who hasn't been out to the board?
*Have I **missed/forgotten somebody/anybody**?*

6 Not you again.
*You've already had a **turn/go**.*
You've been out once already.
You did it last time.
*You had a **turn/go** in the last lesson.*

7 Let's give someone else a chance.
*Let's give someone else a **turn/go/try**.*
Now let's have someone else (try it).
Let someone else have a turn.

---

1 ⌊ Additional phrases.
The rest (of you), wait (for) your turn.
*Not all **together/at the same time/at once**.*

⌊ Notice how the word 'turn' is used:

Please	take turns	reading.
	take it in turns	to read.

---

4 Ⓢ *Is it my turn?*
Am I next?
Shall I start?
Should I go first?

---

6 ⊗ *You were already.* ✗

Student choices

1 Who would like to do this?
Who wants to come out?
Who would like to go first?
Who wants to start?
Who wants to come out and write that for me?

2 Are there any volunteers?
Any volunteers to try the next one?
Anybody willing to clean the board for me?
Is there anybody interested in helping me clear up?

3 Which group do you want to join?
Which team do you want to be in?
Which topic would you like to take?

4 You can decide.
*You can **pick/choose**.*

---

1 ⌊ The choice of phrase will depend on the activity:
*Who **wants/would like** to write that on the board?*
Who wants to be Mrs Brown?
Who would like to read the part of John?
Who wants to act as secretary?

⊗ See Unit 3, Classroom essentials (page 66) for more practice with *want* and *like*.

⊗ *Who comes and writes that for me?* ✗

2 ⌊ *Any volunteers + to +* infinitive:

| *Any volunteers* | *to read (the part of) Sherlock Holmes?* |
| | *to clean the blackboard?* |

Notice the use of the verb *to volunteer* in the following:
*Is there anybody who wants to volunteer **to stay behind/for this**?*

⌊ You can also say how many volunteers you need:
Three volunteers. All right, Toni, Mari and Emile.
I need three helpers. OK, you three.
If nobody is willing, then I'll have to choose somebody.

Ⓢ *Me!*
I'll do it.
Let me do it.

⌊ Notice the short form of question that can be used with *anyone/anybody*. See 🎧 2.3

---

3 ⌊ Typical classroom choices for students include the following:

1 Choosing an English name (with younger students or when doing role play activities):
Which English name do you want?
Which name would you like (to have)?
*Which name do you **like best/prefer**?*
Do you want to be John or Mark?
Which part do you want to play?

2 Choosing a group or team:
Do you want to be in Juan's team?
Which team do you want to be in?
Is there anybody (in particular) you would like to work with?

3 Choosing a topic:
Which subject do you want to work on?
Is there a particular topic you are interested in?

There are too many in this group!

Find yourself a partner

Working in groups

1 Work in groups.

*Get into groups. Three students **in/to** each group.*
For this activity, I'd like you to work in fours.
*Could you **work/get into/make/form** groups of **three/five**?*
*I'd like you to **arrange/divide** yourselves into **two teams/
threes**.*
*I'll **divide/split** the class up into five groups.*

2 Find yourself a partner.

*Work together with **a friend/your neighbour/the person
next to you**.*
You two together, and you two, and so on.
Go and sit with Lahcen and make a pair.
Team up with two other people to make a group of three.
Has everybody got a partner?
*Is there anybody **on their own/left over/without a partner**?*
Haven't you got anyone to work with?

3 Could you join this group?

You'll have to join Julia's group.
Lena and Marco, you can join group 4.
Could you work with Mikael today?
Move over to this group, Melanie.
Can you team up with Sara?
We need one more in this group.

4 Work on your own.

*Work by **yourself/yourselves**.*
Everybody work individually.
Try to work independently.

**5 One of you will read the question, the other one will
answer it.**

One of you will read the story aloud, the rest of you will listen.
*One person in the group is the secretary, the others must
discuss the problem.*
One of you is A, the other (one) is B.

---

1 ⓘ Notice also:
I want you to pair off.

Ⅼ You can also specify the activity:
I want you to do some reading in groups.
I'd like you to work on this in threes.
*Here are some exercises for you to work on in **groups/pairs/threes**.*
This is a task that you will have to cooperate on.

Ⅼ Sometimes it is necessary to rearrange classroom furniture:
*Turn your chair round to **make a pair/face each other**.*
*Turn round so that you can **see/talk to** Mia.*

⊗ See Unit 3, A4 and A5 for more phrases related to the classroom
environment.

⇨ It is often more practical to give all the necessary instructions
for an activity before letting students break up into groups. A
simple demonstration will also speed things up. Try to teach any
language that your students will need to work effectively in a
group; for example, *Is it my turn?*, *Shall I do this?*

---

2 ⊗ *Find a pair.* ✗   *Find a partner.* ✓   *Make a pair.* ✓

3 Ⅼ If necessary, explain why you are assigning students to certain
groups:
We have an odd number (in this group).
We have one too many here.
There are too many in this group.
Four only to a group!
There should only be three people in each group.

Ⓢ *Should I join this group?*
Is it OK if I work with Timo?
Is it all right if I change places with Maya?

---

4 Ⅼ If students are doing a test, you can add:
*Don't disturb **your neighbour/the person next to you**.*
Concentrate on your own work.
There's no need to discuss it with your neighbour.
Don't copy from your neighbour's sheet.
No cheating, please.

Ⅼ If you don't want students to help their fellow students, you can
say:
Don't help her.
*Let her try (it) **on her own/by herself**.*
Just you, Maija.
*You **on your own/by yourself**, Mikko.*
Let's see if he can manage without your help.

---

5 ⊗ *the ~~other~~ ... the other (one) ...* ✗
Notice that in English the word *other* always refers to the
second mentioned person, object or group. The word *one* (for
example, *one of you*, *one group*) refers to the first mentioned
person, object or group.

Ⅼ If the activity in pairs or groups involves different roles, you can
say:

First, you can ...,

... then			*round.*
... after that	*you can*	*change*	*parts.*
... later on		*swap*	*over.*

It is useful to add:
*Make sure everybody **gets/has** a turn/go**.*

Classroom etiquette

The classroom is a lively environment, full of events and interaction, some predictable, some surprising. A lot of classroom situations offer the students a chance to hear and use phrases that are useful in the real world beyond the classroom walls. This is especially true of those phrases related to everyday social politeness. If you use such phrases with your students in a natural way, without exaggeration, the language in the classroom will come to resemble ordinary social interaction more and more. At the same time the social dimension of language becomes part of the students' language learning experience.

1 Birthdays and holidays
What's the date today?
Happy birthday!
Have a good holiday.
The same to you.

2 Wishes
Bless you!
Good luck!
Congratulations!

3 Thanking
Thank you.
Here you are.
Thanks for your help.

4 Apologizing and not catching what someone has said
Sorry.
That's all right.
Pardon?
I'm sorry to hear that.

5 Leaving the classroom
Excuse me for a moment.
Excuse me, could I get past?

Points to think and talk about

1 An important part of English language learning in school is the study of English-speaking cultures. What kind of British or American festivals, for example, could you present to your students? Would it be useful to celebrate these as part of your annual teaching programme? Would the age of the students influence your choice?
2 Which aspects of everyday life and social interaction in English-speaking cultures do you think your students find strange? Is it important to teach these aspects?
3 How would you explain these cultural differences to your students?
4 As a teacher of English, should you follow the etiquette rules of your own classroom culture, or try to introduce those associated with English-speaking cultures?
5 How does your own culture and language express politeness? Do you think it differs from typically British or American usage?
6 Is it the custom to celebrate students' birthdays at school?
7 And what about the achievements of individual students (for example, playing in a soccer team)?
8 Do you consider yourself a speaker of British or American English? Do you encourage your students to use a particular variety?
9 Do you think it is a good idea to allow your students to hear all possible varieties of English?
10 In an advanced class, would you teach the key differences between the varieties of English?

Language to think about

1 Think of some occasions in the classroom when you might say
   a *Thank you*
   b *Sorry*
   c *Good luck!*
   d *Excuse me.*
2 When would you use *same to you*?
3 How do you use the phrase *help yourself* in English?
4 Is *here you are* the same as *you are here*?
5 Think of the typical holidays in your school's annual calendar. What would be an appropriate wish or greeting for each of them?
6 *Mind* is a very useful word in English. How many different ways of using it can you think of?
7 What would you say to your class if one of your students had won a national sporting championship?
8 Can you use *whether* correctly in English?

Classroom English vocabulary to collect

1 The job titles of the people who work in your school. (For example, *caretaker, nurse*)
2 Some of the special events and days in your school year. (For example, *summer holidays, school reports, graduation*)

B1
Birthdays and holidays

1 What's the date today?
What day/date is it today?
What's today's date?
What's special about today?
What makes today a special day?

2 Happy birthday!
Many happy returns (of the day), Tessa.
Rebeca has her/a birthday today.
Anna is twelve today. Let's sing 'Happy Birthday'.
Congratulations on your 18th birthday, Jeanne.

3 Have a good holiday.
I'd like to wish you all a very happy holiday.
Have a good holiday!
Merry Christmas (to you)!
Have a nice Christmas!
Enjoy your Christmas!
I hope you all have a good Christmas.
All the (very) best for Christmas and the New Year.
Happy New Year/Easter/May Day!
Enjoy your autumn break.
Have a great vacation! (AE)
Make the most of your winter holiday.

4 Thank you. The same to you.
Thanks, same to you.
Likewise. Thank you.
And you!
You, too.

---

1 📖 In British English dates are read aloud as follows:
December 9th = December the ninth.
9th December = the ninth of December.
Compare with: *December nine (AE)*

In modern usage, the dates are written:
9 December, 2006 or *December 9, 2006*
Short forms are: *9/12/05 (BE), 12/9/05 (AE)*.

📖 Correct replies to the question *What date is it?*:
It's December the 9th today.
Today is the 9th of December.
Today's date is December the 9th.

---

3 📖 *Season's greetings* (especially in writing) is suitable for non-Christian or multi-faith classes.

4 ⨂ Thanks, the same ~~for~~ you. ✗ *Thank you, ~~the same~~. ✗

B2
Wishes

1 Bless you!
(God) bless you!
Gesundheit! (AE)

2 Good luck!
Best of luck!
Break a leg! (AE)
I hope you win/do well.
I hope you get through/pass the test.
Best of luck with/for your driving test!

3 Congratulations!
Well done!
Congratulations!
Good job! (AE)
Way to go! (AE)
I think we should congratulate Matti on winning a silver medal.
I'd like to offer my congratulations to you all on passing the exam.

---

1 📖 In English-speaking cultures, these expressions are used when someone sneezes. They indicate that you are concerned about the other person's health. You can add to this with:
I hope you're not catching/getting a cold.
It sounds as though you're getting the flu.

---

3 ⓘ *Give me a high five! (AE)*.

📖 Sometimes, though, you will have to offer your commiserations:
Hard/Tough/Bad luck!
Never mind!
Better luck next time!
Too bad!
What a pity/shame!
That's life.
That's the way it goes.

Thanking

1 Thank you.
Thank you very much.
Many thanks.
*Thanks **a lot/a million**.*
Thanks for that.
Thanks for the idea.

2 Here you are.
There you are.
Take this.

3 Thanks for your help.
Thanks for helping.
*It was very **kind/nice/good** of you to help. Thank you.*
I (really do) appreciate /əˈpriːʃeɪt/ your help.
I (really) am very grateful for your help.
*That's **lovely/fine/great**. Thank you.*

---

1 ⓘ In colloquial British English, notice:
Cheers.
Ta. /taː/

⅃ Notice the following uses of *thank you*:
Enjoy your holiday! – Thank you, I will.
*Have some more. – No, I won't. **Thank you anyway/Thanks all the same**.*

Ⓢ Typical replies include:
That's all right.
Not at all.
Don't mention it.
Think nothing of it.
You're welcome.
Any time.
No problem.
Be my guest.

---

2 ⅃ Use these phrases when giving or handing over something.
Other phrases:
One for you.
This is for you.
Take it. It's for you.
Here it is.

ⓘ You will also hear:
There you go.

⇒ Make frequent use of these phrases when you are handing out material, exercises and handouts, and encourage the students to use them.

⅃ If you want the students to take a copy from a pile, you can say:
Help yourself to a copy (from the pile).
***Grab/Get/Find** (yourself) a handout.*

Or ask a student to help:
*Take **one/this** to Sam, please.*
Pass this back to Beatriz, please.
*Could you **give/take** this book to Felix, please?*

⊗ Remember not to use *please* on its own when you are giving or handing over something. However, you can use *please* with an imperative, for example:
Help yourself, please.

3 ⅃ *Thank you + for (doing) something:*
Thank you for cleaning the blackboard.
Thank you for your help moving the desks.

⅃ Notice these phrases:
Thank you for lending me your book. = Thanks for the loan of your book.
*I'd be **grateful/thankful** if you could help me.*
This is all thanks to you.
Thanks to you, we got the computer to work.

⇒ There is a whole range of small classroom jobs that you can ask the students to help you with: distributing and collecting handouts and exercises, cleaning the board, delivering messages to other teachers, tidying up after a lesson, opening and closing windows, putting lights on and off, operating equipment, and carrying it back to the staffroom. All of these tasks are natural contexts for asking and thanking.

Apologizing and not catching what someone has said

1 Sorry.
I'm **very/terribly/awfully/so** sorry (about that).
I am sorry.
Sorry, that was my fault.
I (do) beg your pardon.

2 That's all right.
It doesn't matter.
It's **alright/OK**.
No problem.
No **damage/harm** done.

3 Pardon?
Sorry? | What was that (again)?
What? | What did you say?
I beg your pardon? | Excuse me? (AE)
I'm sorry. I didn't (quite) **hear/catch** what you said.

4 I'm sorry to hear that.
Oh dear, that's a pity.
What a **pity/shame**.

1 Ⓛ Apologies generally use a falling intonation.

Ⓛ You may have to apologize for mistakes in handouts, textbooks, and on the board:
I'm sorry. I've made a mistake on the board.
There's a spelling mistake in exercise 5.
There's a misprint on the handout.
I'm sorry, I didn't notice it.
It should **say/read/be**:
The correct version is:

3 Ⓛ These questions are used to check that you have heard or understood correctly. They use a high rising intonation. Notice that the main sentence stress in the phrase *What did you say?* is on the word *what*. See 🎧 2.1.

Ⓛ Expressions with the same basic meaning include:
I missed that. What did you say?
I missed the beginning of what you said.
Sorry, I **can't/couldn't** hear you.
Speak up.
Could you repeat what you said?
Could you say it a little louder?
Could you speak more slowly, please?

If the class is noisy, you may have to add:
The rest of you, **keep/be** quiet.
I can't hear **for the noise/with all this noise**.

⨠ See Unit 3, B2 for more phrases dealing with classroom noise.

4 Ⓛ If you are not feeling too well, you can apologize to the students in advance. Notice the use of *I'm afraid* and *I'm sorry*.
I'm afraid I'm not feeling **very/too** well today.
I'm afraid I can't speak any louder.
I seem to be losing my voice, I'm afraid.
I'm sorry, I have (a bit of) a headache. /ˈhedeɪk/

Leaving the classroom

1 Excuse me for a moment.
Would you excuse me for a **while/moment**?
Please excuse me. I've just got to go next door for a moment.
I'll be back in a moment.
Carry on with the exercise while I'm away.
I'll leave you to it.

2 Excuse me.
Excuse me. Could I get past?
May I pass, please?
Do you mind moving?
Could you step aside, please?
Could I just squeeze past? Thank you.

1 🔊 Your students, too, may have to leave early. When appropriate, help the students to use the following phrases, for example:
Could I leave ten minutes before the end?
Do you mind/Is it all right if I leave at twenty to?
Can I go to the **toilet/loo**?
Can I use the **bathroom/washroom/restroom**? (AE)
I'm not feeling very well.
I have to go and see the school nurse.

2 Ⓛ In the classroom situation, *excuse me* is used:
—when asking politely to get past somebody;
—when going between two people who are talking to each other;
—when gaining attention before asking a question;
—when apologizing (especially AE).

Notice also:
Sorry to bother you, but ...

Ⓛ There are more direct and less polite expressions:
Mind out!
Mind out of the way.
Out of the way now!
Get out of **my/the** way.
You're in **the/my** way.
Shift!
Move!
Budge!

Ⓛ The following may also be useful in a typical classroom:
You're blocking the **way/aisle**. /aɪl/
I can't get past for your bag.
Make room for another seat.
Stand to one side.

🗩 You're ~~on~~ the way. ✗

SECTION C

We believe in the motto 'Success breeds success'. Motivation and constant encouragement are central to successful learning, and probably even more so in language learning. That's why it is important to give positive feedback and support to all of your students as often as possible. The short, simple phrases in this section help the lesson to move forward fluently and efficiently, but at the same time they create a positive and encouraging atmosphere. The phrases can be used with the whole class, or with groups, or with individual students. The important thing is to encourage every individual student equally and fairly. This reinforces class solidarity and helps to shape your own classroom culture.

1 Saying yes
Yes.
That's right.
Excellent.
Well done.

2 Encouraging
Not quite right.
Have another try.
There's no hurry.
That's better.
Keep it up.

3 Saying no
No, that's wrong.
Could be.
You tried your best.

4 Complaining
Come on!
You can do better than this.

Confirming and encouraging

Points to think and talk about

1 Think back to your own language learning experiences. What sort of feedback did your teacher(s) give you?
2 Now think about yourself as a teacher. Do you think you give more positive or more negative feedback?
3 Which language do you use to give feedback and encouragement?
4 Do you think there are cultural differences in how much positive feedback teachers give to their students? Is public praise (or even shaming) a part of your classroom culture?
5 Do you give feedback differently, depending on whether you are dealing with individual students, pairs, groups, or the whole class?
6 How can you tell whether the feedback you give is effective? How could you make it even more effective?
7 Recasting is a useful technique when correcting a student's mistakes. Instead of drawing attention to the mistake and interrupting the student, you repeat or rephrase what the student intended to say in a correct form, as part of the conversation. For example, the student says *I did went to cinema*. Your reaction: *OK, that's great. I went to the cinema, too. What did you see?* What are the advantages of this technique?
8 Which are more important to correct, mistakes in structure (for example, verb forms, prepositions, articles) or mistakes that affect communication (for example, mispronunciations, use of the wrong word)? Does it depend on the type of activity? Which do you focus on?

Language to think about

1 If a student answers a question correctly, what do you say?
2 And if the answer is wrong, what do you say?
3 How many different ways can you think of for saying *Good*?
4 How would you encourage a student not to give up on a difficult task?
5 When would you tell the students to *pull their socks up*?
6 What do you say if you're not sure whether a student's answer is correct?
7 When would you say: *That was spot on!*?
8 What signs and gestures could you develop to encourage students and to signal that their answers are correct?

Classroom English vocabulary to collect

The typical events of a normal school day. (For example, *break, lunch hour*)

Saying yes

1 Yes.
Good.
Fine.
Right.

2 That's right.
(You're) quite right.
Right you are.
Correct.

3 Excellent.
(That's) very good.
Very nice.
That's great/brilliant/fantastic.

4 Well done.
Excellent/nice/good work.
Nicely done/read.
You managed very well.
You did a good job there.
You made a very good job of that.
I was pleased with the way you did that exercise.

---

1 Ⓛ These single words simply confirm that the student's answer is correct. They do not in themselves carry a strong message of encouragement or praise. Very often, for example in checking an exercise, you can simply nod and say *hm-hm* or *uh-huh*.

2 Ⓛ If you are explaining or demonstrating something and you see that a student has grasped the idea, you can say:
Yes, you've got it.
You've got the idea/point.
That's it.
Exactly.

Ⓘ *(That was) spot on!* = That was exactly right.
You've cracked it = You've understood the idea.
Bingo! = You've understood, you've done it correctly (and I'm pleased).
You seem to have got the hang of it.

Ⓛ Other longer expressions:
That's exactly the point.
That's just what I was looking for.
That's precisely the answer I wanted.

Ⓛ If the student is carrying out an activity correctly, you can say:
That's the way.
That's the way to do it.
That's it.

---

3 ⇒ There are many expressions you can use to encourage and reward your students. You may find some of them inappropriate for your own class, but remember that in foreign language teaching they are a vital part of motivation and help to create a different world for learning. The key thing is to use them systematically and equally, especially when circulating in the class.

Ⓘ How you use the following expressions of praise will depend on many factors: the age of your students, the general atmosphere in the class, and the type of activity:

Marvellous!	*Nice work!*
Magnificent!	*Great stuff!*
Fabulous!	*I like that*
Sensational!	*Cool!*
Wonderful!	*Right on! (AE)*
Terrific!	*Way to go! (AE)*
Wow!	*Awesome! (AE)*
Outstanding!	*Good job! (AE)*
Nice going!	

With younger and primary students you can say:
*Good **boy/girl**!*

Ⓛ Use the following to give more precise feedback:
That sounds good to me.
I can't see anything wrong with that.
Perfect!
That's perfectly correct.
There's nothing wrong with your answer.
You're absolutely right.
What you said was perfectly all right.
You didn't make a single mistake.
Couldn't be better.
I couldn't have given a better answer myself.

⊗ Very ~~well~~. ✗

Do not use *Very well*, when you mean *Very good*.

---

4 Ⓘ *Nice going!*
Good for you!
You did it!
Not (too) bad!
Good thinking!

⇒ It's a good idea to finish each class with some general positive feedback and encouragement. See also Unit 1, C3, note 4.
I'm really pleased with you.
You've all tried really hard today.
What a great piece of work from everybody!
*That was a **wonderful/first-class** piece of work.*

Well done!

Encouraging

1 Not quite right.
Almost (right).
That's almost it.
*You're **almost/nearly** there.*
You were almost right that time.
Nearly.
*You've **almost/just about** got it.*
You're so close.
***Good/Nice** try.*

2 Have another try.
*Have another **go/look**.*
It doesn't hurt to try.
Do your best.
Think about it again.
Are you sure?
Are you happy with your answer?
(Do you want to) try (it) again.
What should the answer be?

3 There's no hurry.
*There's no need to **rush/hurry**.*
We have plenty of time.
Take your time.
In your own time.
Take it easy.
Take it a little more slowly.
Not so fast.

4 That's better.
That's (so) much better.
That's a lot better.
That's (a bit) more like it.
That's a real improvement.
I knew you could do it!

5 Keep it up.
Keep up the good work.

---

1 ⓘ *You're on the right **lines/track**.*
You're halfway there.
*Just one **little slip/small mistake**.*
One more time and you'll have it.

Ⳑ Use these phrases to encourage your students to try:
Maybe this will help you.
What if I give you a clue?
I'll help you if you get stuck.

Or you can warn them about possible problems:
*This one seems to **have given/be giving** everybody a lot of trouble.*
*This is a **tricky/nasty** one.*
*I'm not surprised you **got this one wrong/found this hard**.*

2 Ⳑ Other encouraging expressions:
Go on. Have a try.
Have a guess if you don't know.
Take a guess at it.
Don't give up.
Go for it! (AE)

ⓘ *Have a **go/bash/shot/crack** (at it)!*
*Give it a **bash/shot/go/try**.*
*Do you want to **take/have** another **try/shot/bash/crack** at it?*

---

3 Ⳑ You may be more interested in getting the student to communicate than in accuracy:
*Don't worry about **the spelling/your pronunciation**.*
*The **main/most important** thing is to speak.*

---

5 ⇨ More general encouragement and feedback can be given to individuals while you are circulating and to the whole class:
*You read **very/really/quite** well.*
You have (a) very good pronunciation.
*Your pronunciation is **very good/excellent/outstanding/fantastic**.*
You sound very English.
*You **speak/read** very fluently.*
You've been working hard and it shows.
I can tell you've been practising.
All your hard work is paying off.
You deserve a pat on the back.
You have all made a lot of progress.
You're getting better all the time.
You've improved no end.
I'm really impressed with your progress.

Older students will appreciate more detailed individual feedback on their progress and skills:
*You still have some trouble with **your spelling/irregular verbs**.*
You find it difficult to read aloud.
Reading aloud is difficult for you.
You need some more practice with these words.
You'll have to spend more time practising this.

Remember, though, to add an encouraging comment:
*Not to worry, it'll **improve/get better/get easier**.*
Don't worry about it. It'll get better in time.
Hang (on) in there! = Don't give up.

⇨ Some teachers like to put encouraging mottos on their classroom walls, for example:
Believe in yourself!
Never give up!
Keep trying!
Practice makes perfect!
Always do your best.

Saying no

1 No, that's wrong.
Not really.
Unfortunately not.
I'm afraid that's not quite right.
You can't say that, I'm afraid.
You can't use that word here.
Good try, but not quite right.
Not exactly.
That wasn't the answer I was looking for.

2 Could be.
It depends.
It might be, I suppose.
In a way, perhaps.
Sort of, yes.
Well, er …

3 You tried your best.
Nice try anyway.
Don't worry about it.
Don't worry about making mistakes.
*You learn **through/from** your mistakes.*

---

1 ⇨ Recasting is a technique for correcting students' errors (see page 36). Its main benefit is that it takes attention away from the actual error and encourages the student to speak.

  ✗ That was a wrong answer. ✗

  Although there may be several wrong answers, English tends to use the definite article with *right* and *wrong*.

---

2 ⟫ You can ask for additional ideas and suggestions. See also Unit 4, C5:
Has anybody else got an answer?
*Any **more/other ideas/suggestions**?*
*Did anybody come up with **another answer/something else**?*

Pull your socks up!

Complaining

1 Come on!
Try harder.
You can do this!
A bit more effort, please!
Come on with you!

2 You can do better than this.
Is that the best you can do?
Better than that!
Can't you do any better than that?
I'm sure that's not the best you can do.
I think there's (some) room for improvement.
I know you're capable of better work.

---

1 ⓘ *Pull your socks up! = Try to improve.*
   ***Wake/Buck** your ideas up!*
   Put some effort into it!

  ⌐ If you are disappointed with a student's work, you can say:
   That wasn't very good, was it?

I was	rather somewhat a bit	disappointed	with	that. your work.

I wasn't	too very	happy satisfied pleased	with	the way you did that. what you wrote.

⇨ In addition to giving positive feedback, you should also be ready to push your students to accept new challenges, especially if you believe them capable of better or more demanding work. In such cases you need to provide inspiration rather than open criticism. The following phrases may be useful:
This group has some good ideas, but what about over here?
Some of you are working very well, but some others need to try harder.
I'd like you all to think about this, not just one or two of you.

---

2 ⇨ If you have expectations about how something should be done, you must communicate these expectations clearly to the students, as well as giving precise instructions. The following expressions are typical:
I hope you do it better next time.
There will be no interrupting from now on.

In future	I want		bring your textbook.
When you try this again	I would like		prepare some questions.
The next time we do this	I expect	you to	read the passage at home.
	I shall expect		learn the vocabulary.
Next time From now on	I prefer		do your homework on time.

Classroom essentials

ASKING QUESTIONS (1)

Yes/No questions

1 Asking questions in the classroom

In your work as a teacher, you have to perform various roles. In Unit 1 we looked at your role as a *ringmaster* (i.e. organizing learning and giving instructions), but you also spend a lot of time in the role of a *quizmaster* (i.e. asking questions and responding to answers). This is also a very important role since effective use of question-and-answer techniques has always been a fundamental part of the teaching and learning process.

A traditional way of classifying questions in language teaching is according to the grammatical form of the question, so-called *Yes/No, Or,* and *Wh-* questions:

Yes/No   *Have you finished?*
Or   *Do you prefer working in pairs or on your own?*
Wh-   *Who would like to write that up for me?*

But classroom questions can be classified in a number of other ways. For example, according to who asks the question: the teacher or the student. The question *Why is this wrong?* has a very different meaning if one of your students asks it. We should try to remember that students' questions can often be just as valuable for learning as those that you ask. Students' questions, for example, may highlight problems that you have overlooked in planning the lesson.

Another perhaps more valuable approach to classroom questions is to divide your questions into three main types according to how closely they resemble question-asking in the real world, as follows:

A Questions where you do not know the answer beforehand. For want of a better term, such questions can be called **authentic questions**. Typical examples can be found in normal classroom situations (for example, organizational problems) or when you are asking for new information, opinions, and reactions:

Has everybody got a book?   *Are you all ready to begin?*
Who hasn't finished yet?   *Do you agree with Selma or Pedro?*
Who is your favourite singer?   *What did you think of that story?*

B Questions where you know the answer in advance, although a student is initially expected to supply it. You may also be looking for answers in line with a particular argument. These can be called **pedagogical questions** (sometimes called **display questions** because students have a chance to display their knowledge). Typical examples of this type are language-related and comprehension questions:

What's the past tense of 'to go'?   *Is this correct?*
What's the answer to number 2?   *Are the men running or walking in picture 1?*

C In addition, you may sometimes ask questions where it is not clear whether you are asking because you don't know the answer and are interested, or whether the question merely rehearses an everyday situation or language structure. These questions could be called **rehearsal questions**.

How are you feeling today, Mark?   *Is it raining today?*
What is the date today?

As a language teacher, you should be interested in increasing the amount of genuinely communicative language in the classroom. For this reason, type A questions, authentic questions, are crucially important. You will have noticed that the questions listed in Units 1 and 2 of this book are precisely of this kind. Nevertheless, it is probably true to say that pedagogical and rehearsal questions, particularly those based on unit texts and textbook activities, predominate in the classroom. We will take a closer look at these and questioning techniques in Units 4 and 6.

The grammar of questions in English is complex and experience shows that this is an area where mistakes frequently occur. In this unit we examine *Yes/No* questions and question tags.

2 Normal and abbreviated *Yes/No* questions

- *Yes/No* questions are usually said with a high-rising intonation on the tonic syllable:

Can you swim?	*Doesn't Watson like lettuce?*
Is it going to rain?	*Don't you know the answer?*
Was that too easy?	*Haven't you finished yet?*

» See 🎧 2.2.

- Notice the word order in the alternative longer negative form:

  Does Watson not like lettuce?
  Do you not know the answer?
  Have you not finished yet?

- Notice that *Yes/No* questions related to everyday classroom management are very often abbreviated, with the main verb disappearing. This applies to both affirmative and negative questions:

Does anybody want to try number 1?	→ *Anybody want to try number 1?*
Is there anybody who hasn't got a book?	→ *Anybody not got a book?*
Does anybody not understand?	→ *Anybody not understand?*

» See 🎧 2.3.

- Sometimes abbreviation reduces the question to just one or two words. Notice the high rising intonation:

Can anybody do this?	→ *Anybody?*
Have you finished?	→ *Finished?*
Are you having problems?	→ *Problems?*
Are there any volunteers?	→ *Any volunteers?*
Are you having difficulties?	→ *Having difficulties?*

» See 🎧 2.3.

3 Question tags

- Question tags (*isn't it?*, *haven't you?*, etc) are very much a part of everyday spoken English and as such they should be used in the classroom. Notice the differences in intonation:

- A falling intonation on the tag itself suggests that you are stating a fact and that you assume your listener will agree:

  Well done, everyone. That wasn't so difficult, was ↘it?
  If I remember correctly, we finished this exercise last time, didn't ↘we?

- A high-rising intonation on the tag suggests surprise or that it is a genuine question:

  You all look confused. It wasn't so difficult, ↗was it?
  Surely you remember! We did this last time, ↗didn't we?

» See 🎧 2.4–2.6

- There is another question form that resembles the high-rising tag, but it is simply an alternative word order for asking the same question. Once again, there are two possible intonation patterns: falling (you expect the answer 'yes') and rising (you are really asking). Notice that these questions can also be abbreviated:

  Have you finished? = *You've finished, have you?* = *Finished, have you?*
  Are you listening? = *You're listening, are you?* = *Listening, are you?*
  Did you enjoy that? = *You enjoyed that, did you?* = *Enjoyed that, did you?*

» See 🎧 2.7

4 Indirect *Yes/No* questions

It is very typical in classroom question-and-answer activities to use indirect questions beginning with phrases like *Can you tell me ...?*, *Does anybody know ... ?* Word order in indirect questions can cause problems. For indirect *Yes/No* questions, notice:

> the use of **if** or **whether**,
> normal positive word order:

Direct question	Indirect question		
Are we on page 27?	Can you tell me		we are on page 27?
Is Juan ill?	Can anyone tell me		Juan is ill?
Is Carole at school today?	Do you know		Carole is at school today?
Did Elke miss her bus?	Does anybody know	if	Elke missed her bus?
Has Juris been absent?	Do you happen to know	whether	Juris has been absent?
Will it rain tomorrow?	Have you any idea		it will rain tomorrow?
	Can you guess		
	Hands up if you know		

- Notice than in everyday speech we quite often split the question into two parts and use question word order:

  Tell me, are we leaving straightaway?
  Will it rain tomorrow? Have you any idea?

Practice

🗣 **1** Expand the following abbreviated *Yes/No* questions into full questions.

1 Understood?
2 No pencil?
3 Problems?
4 Finished?
5 Anybody done question 7?
6 Anybody not finished?
7 Questions?
8 Anybody not know the answer?
9 The next one. Anders?
10 Not got a book?
11 Difficult?
12 Not listening?

2 Re-express the following questions as indirect *Yes/No* questions. Remember to use *if* or *whether*. Begin your question with a suitable phrase; for example, *Can you tell me, Does anyone know, Have you any idea.*

1 Does Aleksi speak Spanish?
2 Is she leaving next Saturday?
3 Have we done this exercise already?
4 Will Anne be away next time?
5 Did we stop on page 45 last time?
6 Had this ever happened before?
7 Did he do well in the test?
8 Is Riga the capital of Latvia?
9 Does Laura have a driving licence?
10 Will Tim be playing in next Saturday's match?

3 Now ask the same questions as in exercise 2 and use a tag question. *Aleksi speaks Spanish, doesn't he?*

4 Go through the phrases in section A again and notice how many authentic questions there are. How many authentic questions can you find in Unit 1, sections B2, B4, and C6?

RECORD 5 Record yourself teaching a class. Listen to the recording and count the number of authentic questions that you asked. Did you ask all types of questions (*Yes/No, Or* and *Wh-*)? Did you ask any indirect *Yes/No* questions?

Exercises and activities

1 Prepositions and vocabulary

See the OUP website http://www.oup.com/elt/teacher/pce.

2 Rephrasing

Below there are twenty typical classroom phrases. Try to make another phrase that has more or less the same meaning, but use the word (or another form of it) given in brackets at the end. You can find the answers in Sections A–C, either in the list of phrases or in the notes. The relevant section number is given after each question.

EXAMPLE   You, too, Ralf. (join)
             You join in with the rest of us, Ralf.

1 There's no need to rush. (time) C2/3
2 I'd like you to get into two teams. (divide) A4/1
3 I'm sorry, I didn't notice that at all. (overlook) B4/1
4 All right. When you're ready, Laura. (time) C2/3
5 It's all the same to me which group you join. (difference) A3/4
6 What you said was perfectly correct. (single) C1/3
7 Have I missed somebody? (turn) A2/4
8 Excuse me, do you mind moving? (squeeze) B5/2
9 Let me see more of this good work! (up) C2/5
10 You've improved a lot. (like) C2/4
11 You found this one difficult. (trouble) C2/1
12 If you can't hear, come a bit closer. (front) A1/1
13 You try it on your own, Mats. (yourself) A4/4
14 Let's read. One after the other, please. Lena, you start. (turns) A2/2
15 Nicely done. (job) C1/4
16 I'll be back in a moment, so don't stop working. (carry) B5/1
17 It's May 7th today. (date) B1/1
18 You need some more practice with this. (spend) C2/5
19 OK. It's alright. (damage) B4/2
20 Would someone like to clean the board? (volunteer) A3/2

3 Classroom scenario

Passages A–E below describe different situations of an English lesson. At the places numbered, try to think what the teacher could say in the situation. You are free to invent any extra information where necessary. Remember to be motivating and encouraging.

A It is the last lesson before the winter holiday. At the beginning of the lesson you apologize — you're coughing and your head is aching (1). One of the students sneezes (2). Hopefully the annual flu epidemic hasn't started! (3). At the start of the lesson, you hear that the class has a volleyball match against 9A the next day. You wish them luck (4). You also remember that Norbert has his 16th birthday today (5).

B Your plan is to begin with a short video about winter sports (6). As you're moving the TV, you accidentally tread on Margarete's foot (7). Now you just have to check that the screen is visible right round the class (8) and that even the students at the back can follow the sound (9). Three students near the window can't see because of the sun. You solve this problem (10).

C After showing the video, you invite the students to talk about their own winter hobbies. The topic seems to interest them, but you remind them that it's difficult to follow if they all talk at once (11). You decide to let them prepare something in pairs for five minutes (12). You will circulate and listen. You encourage Susanna, one of the quieter students, to say something (13). At the end of the five minutes, you ask Minna to talk about her hobbies. She speaks so quietly that you can't really hear what she is saying (14). You want to hear all the students speak, so when Piia puts her hand up for the second time, you have to choose someone else (15). At the end of the discussion, you check that everybody has contributed at least once (16).

D You check key vocabulary from the video on the board, and then ask for someone to clean the board (17). You thank the student who volunteers (18). The next stage of the lesson is some group work. You want them to work in fours (19). Ruyd isn't sure which group he belongs to, so you let him decide it himself (20).

E You finish the lesson with a short role-play activity. The students work in pairs, one is the customer in a sports shop, the other the salesperson (21). The customer should ask some questions about a product. After three minutes the roles are reversed (22). You circulate. Uwe's pronunciation impresses you (23). Anton and Dirk seem to be having difficulty. You encourage them (24). The bell rings. You thank the students—they worked very hard (25). Finally, as it's the last lesson, you say an appropriate goodbye (26).

4 Role-play

Divide up into groups of four or five. Choose some suitably easy exercises from a textbook (or use those on the OUP website). One member of the group acts as the teacher and goes through one exercise. The other members of the group play students with very different language skills. They can agree on this amongst themselves. The teacher's role is to give feedback on the students' answers—to confirm correct answers, to recognize excellent answers, to identify mistakes, and to encourage weaker students to try again. Change roles so that every member of the group has a turn as the teacher.

5 A board game: The Blackboard Jungle

For this game you will need copies of the game on page 46 and two dice. Each player will also need a counter or marker (for example, a coin or button). Decide who will start. The first player throws one of the dice. This shows how many spaces to move on the board. The player then throws again, but this time using both dice. The player multiplies the numbers on the dice, and does the task which has the corresponding number in the list below. If the other players think the task was performed well, the player can move to the new space. If the player lands on a shaded space, one dice has to be rolled again. The result can be seen in the list below called 'Chance'. The winner is the first player to reach the Finish line. If a player gets the same task twice, he can throw the dice again.

Tasks

1 Think of two replies for when a student says *Thank you*.
2 Think of two classroom situations where you could say *It's alright*.
3 Think of two classroom situations where you could say *What a pity!*
4 Ask two questions containing the word *whether*.
5 Think of two phrases that contain the words *odd* and *even*.
6 What would you say if you suddenly developed a splitting headache?
8 Think of three other ways of saying *Very good*.
9 How would you check that everyone can hear and see OK?
10 Think of two phrases that contain the words *shot* and *bash*.
12 What would you say if you had forgotten the date?
15 Think of two other ways of saying *I missed that*.

16 Think of two ways of telling the class to divide into twos.
18 What would you say if you think you forgot to give a turn to everybody?
20 Ask a question with the tag *have you?*
24 Think of something appropriate to say just before school breaks up for the summer holiday.
25 What would you say if you had to leave the classroom for a few moments?
30 Describe a situation in real life when you would say *Mind out*. And one in the classroom.
36 Think of two ways of thanking your class for their hard work.

Chance
1 Go back one space.
2 Have another go.
3 Miss your next turn.
4 Go forward one space.
5 Stay where you are.
6 Swap counters with the person on your left.

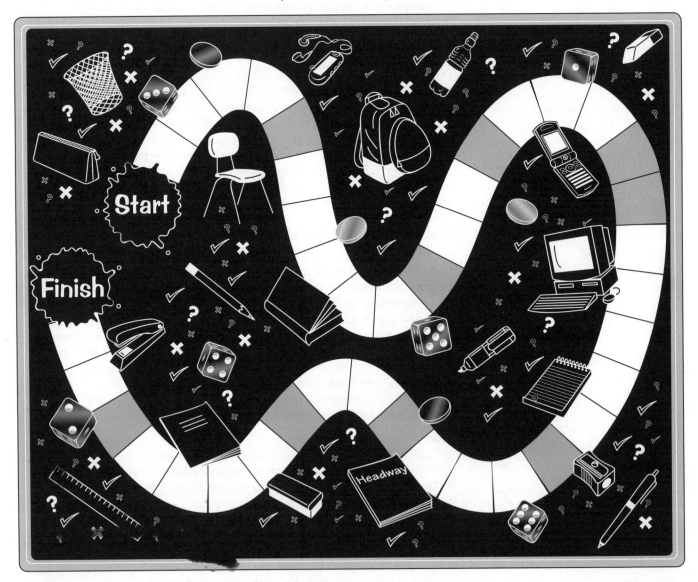

Photocopiable © Oxford University Press

Audio practice

1 Classroom intonation

2.1 Listen to the following phrases and decide whether the intonation is falling (an apology or question) or rising (a request for repetition). Then repeat the phrases.

1 Sorry.
2 What did you say?
3 What was that?
4 Excuse me.
5 I beg your pardon.
6 Sorry.
7 I beg your pardon.
8 Excuse me.
9 What did you say?
10 Where were you?

2.2 The following sentences all have rising intonation. Decide where the main sentence stress (= tonic syllable) is. Then listen and repeat.

1 Could I get past?
2 Do you mind moving?
3 Can you all see?
4 Am I speaking loud enough for you?
5 Do you want to try it again?
6 Are you sure about that?
7 Would you excuse me for a moment?
8 Could you step aside, please?
9 Is that the best you can do?
10 Could you repeat what you said?

2.3 Turn the following *Wh-* questions into *Yes/No* questions. Then reduce them to just a few words. Remember the rising intonation. Then listen and check.

EXAMPLE
Who didn't hear? → *Is there anybody who didn't hear?* → *Anybody not hear?*

1 Who needs help?
2 Who hasn't finished?
3 Who wants to try the next one?
4 Who would like to help me?
5 Who's left over?
6 Who didn't get the idea?

2.4 Listen to the question tags in the following sentences and decide if the intonation is falling or rising.

1 We didn't manage to do everything last time, did we?
2 That was easy, wasn't it?
3 You did this exercise last time, didn't you?
4 You've got the idea, haven't you?
5 We looked at this last time, didn't we?
6 That was a lot of work, wasn't it?

🎧 **2.5** Read out the following sentences aloud and add a falling question tag. In other words, you expect your listener to agree with you. Then listen and check.

1 That was easy.
2 We started the new unit last time.
3 This group was going to start.
4 This isn't so easy.
5 We haven't started exercise 7 yet.
6 You haven't had a turn yet, Toshie.

🎧 **2.6** Read out the following sentences aloud and add a rising question tag. In other words, you are really asking a question. Then listen and repeat.

1 You've all had a turn.
2 I returned all your essays.
3 That wasn't too much work.
4 You all received my email message.
5 I haven't left anybody out.
6 We've completed exercise 5.

🎧 **2.7** Read out the following *Yes/No* questions. Then use the tag word order (see page 42). Remember the rising intonation. Finally try to make a shortened form of the same question. Then listen and check.

EXAMPLE:
Have you finished? → You've finished, have you? → Finished, have you?

1 Are you starting the next exercise?
2 Do you want to go last?
3 Are you having difficulty with this one?
4 Do you understand what to do?
5 Have you already done the exercise?
6 Would you like to start?
7 Did you enjoy working in groups?
8 Do you get the idea?

2 Key sounds

🔊🎧 **2.8** Identify the sibilant sound or sounds (s z ʃ ʒ tʃ dʒ) in the following list of words. Then read them out loud. Then listen and repeat.

1	sheet	11	noise
2	cassette	12	join
3	enjoy	13	excuse (verb)
4	much	14	sure
5	easy	15	close (adjective)
6	projector	16	version
7	choose	17	manage
8	mention	18	question
9	television	19	use (noun)
10	catch	20	damage

🔊🎧 **2.9** Identify the sibilant sounds in the following sentences and read them out. Then listen and check.

1 Make sure you use as much English as possible.
2 Did you manage to finish the job?
3 Ask each other some questions and then change over.
4 Arrange the chairs in a circle.
5 Now you have a chance to choose which exercise you do.
6 Then you should show your answer sheet to your partner.

3 Word stress

🎧 **2.10** Say the following words aloud and mark the stressed syllable.
There are three types:

1 words stressed on the first syllable (for example, 'schedule);
2 words stressed on the second syllable (re'lax);
3 words stressed on the third syllable (elec'tricity).

Then listen and repeat.

1	transparency	11	handout
2	misprint	12	divide
3	cassette	13	progress (noun)
4	arrange	14	CD
5	cooperate	15	volunteer
6	interrupt	16	terrific
7	damage	17	independently
8	mistake	18	secretary
9	volume	19	appreciate
10	individually	20	overhead (noun)

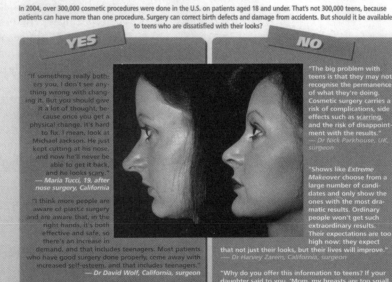

DEBATE

SHOULD TEENS HAVE COSMETIC SURGERY?

In 2004, over 300,000 cosmetic procedures were done in the U.S. on patients aged 18 and under. That's not 300,000 teens, because patients can have more than one procedure. Surgery can correct birth defects and damage from accidents. But should it be available to teens who are dissatisfied with their looks?

YES

"If something really bothers you, I don't see anything wrong with changing it. But you should give it a lot of thought, because once you get a physical change, it's hard to fix. I mean, look at Michael Jackson. He just kept cutting at his nose, and now he'll never be able to get it back, and he looks scary."
— Maria Tucci, 19, after nose surgery, California

"I think more people are aware of plastic surgery and are aware that, in the right hands, it's both effective and safe, so there's an increase in demand, and that includes teenagers. Most patients who have good surgery done properly, come away with increased self-esteem, and that includes teenagers."
— Dr David Wolf, California, surgeon

"Is your child being mocked because he or she has a big nose or teeth that stick out? Have they been called "pizza face" because of acne, or been made fun of because of a birthmark? If you deny your kid a normal life by refusing to give them corrective surgery, then you are the one who is unfit and cruel."
— Cosmetic Surgery & Beauty Network website

"Doctors believe that for some teenage patients cosmetic surgery can benefit their physical and emotional development. The surgeon must make sure that the teen selects the right operation. Nose reshaping is the most common procedure requested. The nose has completed most of its growth by 14 in girls and 16 in boys."
— Dr Patrick Hudson, New Mexico, surgeon

"If any part of you takes away your self-esteem, then why live like that? The longer you go on living like that, the more it's going to affect you and bring you down. There is something you can do about it. I would do it ten times over."
— Matt Schlepp, on MTV's I Want a Famous Face

NO

"The big problem with teens is that they may not recognise the permanence of what they're doing. Cosmetic surgery carries a risk of complications, side effects such as scarring, and the risk of disappointment with the results."
— Dr Nick Parkhouse, UK, surgeon

"Shows like Extreme Makeover choose from a large number of candidates and only show the ones with the most dramatic results. Ordinary people won't get such extraordinary results. Their expectations are too high now: they expect that not just their looks, but their lives will improve."
— Dr Harvey Zarem, California, surgeon

"Why do you offer this information to teens? If your daughter said to you, 'Mom, my breasts are too small, I want implants,' would you make her an appointment with the surgeon, or assure her she's beautiful the way she is? Any parent who agrees that their kids should have surgery to be ideal, is an unfit parent."
— anonymous parent on pro-surgery web forum

"I think there's an overindulgence in this surgery, and TV shows like I Want a Famous Face are making it worse. Patients are not carefully researching the moral and ethical standards of their surgeons. It's best if they find a surgeon who can talk about all the issues that surround adolescents, including whether or not having a smaller nose can bring happiness."
— Dr Frederick Lukash, New York, surgeon

"You are doing a mature operation on immature people. We all want the perfect body, the new sports car, the wonderful boyfriend or girlfriend, and we want them now. But you can't have them now. And you shouldn't have them now."
— Dr Tom Geraghty, New York, surgeon

to **bother** (v) to annoy
breast (n) a woman's mammary gland
to **deny** (v) to refuse to give or allow
overindulgence (n) the act of allowing oneself

to have too much of something enjoyable
to **scar** (v) to leave a permanent mark on the skin
scary (adj) frightening
self-esteem (n) a good opinion of oneself

unfit (adj) incompetent; U.S. legal term used to describe dangerous parents whose children can be taken away from them by the state

From *Speakeasy* magazine, Sept. 2005

4 Live lessons

You will hear some short extracts from different classroom situations. Listen to each extract and then answer the questions. Live lesson transcripts can be found on page 166.

🎧 2.11 Making groups

1 There are fourteen students present. Is there full attendance?
2 How does the teacher divide them up?
3 How does the teacher make the last group the same size as the others?
4 Fill in the missing words:
a It _____ better if we have a group of four.
b You _____ over here.
c I'm going to _____ you.

🎧 2.12 Working in groups

The class is using a magazine article to talk about teenagers and cosmetic surgery (see page 49).

1 Mark the statements as true (*T*) or false (*F*).
a The students must list only the advantages of cosmetic surgery.
b The students are only allowed to work in pairs.
c Preparations can take between five and ten minutes.
d A bell will ring when time is up.
e There should be one secretary in each group.
f The class will begin by reading a text on cosmetic surgery.
g The students must only use English.

🎧 2.13 Giving turns

1 Which of the following words does the teacher *not* use when confirming her students' answers?
   Great! Exactly! Perfect! Fantastic! Marvellous! Super!
2 Where are Alan and Hugo probably sitting?

🎧 2.14 Giving feedback

1 What aspect of English grammar is the class studying?
2 How does the teacher deal with the problem of the mobile phone?
3 What word does the teacher use?
   a) conflagrate; b) confiscate; c) complicate.
4 What are the roles of English and Finnish in this extract?

🎧 2.15 Inviting answers

In this lesson the teacher has asked her students to read out sentences that they have made up using some new vocabulary. Brett, a native speaker, is sitting in on the class.

1 What word has the student used in her sentence?
2 Why is the teacher pleased with her students' sentences?
3 Is the teacher serious when she says *We have to punish you.* How do you know?
4 What is special about the way the teacher says the following phrases: *No more. You've done it. No idea.*

🎧 2.16 Encouraging

1 What does the teacher encourage her students to do?
2 Does the teacher actually say that the student's suggestion is wrong?
3 How does the teacher use the situation to develop vocabulary?

Managing the classroom **3**

3

SECTION A

The classroom environment itself plays an important role in students' language learning. A positive classroom environment offers opportunities for students to use English and encourages them in their learning. Creating a positive environment includes two aspects: the material (for example, how the furniture is arranged, what is displayed on the walls); and the immaterial (the relationship between the students and teacher, the atmosphere created by the teacher). Different environments can support different types of interaction and create different types of learning opportunities—from practising set phrases to using language spontaneously.

1 Keeping the classroom comfortable
Phew! It's warm in here today.
Open a window, please.
Can you see the board OK?
Let's open the curtains.
Please turn on the lights.
That's better.

2 Keeping the classroom safe
Please put your things under your desk.
Please move the broken desk out of the way.
Be careful!
What a mess!
Put any rubbish in the bin, please.

3 Making space
We need to make some space.
Please find yourself a space.
Does everyone have enough room to move?
Please leave enough space for us to get through.

4 Moving around in the classroom
Sit down, please
Stand up.
Come to the front.
Go back to your seat.
Bring out your work, please.

5 Moving furniture
Today we'll have a change.
We need to move the desks.
Please help me move the TV stand.
We have to put the furniture back.

6 Hands and gestures
Hands up, please.
Is your hand up?
Don't be afraid to put your hand up!
Hands down, thank you.

Managing the physical environment

Points to think and talk about

1 If you could design your ideal classroom, what would it look like? How would it differ for adult learners, and for young teenage learners?

2 Think about different ways the surroundings of the classroom can be used to support the use of English. If, for example, you had an English notice board, what could you display on it?

3 Draw a sketch of your classroom (or of a classroom you are very familiar with). How could the available space be used differently? For example, would it be possible to have a reading corner, a culture corner, or a computer?

4 Sometimes even inconveniences in the classroom can provide rich opportunities for language development. Think of some of the problems that can occur in the classroom environment; for example, the sun is shining in through the window so that the students can't see the board. How can these problems be made into language learning opportunities?

5 List some of the benefits and uses of different seating arrangements – rows, circles, semi-circles, groups of desks, no seats at all. When can different arrangements be used? Is the age of the learner a factor? What are the problems with rearranging furniture?

6 How often do your students get up out of their seats during a normal lesson and move around; for example, to fetch materials or to come to the board? How can you use these occasions to enhance students' language development?

Language to think about

1 You need three volunteers to come and stand at the front of the classroom. Think of different ways of saying this to the students.

2 What would you say to get the students to rearrange themselves into groups of three?

3 Imagine you had rearranged the classroom for a drama lesson but you wanted the furniture back in its right place at the end of the class. How would you ask the students to help you?

4 You see one student struggling by herself/himself to move a desk. How would you ask another student to go and help her/him?

5 Students keep shouting answers out and it is difficult to know who said what. What can you say to the students to get them to put their hands up rather than to shout out?

6 It is a hot summer's day and the classroom is far too hot to work in. What could you say to get the students to help you improve the classroom conditions?

7 You are not sure if a student keeps putting his hand up or not. What can you say to him?

8 How would you invite the students to come to your desk to have their work marked and to return to their seats again without disturbing the others?

Classroom English vocabulary to collect

The names of classroom furniture and fittings (e.g. *notice board*, *radiator*)

Key to symbols:		
ⓘ Idiomatic phrase	⇨	Pedagogical pointer
Ⓢ Student reply	⊛	Cross-reference
ⓧ Typical mistake	⌨	Listen to the CD
Ⓛ Language comment	RECORD	Record yourself

Keeping the classroom comfortable

1 Phew! It's warm in here today.
*It seems to be too **hot/cold** in here.*
*It's very **warm/stuffy** in this classroom, isn't it?*
*Isn't it really **cold/freezing**?*
*Don't you think it's **quite/somewhat/a bit** chilly today?*

2 Open a window, please.
Please close the window.
Could you open the door?
*Let's **have/keep** the door open.*

3 Can you see the board OK?
Is the sun shining on the board?
Is the sunlight reflecting on the board?
*Is the sun **dazzling/blinding** you?*

4 Let's open the curtains.
How about drawing the curtains?
*Shall we pull the blinds **down/across/back/up**?*
*Ask Sam to **close/open/adjust** the blinds.*
*Please let the blinds **down/up**.*

5 Please turn on the lights.
*Oh, this classroom is too **bright/dark/dim**.*
*Let's switch **off/on** the lights.*

6 That's better.
(Is that) any better?
How's that?
That's more like it.
*That feels **a lot/much** better.*
That's an improvement.
That's the best we can do for now.
Well, we'll just have to manage with things as they are.
I don't think we'll be able to do anything about this now.

---

1 ➪ Making sure the classroom environment is a comfortable place to work is an important part of creating a positive learning atmosphere. It also provides a good opportunity to introduce some useful vocabulary, for example:
chaotic /keɪˈɒtɪk/
cramped
crowded
humid /ˈhjuːmɪd/
messy
smelly
squashed /ˈskwɒʃt/
sticky
stuffy
untidy

🔔 Additional phrases include:
***Are you/is anybody** too **warm/hot**?*
*You seem to be too **hot/cold**.*
Tell me if you're uncomfortable.
Let me know if it's too stuffy.
***Do/Just** say if it gets too hot.*

1 🔊 Students can answer using the following phrases:
*I'm **too hot/boiling**.*
I'm OK, thank you.
*I'm **a bit cold/freezing**.*
It's fine now, thanks.

🔔 You can also make adjustments to the temperature:
*Is the **fan/heating** on?*
*Could you check (that) the radiator's **on/off**?*
Please put the fan on.
Let's (try to) adjust the air-conditioning.
*Please turn the heating **up/down**.*

---

2 🔊 Students might find they cannot carry out the instructions for different reasons:
*It's **stuck/broken**!*
*It won't **open/close**.*
I can't do it.
It's already open.

---

3 🔔 Please notice the following:
I can't see for the sun.
I can't see because of the sun.
I can't hear for the noise.

---

5 🔔 You may have technical problems with lighting. See also Unit 5, A3:
What's wrong with that light?
Is that light working?
Will that light come on?
*I wonder if we can stop that light from **flickering
/flashing on and off**.*
This light seems to need a new bulb!

❌ *Close/Open the lights.* ✗

It seems a little cold today

Keeping the classroom safe

1 Please put your things under your desk.
Make sure your bags are under your seats, please.
*Don't leave your bag lying in the **way /aisle**.* /aɪl/
Move your bag so that no one can trip over it.
That's not a good place for your bag, is it?

2 Please move the broken desk out of the way.
*Let's put this **broken/damaged** chair to **one/the** side.*
*Don't **touch/sit on** that broken chair.*
Tuck your chair under the table.
Don't lean back on your chair.

3 Be careful!
Mind!
Watch out!
Look out!

4 What a mess!
This looks really untidy!
Let's tidy up before we begin.
Let's try to sort out the classroom before we start.

5 Put any rubbish in the bin, please.
Do pick the rubbish (up) off the floor.
Get rid of that rubbish (on the floor), please.
Don't leave any rubbish lying around.
Put your trash in the trash can. (AE)

3 　There might be occasions when the following phrases are necessary, especially if the classroom is new to the students or if equipment has been brought into the room which isn't usually there:
Mind you don't bang your head.
(Be) careful not to trip up.
Watch (out) for the lead.
Look out for the cable.
Mind the step!

　These idiomatic phrases might also be useful:
Duck! (= Keep your head down.)
That was close!
Phew! That was a near thing!
That was lucky!
That could have been nasty.

　You may even have to use the following:
*There's going to be a **fire/evacuation** drill today.*

5 　These phrases can of course be used at the end of the lesson to tidy up the room before the students leave. See also Unit 1, C6.

Making space

1 We need to make some space.
*We need a large space in the **middle/centre** of the classroom.*
Let's make a nice big space (at the front of the classroom).
Each group needs its own space (to work in).

2 Please find yourself a space.
*Please find yourself a **spot/place**.*
Make sure you each have enough space (around you).
Everybody spread out.
Stand well apart from each other.

3 Does everyone have enough room to move?
Make sure you give your neighbour plenty of space.
Please leave some space for your neighbour as well!
*Please check everyone has enough **space/room**.*
Is everyone able to stretch out their arms without touching someone else?

4 Please leave enough space for us to get through.
Can you make enough room for someone else to sit here too?
Please leave (enough) space for me to be able to squeeze through.

---

1 ⊗ For actual instructions about moving furniture refer to A5.

2 ⇨ If students know what activity is about to take place, it will help them to gauge how much space they need or should create.
Do you need that much space?
Don't take up all the space!

3 　Special situations may require special instructions:
Do you all have enough space for your equipment?
Please leave one empty space between you and your neighbour when we have the test.
Make sure you have adequate space for your poster.

Moving around in the classroom

1 Sit down, please.
You may sit down now.
Take your seat(s).
Find yourself a seat.
You are welcome to sit.
Sit in your seats.
Sit properly.

2 Stand up.
Go and stand there.
Please stand by the door.
*Come and stand **here/by the board**.*
Stand facing (the rest of) the class.

3 Come to the front.
*Come **over/out/up** here.*
*Come and sit **at/near** the front.*
Come to the back of the class.
*Come **closer/nearer** to the **television/screen/board**.*
Follow me.

4 Go back to your seat.
Go and sit down again.
Return to your own place, please.
*Sit in your **original/normal** seat, please.*
Please return to your seat quickly and quietly.
Go back to your place without disturbing anyone.
Change places with Salim.

5 Bring out your work, please.
Bring out what you have done.
*Bring your work to me to **check/look at**.*
Let's see what you have been working on.

---

1 Prepositions:
    *to sit on a **bench/stool/chair**.*
    to sit on/in a seat.
    *to sit in your **seat/place**.*
    *to **sit/kneel** on the floor.*
    to sit at your desk.

Notice the rather formal phrase:
    Please be seated.

---

2 Related idioms include:
    On your feet!
    Up you get!

---

3 Further directions might also be useful:
    Come here and (turn to) face the class.
    Come closer so that you can see better.
    Move to the side so that you can see more easily.
    Let's stand and stretch before we continue working.

Reasons for teachers moving around the classroom may include:
    I'll come round to each of you to check your work individually.
    I'll be coming (round) to the different groups to answer any questions.
    I'll circulate (round the class) to see how you are going on.
    I'll give you further instructions when I come to your group.

To encourage students to move more quickly you might say:
Hurry up!
Quickly now!
Be quick!

The opposites are:
Slow down!
What's the rush?
Calm down.

Other idiomatic expressions are:
We haven't got all day.
*Get **moving/cracking/weaving/cooking**.*
Let's see some action.
Look lively!
Don't hang about.
Get on with it
Chop, chop.
Stop dawdling.
Don't dawdle.
Let's jump to it.

---

4 The following phrases might be useful, not only with younger students but also for introducing some exercise during a long session:

Turn around (anti/clockwise).   *Stand up straight.*
Stand on one leg.   *Bend down.*
Hop up and down.   *Bend your knees.*
***Jump/Run** on the spot.*   *Wave your hands in the air.*
Stamp your feet.   *Clap your hands.*
Touch your toes.   ***Snap/Click** your fingers.*
*Take one step **forward/backward**.*   *Hold hands.*
Take one step sideways.   *Link your arms.*
Kneel down.   *Let go of each other's hands.*
Get down on your hands and knees.   ***Nod/Shake** your head.*
Stand with your feet apart.   ***Pat/Rub** your head.*
Stand with your feet together.   *Point to your **mouth/nose**.*

Other instructions involving movement:
    Please go and fetch some scissors.
    Go and collect the equipment from the back of the class.
    Please collect a textbook and then return to your seat.

A5

Moving furniture

1 Today we'll have a change.
Let's do things differently today.
(There's) a change to the normal arrangement today.
It's time for a change!

2 We need to move the desks.
*We need to move the tables around (for) this **lesson/***
 ***afternoon/session**.*
We have to rearrange the desks today.
Please push your desks to the side.
*Move your seats **in/out/back/forward/this way/that way**.*
*Try to **move/push** your desks **forwards/backwards/sideways**.*
*I want you to move your chairs to the **back/front** (a bit).*

3 Please help me move the TV stand.
I need some help with (moving) this.
Could someone give Pablo a (helping) hand with the desk?
Can you help David to move the (extra) desk?
*Could you give **me/him/her/us** a hand, please?*

4 We have to put the furniture back.
Put the desks in their original rows.
Return the chairs to their regular places.
*Move your seats back **to where they were/they came from**.*
*Please put your desks into the normal **groups/arrangement**.*
Put everything back where it belongs.
Return your seat to its original position.
Please make sure the desks are straight.

---

2 ⌂ You might want to add the explanation for moving the desks:
We need to move the desks for the activity later today.
We need to arrange the desks for the drama presentation.
Please move your desks so that you can all see the television easily.

 ⌂ Other more detailed instructions include:
*(Let's) **form/create/make** three big tables.*
(We need to) arrange the tables in groups of four.
*How about turning your **desk/table** round so that it faces **the***
 ***front/your partner**?*
*We only need to have three rows of desks in the **middle/centre** of*
 the room.
Please put the desks and chairs around the outer edges of the room.
Please place (all) the chairs in a circle.
*Let's **make/get into** a circle.*
*Could you rearrange your desks to create a **horseshoe/semi-circle**?*

 ⌂ It might be useful to say how much movement is required:
Please move your desk back a little bit.
Please move your chair right back.
Please put the tables right out of the way.
We need to create as much space as possible.

---

4 ⊗ *Furnitures* ✗ *Notice also homeworks* ✗, *equipments* ✗.

 ⇨ Wherever possible, arrange the furniture to allow for easy
 movement. This will help create a relaxed, pleasant atmosphere.

A6

Hands and gestures

1 Hands up, please.
Put your hand(s) up.
Please raise your hand.
Put your hand up (high).

2 Is your hand up?
*Please **raise/put up** your hands so that I can see them clearly.*
That's it, hands right up if you know the answer.
*I'm sorry, but I didn't see your hand **up/raised**.*

3 Don't be afraid to put your hand up!
Don't be shy! Hands up if you know the answer!
Come on, be brave and put your hand up if you have a
 question!
Always the same hands up!
Let's see some different hands up for a change.
Who hasn't put their hand up?

4 Hands down, thank you.
*Thank you, hands down **again/now**.*
OK, everyone, you can put your hands down now.

---

1 ⌂ You might want to add when or why the students should raise
 their hands:

Please raise your hand	when you	know the answer. **finish/have finished** your work. want the next task.
Put your hand up	if you	get stuck. encounter any difficulties. have any questions. need any help. have a problem.

 ⊗ Don't confuse the verbs *raise* and *rise*:
Raise /reɪz/ *(raise-raised-raised)*
Please raise your hands.
Rise /raɪz/ *(rise-rose-risen)*
Would everybody rise, please?

---

2 Ⓢ A raised hand may mean that a student has a question:
Excuse me, can I ask something?
Sorry, I have a question.

 ⌂ If you don't want to respond immediately to a raised hand, say:
Not now. I'll come back to you later.
Just one moment. I'll get to you in a minute.

4 ⌂ There are some other useful phrases connected with gestures:
Fingers crossed.
Let's keep our fingers crossed all goes well.
I'll keep my fingers crossed for you.
Touch wood (BE). Knock on wood. (AE)
Please nod your head if you understand.
Please shake your head if you haven't got the idea.

 ⌂ Notice that the 'thumbs up' gesture in English does not mean
 'good luck'. It just shows that all is well or that the message has
 been received and understood. Shrugging your shoulders is a
 non-committal 'I don't know' or a somewhat rude, 'I don't care'.

3

SECTION B

Of course, the classroom is not only the physical environment. Each group of students has its own unique character, which is made up of the individual personalities in the class and the teacher him/herself. How you manage this less tangible dimension of the classroom environment is just as important as managing the physical elements. Looking after the learning environment is a complex skill and covers a broad spectrum of considerations. This section can do no more than briefly look at three key aspects: 1) identifying learner types; 2) gaining attention; and 3) dealing with problem situations.

1 Different learner types

Let's think about different ways of learning.
Do you remember better when you read a text or listen to a lecture?
Do you agree with the results of the questionnaire?
How many visual learners do we have?
So the majority of you are visual learners.

2 Gaining attention

There's too much noise.
Quiet, please!
Stay where you are.
Look this way now.

3 Giving instructions

Please listen for the instructions.
I'll just review the instructions.
Did everyone hear what I said?
Are you with me?
You'll find all the instructions on this sheet.

4 Coping with problems

Stop that.
Settle down.
Behave yourselves!
Don't disturb the others, please.
What are you doing?
There will be trouble.
What's the matter?

Managing the learning environment

Points to think and talk about

1 What, in your opinion, does 'managing the learning environment' include? What makes a positive learning environment for you? How can this be created?
2 Find and complete a learner styles inventory (see Useful reading and resources, page 171) and discuss the results with a partner. Does your personal learning style have any effect on the type of tasks you choose to do in the classroom?
3 Discuss what level of noise is acceptable in your classroom and different tactics that can be used to gain students' attention.
4 How can instructions be presented effectively so as to avoid repeating them unnecessarily?
5 What is the disciplinary policy of your school? What different disciplinary actions have you seen used in the classroom? What has been the most effective in your opinion, and what would you be comfortable using?
6 What types of positive or negative behaviour do you most readily expect to find in the classroom? How does this alter with the age of the students?
7 When can misbehaviour be dealt with in the foreign language and when should it be dealt with in the mother tongue?
8 There can be many reasons why a class or individual students find it hard to get down to work. Make a list of the different problems. What different approaches can you use to cope with these problems in the classroom?

Language to think about

1 Explain or describe in English the classroom environment you would like to create for your students.
2 Take it in turns to gain the attention of a loud group of students engrossed in a discussion not related to the topic of the lesson.
3 The class are working away rather noisily, but the end of the lesson is coming and you need to set their homework. What can you say to gain their attention?
4 What kind of phrases would you use to show your displeasure at some classroom behaviour?
5 Do you know the meaning of: *Give it a rest, Stop dawdling, Don't daydream,* and *Stop fidgeting*?
6 All afternoon the class has been unsettled. What can you say to them to find out what is wrong?
7 What would you say to a group of students that has worked much better than usual throughout your lesson and produced a surprisingly good piece of group work?

Classroom English vocabulary to collect

1 Verbs to do with creating a good classroom environment. (For example, *to inspire, to motivate*)
2 Words used in school rules and mission statements. (For example, *respect, equality*)

Different learner types

1 Let's think about different ways of learning.
*What **kind/type/sort** of learner are you?*
Today we are going to do a questionnaire.
Today we are going to find out what kind of learner you are.
Do you know what a visual, audio, kinaesthetic learner is like?

2 Do you remember better when you read a text or listen to a lecture?
What is your preferred learning style?
Are you a visual, auditory or kinaesthetic learner?
Is it easier for you to work with written text or to be 'hands-on'?

3 Do you agree with the results of the questionnaire?
Do you think the results are correct?
Have you noticed that you prefer reading to listening?
How do these results reflect your own learning experience?

4 How many visual learners do we have?
Who has found they are a kinaesthetic learner?
Who is a combination of visual and auditory?

5 So the majority of you are visual learners.
There's a minority of auditory learners in this class then.
There's an even split between auditory and kinaesthetic learners.

1   There are numerous learner style questionnaires available. See Useful reading and resources (page 171). Useful phrases:
*Have a go at this **inventory/questionnaire**.*
Fill in the following questionnaire to find out what kind of learner you are.
Answer the following questions to discover how you learn.
Carefully read through each statement and tick the 'agree' or 'disagree' box.
*Read each question and **check/mark** whether you agree or disagree.*
Circle the option which applies the most to you.
Underline the answer that you most agree with.

⇨ Knowing what kind of learners you have in your class can help in the design and implementation of different activities. In addition, if students themselves actually know how they learn, it should give them confidence in approaching different tasks and help them to anticipate difficulties.

2 ⇨ *Visual* learners learn more readily when information is presented in a visual form, *auditory* learners are able to remember information that is heard and *kinaesthetic* learners learn best when they are physically involved in the learning process, for example, through acting out. Nevertheless, learners should also be exposed to information that uses different senses even if they have a particular learning preference.

4 ⇨ It is natural for visual learners to prefer tasks that require them to visually access information. Students may need encouragement to think how to approach tasks that rely on other methods of decoding information. Identifying strengths helps to overcome weaknesses.
If you are a kinaesthetic learner, how could approach the following task?
If you are an auditory learner, what task would help you process this text?
If you are a visual learner, how can you prepare for a listening task?

Gaining attention

1 There's too much noise.
What a (lot of) noise!
*I'm **sorry/afraid** you're (a little bit) too noisy now.*
*This level of noise is **too much/not acceptable**.*
*I can't hear **for/with** this **noise/racket/din**.*
Is there a reason for this amount of noise?
Keep your voices down.
If you've got something to say, say it to me.
Stop shouting!
I can't hear myself think!

2 Quiet, please!
Ssshhh! Thank you.
Be quiet!
***Quieten down/Quiet now**, please.*
Let's have some quiet now.
Could I have a bit of quiet, please?
I'd like you all to be quiet for a moment.
I'm waiting for absolute quiet.
***Hush a bit/Silence**, please.*
Stop talking (for a minute) now.
*No **talking/chatting** now.*

3 Stay where you are.
Don't move.
Nobody move.
Don't anybody move.
***Stand/Be** still, please.*
*Stay in your **seat/place**.*

4 Look this way now.
Look over here.
*Look **at/towards** the board.*
Turn (round) to face me, please.
Look at your teacher.
Face the front and listen carefully.
You need to look and listen, please.

1   When the level of noise drops to an acceptable level, you could say:
Thank you, that's much better.
Good, let's keep it like this.
(Much) better. Now we can all get on with our work.

2 ⇨ Try not to end up competing with the students for attention. Think of inventive ways to gain their attention; for example, flashing the lights on and off. If you know the noise level will rise with a certain activity, it might be useful to arrange a signal or a time limit with the students before they begin so they know when to be quiet again.

  With some students the following reminders might be useful:
***Switch/Turn** off your **mobiles/mobile phones/cell phones** before we start.*
*Please make sure your phones are **switched off/on silent** before we begin.*

Giving instructions

ᒻ The following instructions are far more abrupt:
Shut up!
Shut up, all of you!
Shut it!
Mouths shut.

ⓘ Other ruder phrases include:
Zip it!
Put a sock in it!

ᒻ Sometimes it is enough to place your forefinger vertically across your lips.

---

4 ⊗ *Look at̶ here.* ✗

ᒻ It might sometimes be appropriate to direct students to look in a different direction:
*Look (to the) **left/right**.*
*Look to the **front/back**.*
*Look **forward/straight ahead/in front of you**.*

ᒻ Note that *look* and *listen* can both be used in the following phrases:
***Look/Listen**, you need to concentrate now.*
***Look/Listen**, I think we can finish for today.*

ᒻ *Look here* and *Listen here* on their own can be warnings, meaning something like *That's it, I've had enough*.

ⓘ Other useful phrases related to *eye* include:
All eyes on me!
***I'm keeping/I've got** my eye on you.*
Remember, I have eyes in the back of my head!

⇨ The following phrases are more appropriate when interrupting students who are concentrating on a given task. You may need to give them further instructions or tell them how much time there is available:
Stop what you are doing and look at me.
Pens down and look up for a moment, please.
*I'm sorry to interrupt, but could you look **this way/at me** for a moment.*
*Could I **interrupt/disturb** you?*
Can I have your attention?
Pay attention now.
Your attention, please.
*Everybody **turn/face** this way for a moment.*

I'm waiting for absolute silence...

---

1 **Please listen to the instructions.**
I need to give you some more instructions.
Listen so that you know what to do.
*I hope everyone is **paying attention/listening** now.*
You need to pay attention to what is being said now.
It is important that I have your full attention now, please.
Listen up! (AE)

2 **I'll just review the instructions.**
Let me recap what you have to do (before you begin).
*I'll go **over/through** the instructions **again/one more time**.*

3 **Did everyone hear what I said?**
Did everyone catch that?
Did you all get that?
Has everyone got that?
***Were the instructions/Was that** clear?*

4 **Are you with me?**
(Is everybody) OK so far?
Are you following?
Do you get the idea?

5 **You'll find all the instructions on this sheet.**
I've written the instructions on the board.
Remember to check the instruction sheet.
Please follow the instructions I've given you.

---

1 ⇨ It is very important to have the students' full attention before giving instructions. Make sure you don't give the students too many instructions at once, nor too few! If students clearly understand what they are doing (and why), they can then focus on the learning activity. You are then free to support the learning taking place rather than repeating the same instructions unnecessarily.

ᒻ Useful phrases to gain students' attention include:
Hey!   *Wakey-wakey!*
Hoy, you there!   *Wake up there!*
You three (over) there!   *Are you with **us/me**?*

2 ⇨ Asking a student to repeat the instructions is often useful. It confirms that they have understood what they are supposed to do and provides another opportunity for the students to hear the instructions. Useful phrases:
Let me check you all understood what we have to do.
Do you all understand what you have to do?
Please repeat the instructions for me, Celine.
Could you tell me what the instructions were?
Give me a summary of what I said.
OK, Petri, tell me, what we are doing, please?
What do you have to do next?
What's the next step, Francis?

4 Ⓢ Encourage students to ask:
What do we have to do?
What are we supposed to do?
Could you repeat the instructions, please?
*I still don't **understand/get it**.*
One more time, please.

---

5 ⇨ Even if you provide the instructions in writing, it is worth going over the key points of the task orally, at least briefly.

Coping with problems

1 Stop that.
That'll do (now).
That's enough of that.
No more of that.
Stop everything, please.
I've had enough of that, thank you.

2 Settle down.
(Let's) calm down (now).
Take it easy, everyone.
*Don't keep **fidgeting/mucking about**.*
Let's hope there are no more interruptions.

3 Behave yourselves!
*Stop **messing/fooling** around.*
*No more **fooling/clowning/mucking/messing** about.*
Don't play the fool, (please).
Don't waste time.
*Don't **push/shove**.*
*No **pushing/shoving/fighting**!*

4 Don't disturb the others, please.
*Don't **distract/keep interrupting** your neighbour.*
Don't keep bothering him.
No copying from your neighbour.
No cheating.
*Work **on your own/by yourself**.*
*Please ask me if you have any **questions/problems** (rather than your neighbour).*

5 What are you doing?
What's happening over there, Stefan?
What's going on at the back of the class?
Simon, what are you doing out of your seat?
Why are you out of your seat, Ahmed?
Get down from there immediately!

6 There will be trouble.
You will end up in trouble if you continue like this.
We won't be able to play the game if you carry on like this.
*You will **miss/go without** your break if you continue to mess around.*
If you go on like this, you'll have to change places.
I'm getting tired of this.
How many times do I have to tell you?
This is my final warning.

7 What's the matter?
Is there anything I should know?
Let's talk about what's wrong.
Why do you seem so unsettled today?
What seems to be the problem today?
*What's stopping you from getting **down to/on with** your work?*
Where shall we go from here?
Please see me afterwards.

---

1 Even if students don't exactly understand the words or expression used, your tone of voice will clearly indicate the meaning.

ⓘ Useful idioms include:
Give it a rest.
Leave it be.
Cut it out.

---

3 There might be other disturbances:
*Leave **that/him/her** alone.*
*Stop fiddling with **the switch/your pen**.*
Don't daydream.
Stop daydreaming.
Please don't tap your fingers.
*Don't **lean/swing** back on your chair.*
Don't put your feet on the desk.
Take your feet off the desk.
*Do not **bang/slam** the lid of your desk.*

Other possible comments include:
*That's not **fair/nice**.*
That's not the way to behave.
You can't behave like that here.

---

5 Students may have a genuine reason for being out of their seats and can reply, for example:
*I'm borrowing **a pencil/ an eraser**.*
I need to sharpen my pencil.
I need to fetch a book.
I have to wash my hands.

---

6 Disciplinary measures will vary according to the culture and practices of different educational institutions:
*I'll have to report your behaviour to your **class teacher/parents**.*
I will have to send you to the head teacher.
You'll have to do some extra work.
You will have to stay behind during the break to finish the exercise.
You'll have to stay behind for detention.

---

7 If classroom problems are serious, use the students' mother-tongue to re-establish order and a sense of direction. It is often better to be 'proactive' rather than 'reactive' as far as classroom management is concerned. See Useful reading and resources (page 171).

Stop clowning around!

3

Using the classroom creatively

Activities in the language classroom, such as quizzes, songs, or drama, can help students to experience English in a different way. At the same time they also overcome their fears of participation since they are concentrating on what they are doing, rather than on the language they are using. Cooperative and creative activities can also help to build a sense of community in the classroom and increase the motivation of the students to use the language. They not only see themselves succeed but they also realize that the language they have acquired in more formal classes also works in non-formal situations.

1 Playing games
Let's play a game.
Get into two teams.
Listen carefully to the rules.
Are you ready?
It's your turn.
One point for this team.
Last question.

2 Songs, rhymes and chants
It's time for a song.
Do you know this song?
Repeat the words after me.
Sing along with the recording.

3 Acting out
Let's act out this dialogue.
Who wants to be the detective?
You have five minutes to practise.
Give yourselves a clap.

4 Preparing and organizing displays
You are going to prepare a poster.
First decide what information to include.
Now try out different designs.
Let's make the display.

5 Using objects and realia
I have something to show you.
I'll give you a clue first.
Look at it carefully.
How would you describe this?

Points to think and talk about

1 What do you think is the role of non-formal activities in the language classroom? How much time should be given to such activities?
2 What different types of games do you play (or have you seen) in the classroom? What benefits have you noticed?
3 It isn't just traditional language games that provide language opportunities in the classroom. Think of a simple board game that could be played in English and discuss what kind of language it requires.
4 Older students might be interested in developing their own board game. What kind of language development opportunities would this offer?
5 The genre of songs is enormous, from traditional songs steeped in tradition to popular songs reflecting modern trends and interests. What different activities can you think of to do with songs, other than singing?
6 How can textbook dialogues be used more creatively or adapted by students so that they 'belong' to the students?
7 Have you used or seen drama activities in the classroom? Describe them. How can a safe environment be created for drama activities?
8 Producing poster displays provides interesting language learning opportunities for students. How does making a display develop receptive and productive language skills? Why is it important to display all your students' work?
9 Exploring culture can provide motivating ways to access language. What aspects of culture would you be interested to explore with your students? How could you introduce these in the classroom?
10 A foreign visitor in the classroom is a genuine opportunity for language use and can greatly motivate students. How would you prepare a class for a foreign visitor? What kind of etiquette would you want your students to follow?

Language to think about

1 How do the following words and phrases relate to playing a game? *a round, a draw, heads or tails?, a tie-breaker, on your marks, your turn.*
2 Present a short song to your group and discuss what language you would need. What cultural features would you need to explain?
3 In a small group think about the process of getting students to design a poster encouraging the use of English in the classroom. What kind of language would you need to use?
4 Choose an object in the room and describe it in detail to your group without telling them the name of the object. How quickly can they guess what it is? What different ways are there to describe an object?
5 Think about the language you would need to get your students to act out a dialogue from the textbook.

Classroom English vocabulary to collect

1 Words associated with playing games. (For example, *dice, counter*)
2 Useful equipment for making a display. (For example, *scissors, glue, cardboard*)

Playing games

1 Let's play a game.
(We'll have) A warm-up game to begin with.
*What about a **spelling/rhyming/counting/guessing** game?*
How about a quiz?
*This is a game with **colours/numbers/letters**.*
*Here's a game to **help with/improve/revise** spelling.*
*This is a **vocabulary/grammar** game.*
*This is **a communication/an information-sharing** activity.*

2 Get into two teams.
We need two teams for this next game.
Arrange yourselves into teams (of three).
***Make/Split into** two groups.*
Form two sides.
Let's divide into four teams.
What's your team called?
*Have you **got/come up with** a name for your team?*

3 Listen carefully to the rules.
Let me tell you the rules.
The rules are as follows:
There are some simple rules to follow.
*Who remembers the rules **for/of** this game?*

4 Are you ready?
Everybody ready?
Shall we begin?

5 It's your turn.
(It's) team A's go.
Who's (on) next?
Whose turn is it?
*Who would like to **try/have a go** next?*

6 One point for this team.
*A point **for/to** team A.*
*The first team **with/to score** ten points wins.*
This team was the closest – two points!
Whoever guesses first gets a point.
Whichever team guesses correctly has another go.
I'll award one point for each correct answer.
The team with the best answer wins a point.

7 Last question.
*Last **go/time**.*
*This is the **last/final** round.*
Time's almost up.
We've run out of time.
Quickly! Time's running out!
Quick now, you don't have many seconds left.
That's the end of the game.
Game over!

1 ⇨ Games have several different roles in the classroom. They can act as good preparatory activities (warm-up games) or revision activities. Games also create a positive classroom atmosphere and help students get to know one another. Games are often used to encourage students to keep working, as in the following: *If we have time, we will play a short game at the end of the lesson.*
If you finish your work in time, we can play a game.

ﾚ Some games will require specific instructions or preparations:
One person will have to come to the front.
One of you will (have to) go out for a moment.
***Stand/Step/Stay/Wait** outside the door and I'll call you (back) in soon.*
*Just **pop/go** out of the room for a **minute/moment/few seconds**, please.*
Someone needs to be blindfolded.
Keep your eyes closed.
No peeping!
You can be question-master.
Please take turns.

ﾚ Some games may also require a dice, cards and counters/markers. Notice the vocabulary:
*to **throw/toss/roll** the dice (to see who starts).*
to throw a six.
*to **shuffle/jumble up** the cards.*
*to **deal/deal out** three cards (to each player).*
to spread out the cards.
*to **put/place** the cards face down.*
to pick a card.
to move your marker (three spaces forward).

ﾚ Note also: *a board game, a crossword, a puzzle, a riddle, a word search.*

3 ⇨ When introducing a game for the first time, it might be necessary to present the rules in the students' mother tongue. Think of a good name for the game. Later it will be easier to remind students of the rules in English. See Useful reading and resources (page 171) for language game books.

4 ﾚ Some competitive or timed games will need a countdown to begin:
On your marks, get set, go!
*Ready, **steady/set**, go!*
On the count of 3, one, two, three!
Begin when I clap my hands.

ﾚ If a coin is thrown to decide who goes first, the following phrases are useful:
*Let's **toss for it/flip a coin**.*
Heads or tails?
Heads team A starts, tails team B starts.

5 ﾚ When a team or an individual is eliminated (out of the game) you can say:
Luisa's out (of the game).
I'm sorry, you are out.
You're out for the next round.
You miss a turn.

Notice also:
She can't go.
He's stuck.
Pass = I can't answer.

Songs, rhymes, and chants

7 With games involving a score, use the following:
Add/Count up your points.
*How many points **have you got/did you get** altogether?*
What is your final score?
*Let's see **what the final result/who the winning team** is.*

Announcing the winner:
The winner!
This team has won!
The winning team!
*It's a **tie/draw**.*
Three cheers for the winner. Hip-hip-hurray!
Will the members of team A take a bow.
*A round of applause for **the winning team/all participants** for doing so well.*

A *tie-breaker* (= deciding question) might be necessary if there is no clear winner.

1 It's time for a song.
Let's sing.
How about (singing) a song?
Do you feel like singing?
Shall we listen to a song?
*What shall we sing **today/next/first**?*
What is your favourite song, Thomas?
*Now I have a **new/pop** song for you.*

2 Do you know this song?
*You might **know/recognize** this song.*
*Who remembers how this song **begins/goes**?*
*You already know this **tune/song**.*
*This **tune/melody** should be familiar.*
Here's a song by The Beatles.
*This song is a **traditional/Christmas** song.*

3 Repeat the words after me.
*Try to **say/sing** the words after me.*
*Listen carefully to the **tune/melody/words**.*
*Try to follow **the words/what the singer is saying**.*
Just listen the first time through.
*Follow the words from **your books/the board/the overhead**.*
First I'll explain the words to you.
*That's a **difficult /tricky** part there.*
*Let's **try/go over** that bit again.*

4 Sing along with the recording.
Join in (with me).
Join in for the chorus.
All together.
Start on the count of four.
*I'll accompany you on **my/the** guitar.*
We'll be singing without any accompaniment today.
We could sing this in a round.

---

2 ⇨ Singing or listening to songs is one way of dealing with pronunciation. Along with jazz chants and other rhymes, songs are also useful for introducing and practising different language structures or new vocabulary. They very often represent modern living language with a wide appeal. There is a host of motivating and creative activities based on music and popular songs. See Useful reading and resources, page 171.

---

4 ⇨ The following phrases might encourage greater participation:
Come on, give it all you've got.
Let's put some heart into it.

And positive feedback is important:
You're all singing very well today.
Well, you seem to be in good voice today.
That sounds very nice, well done.

---

5 ⇨ Younger students often enjoy performing actions with songs and rhymes, but even with older learners they can be useful tools to help remember words, especially for kinaesthetic learners.
Let's try the actions.
This song has words and actions.
Who remembers the actions?
*What actions **do/can** we do here in the **chorus/verse**?*
We need to stand up for the next part.

Acting out

1 Let's act out this dialogue.
*Now we **can/shall** act this conversation (out).*
*Let's dramatize this **story/text/dialogue**.*
How would you act this scene out?
Come out to the front and show everybody else.
Come out and mime your favourite sport.

2 Who wants to be the detective?
*Any volunteers **to be/to play/for** the police inspector?*
*Who wants to **play/read** the part of Lucy?*
*You **are to be/will be** Watson.*
*You can read **this part/the narrator**.*
*Who will **swap with/take over from** Tobias?*

3 You have five minutes to practise.
Let's rehearse.
Practise with the lines first.
*Let's go over some **words/phrases** that might be useful.*
You can use your book (this time).
Try to learn your lines by heart.
*This will be our **dress rehearsal/practice run**.*

5 Give yourselves a clap.
A round of applause for everyone.
A big hand for the actors and actresses.
Some applause for the stars of the show.
Please take a bow. /baʊ/
That was a great performance!

---

1 ⇨ Drama and role-plays can introduce students to a wide variety of language use situations, and at the same time bring an important social dimension to learning. Drama activities also develop fluency, promote interaction, and increase motivation. See Useful reading and resources, page 171.

⇨ Public performance can be very daunting for some students, even in their mother tongue. It is important to set drama activities up appropriately. Give students clear guidelines and ample time to practise. This will increase their sense of security and confidence. It will also support their language learning as they repeatedly review and revise texts.

⇨ Students don't need an advanced level of oral proficiency to try to improvise or to play around with a text. If the students already have the language framework (a text, a dialogue), they can focus on changing words, their tone, or their voice to alter the meaning. Useful phrases:
Try to improvise a little.
Don't be afraid to experiment with the character.
*Imagine what your character **might do/say** (in this situation).*
*What might your character **do/say** under these circumstances?*
How else could we act this scene?
***Imagine/Pretend** that you're a character in the play.*
*Try and act **like/as** the character.*
*Act as if you're **angry/shocked/overjoyed**.*

5 ⌊ Related words: *the prompter, to have stage fright, the audience.*

Preparing and organizing displays

1 You are going to prepare a poster.
*Your task is to produce a **display/poster**.*
Have a go at designing a poster presentation.

2 First decide what information to include.
*What kind of information **should/could** you include?*
What are the most important points to present?
What is the key content of your poster?
What message do you want to share?
What is the message you want to get across to your audience?
*Decide what the **key message/aim** of the poster is.*
The aim is to design a poster presenting the facts about global warming.

3 Now try out different designs.
Come up with as many different ideas as possible.
Play around with different designs.
Try out different presentation options.
*Produce a rough version before you prepare the **best/final** copy.*

4 Let's make the display.
Stick your poster up on the wall.
Bring out your poster and put it on the board.
***Tape/Fix/Pin** it to the board.*
Check that the poster is straight.
***Raise/Lower** the right side a little bit.*
Carefully arrange the different parts of the display.
*Don't make it too **crowded/cramped**.*
Make sure you highlight the title of the display.

---

1 ⇨ Posters are just one public presentation format. Students can also prepare 'big books', certificates, game boards, advertisements, and leaflets. Producing something for public display or distribution encourages students to think carefully about what message they want to give and how to present it. These are very important elements of communication in any language.

⇨ You might want to specify the theme of the posters:
Make a poster warning about the dangers of smoking.
The poster theme is festivals.
We'll use the 'dangers of smoking' as our theme.
The posters will advertise different holiday destinations.

⇨ Make sure all the necessary equipment is available:
What equipment will you need?
*Please **collect/gather** the equipment you will need.*
*The **mounting card/masking tape** is at the back of the classroom.*
Go and fetch some Sellotape and a pair of scissors.

2 ⇨ A poster presentation shouldn't be too text-based, but the text that is included should be carefully constructed and well presented. Students need to focus on the different steps involved in producing text: drafting, editing, and polishing. See Unit 6, B4.

Using objects and realia

3 ⌊ Useful instructions might include:
Draw/Cut out a **square/rectangle/triangle/circle**.
Fold/Cut along the (dotted) line.
Fold/Cut it in half.
Trace around the shape.
Stick it on with glue.
Be careful with the scissors.

4 ⇒ Take time to look at the posters on display and discuss the information presented. This is a very important part of the learning experience. Students can be encouraged to present their work and to explain more about the ideas behind the display. They can ask each other questions and offer different perspectives. Make sure you display all the work and give plenty of individual encouragement.

⇒ One important thing to remember:
It's important/Remember to add your name.
Make sure you sign your work.
Clearly add your name before you finish off.
Don't forget /Remember to write your name at the **top/bottom** of the page.
Put your name in the corner, please.

Remember to add your name

1 I have something to show you.
I've brought something to show you.
Let's see what I have here.
Who would like to see what I have here?
Does anybody know what this is (called)?
Somebody have a guess.
(Try to) guess what I've got with me.
Have a go at guessing what I've got in this bag.
What guesses are there?

2 I'll give you a clue first.
Let me give you some **hints/clues**.
I'll give you a little information about the object before I show you.

3 Look at it carefully.
Have a close look at it.
Study it **carefully/closely**.
I'll hold it up for everyone to see.
(You can pass it round to) have a closer look at it.
Just look, but don't touch.
You can feel it and squeeze it.

4 How would you describe this?
What do you notice about this **object/item**?
It's an interesting shape.
It's quite **small/colourful/unusual**.
It feels **cold/soft**.
It is quite **hard/rough/bendy**.
It's made of **wood/plastic/glass**.
What is it used for?
What can you do with it?
What **job/person** (do you think) uses this item?
Where would you find an object like this?

1 ⇒ The object may be the main focus of the lesson, or it might just be something that leads into the actual lesson.

⟩ For phrases dealing with projected visuals, refer to Unit 5, A4.

4 ⇒ When students guess, even if incorrectly, it's important for them to feel that their contribution is valuable and appreciated. Use the following phrases to respond to suggestions:
Good **suggestion/idea**.
That's an interesting idea.
You are almost right.
(Not quite, but a) good try.
You're along the right lines.
That's right!
Absolutely right.
Well done, you guessed correctly.
I hadn't thought of that!

⟩ See Unit 2, C for more on feedback phrases.

Classroom essentials

GIVING INSTRUCTIONS (2)

Polite ways of asking

In Unit 1 we looked at basic commands and simple requests using *please*. This unit examines the many different ways there are in English of making requests and giving instructions politely. At this point you may be thinking that effective language teaching has little to do with giving your instructions politely. You probably believe that it is part of your role as a teacher to maintain some kind of formal distance between yourself and your students.

A model of English

Nevertheless, you should remember that one of your tasks as a teacher of English is to provide background cultural information on English-speaking countries. A lot of this information is contained in the ready-made textbooks and materials used for teaching English. Another important source is mass media, especially television and film, which not only inform but also shape attitudes. One area of cultural information that may be overlooked is the way native speakers interact and the expectations they have of each other in various situations. For students to understand these skills, they need a model of how English is actually used in the real world. In other words, the way you use English to run your own class should to some extent reflect language interaction in normal everyday situations.

Why it matters

Despite huge changes in society and attitudes in the English-speaking world, politeness is still an essential part of everyday language interaction. You may feel that this politeness is superficial and insincere, but it is a part of the language. Failure to use *please*, for example, may be considered impolite and the result may be misunderstanding and disagreement. You should emphasize this to your students and explain that you will try to model the correct use of polite language in running your classes. This is something that you should do from the very beginning. The good thing is that a language class is a perfect environment for giving polite instructions in a natural and very authentic way.

An alternative world

You may feel that your authority as a teacher is in some way being compromised by the use of polite request forms because they may suggest equality of status. Our view, however, is that other rules can apply in the alternative world of English that you create for your students. In this world of English, instructions are given politely and encouragingly. Besides, if there are serious classroom management problems, you will in all probability switch back to the students' native language and so re-establish the normal teacher–student relationship. As you will see below, there are many ways of expressing politeness in English, including some that are grammatically quite complex. This feature, too, can work in favour of your students because it exposes them to a variety of alternative expressions that are used in similar contexts. With some advance planning you may also be able to introduce particular polite forms in your classroom instructions before they are dealt with formally in the lesson material (for example, *could* and *would*, *do you mind* and *I'd like you to*).

Modal verbs

- Polite instructions often make use of the modal verbs *will, would, can, could* and *may*. By adding *You may* or *You can*, you can make a simple command more polite:

  You may sit down again now, Heidi.   You can leave the door open, Sara.

- One of the most frequent polite forms in English uses questions based on *can, could, will* or *would*. *Could* and *would* are more polite:

  Can you say that again?   Will you pass this to the back?
  Could you join this group?   Would you come and sit next to Milan?
  Could you possibly help me?   Would you get into teams?

- Negative questions can also be used to give polite instructions:

  Won't you come out to the front? Can't you give me a hand?
  Couldn't you join this group for today?

- Notice the use of the conditional clause in these polite phrases:

  Write it on the board, if you would (please).
  Try to concentrate, if you could (please).

- It is very usual for *please* to be added to this kind of request. The word *please* tends to come at the end of the sentence, but it can be placed before the main verb. At the very beginning of the sentence, it may sound more formal:

  Can you write it on the board, please?   Will you look this way, please?
  Could you please do exercise 5 at home?   Would you please be quiet?
  Please could you rearrange the chairs?   Please will you listen now?

⊗ See 🎧 3.1.

Modal tag forms

- There is an alternative and very common polite form which resembles a question tag, but uses a positive–positive question tag, instead of a positive–negative, or negative–positive tag. The first part of the instruction is just a simple command, so the central meaning of the instruction should be clear. This is followed by the tag using a modal, which expresses politeness. This politeness is echoed in the rising intonation.

  Open the window, can you?   Do the next one, could you?
  Try it again, will you?   Clean the board, would you?

⊗ See 🎧 3.2.

- Tag requests often include the word *please*. Such sentences carry a message of politeness in many different ways (intonation, *please*, tag). Notice the different possible places for *please*:

  Please close your books, could you?   Please listen carefully, would you?
  Close your books, please, could you? Listen carefully, please, would you?
  Close your books, could you, please? Listen carefully, would you, please?

- If you want to address your instruction to a particular student, simply add the student's name to the instruction. Notice that the order of the four different parts (1 the instruction, 2 the word *please*, 3 the tag and 4 the student's name) can vary freely. This may be useful because it allows you to use a simple command, then make it polite and natural, and finally to nominate the student.

| Move to one side | could you,
could you,
please,
please,
Anya,
Anya, | please,
Anya,
could you,
Anya,
could you,
please, | Anya?
please?
Anya?
could you?
please?
could you? |

» See 🎧 3.3.

want and would like

- The verbs *want* and *would like* are also useful in giving polite instructions. The first use is in questions like the following:

  Do you want to try the next one?   *Does Toshi want to have a try?*
  Would you like to join this group?   *Would Felix like to open the window?*

- Negative questions sound more encouraging and inviting:

  Don't you want to join in?   *Wouldn't you like to work on this task?*

- A more formal use of *want* and *would like* (often contracted to *I'd*) is seen in the following examples:

  I want you to listen very carefully.   *I would like everyone to join hands.*
  I want you all to try your best.   *I'd like you three to make your own group.*

- Be careful of the following typical mistakes:

  I want ~~that~~ you ... ✗   *I would like ~~that~~ everyone ...* ✗
  Who ~~would~~ come out? ✗

mind and kind

- The phrases *do you mind* and *would you mind* are often used in connection with polite questions and requests. Notice the use of the *-ing* form and the position of *not*.

  Do you mind repeating what you said?
  Would you mind sharing today?
  Do you mind not talking for a moment?
  Would you mind not disturbing your neighbour?

- *Mind* is also used to ask politely in conditional phrases with *if*:

  Do you mind if we keep the door open?
  Would you mind if I switched the lights on?

- *If you don't mind* and *if you wouldn't mind* can be added to simple commands to make them more polite:

  Come and work with this group, if you don't mind.
  Close the window, if you wouldn't mind.

- In formal contexts you will hear two extremely polite forms of request which use the word *kind*.

  Would you be kind enough to lend me your copy?
  Would you be so kind as to hand me the dictionary?
  Go back to your seat, if you would be so kind.

- Additional politeness can also be given to a request by adding *do you think* or *I wonder if*:

  Could you try this again? > *Do you think you could try this again (please)?*
  Could you repeat that? > *I wonder if you could repeat that (please).*

Polite or angry?

- Finally, it should be remembered that even a superficially polite form may nevertheless be used to express annoyance and anger. The situation and your tone of voice will make it clear whether you are being polite or expressing annoyance. The following examples are typical:

  Will you go back to your seat now?   *Can you stop talking for a moment?*
  Do you mind moving out of the way?   *Would you mind shutting up?*
  Sit down, could you?   *Would you be so kind as to stop talking?*

- Another way to express your annoyance is to use the phrase *do you mind?* on its own. If two students, for example, are talking loudly to each other, you can interrupt them by saying:

  Do you mind? I'm trying to explain something.

Practice

1 Re-express the following instructions in two ways, using the clue words given in brackets.

EXAMPLE:
Go back to your place. a) mind; b) would
a) Do you mind going back to your place?
b) Would you go back to your place, please?

1 If you want, you can come and sit at the front, Emilia. a) like; b) could
2 OK, where shall we start? How about Mari? a) wonder; b) mind
3 Read three lines each, everybody. a) want; b) like
4 Suzanne, I think it's your turn to come out to the front. a) could; b) mind
5 Help me with the CD player, Arminda. a) think; b) kind
6 Anyone willing to clean the blackboard for me? Emil? a) not mind; b) kind enough
7 For today, please work in pairs. a) like; b) think
8 Please don't shout, Toni! a) mind; b) could
9 Pass me that dictionary off the shelf. Alex. a) so kind; b) think
10 Change places with Miriam, Rubén. a) like; b) mind
11 You can work with this group. Is that OK? a) like; b) want)
12 Collect in the test papers, Natalia. a) wonder; b) could

2 Do this exercise in pairs or groups. You will need two dice. The first player throws both dice at the same time and then adds up the scores. That score shows which of the sentences in exercise 1 above is to be used (2–12). The player then throws one of the dice again. This score tells the player how many different ways (1 to 6) he or she must use to re-express the same idea politely. There is one point for each correct alternative. The other players must decide whether the answer is correct or not. The first player to get 30 points is the winner.

RECORD 3 Think of all the stages involved in performing some simple everyday action (for example, making a cup of tea, taking a shower, using a microwave, tying a shoe lace, etc.). Record yourself giving polite instructions to somebody who is unfamiliar with these routines. Use a variety of polite forms.

Exercises and activities

1 Prepositions and vocabulary

See the OUP website http://www.oup.com/elt/teacher/pce.

2 Rephrasing

In each pair of sentences, the second one has its words jumbled up. Rearrange the words so that the second sentence means more or less the same as the first one.

EXAMPLE:

What are you doing at the back?   over on going there what's
What's going on over there?

1   Go back to your seat.   down and sit again go
2   Be quiet.   of bit could a quiet have I
3   Look this way.   face round front turn and the
4   Bring out your work, please.   out your look me at bring for here work to
5   Please hurry. There isn't much time.   all haven't hurry got up we day
6   What was your score?   get many how you altogether points did
7   Be careful of the lead.   the over don't cable trip you mind
8   Put your chairs back.   to belong they seats your return where
9   Today we have to rearrange the desks.   your to this round we tables time move need
10 Listen carefully.   your important full that have is attention I it
11 Ssshh!   noisy down you're bit keep little too voices your a
12 Put your name on it.   the the name please remember page of your at top add
13 Any volunteers for Dr Watson?   Watson of like the play would to part who Dr
14 Hands up if you have a problem.   need your if put help up you any hands
15 Tidy the classroom.   please pick rubbish the all up the off floor

3 Situations

Work in groups. One of the group members chooses one of the situations described below and reads it aloud. The others write down a suitable phrase for the situation. After this all the members of the group compare their suggestions and choose the best or most suitable one. The winner is awarded one point. After each round, change the person who chooses the situation.

1   The midday sun has been streaming into the classroom and now the classroom is too hot.
2   You have to give further instructions to the class but the students are working in groups and are discussing loudly.
3   During a game you have to ask a student to step outside of the class for a few minutes.
4   The desks need to be rearranged for a discussion.
5   It is the end of an art lesson and the classroom is a real mess.
6   You need help to move the OHP from one side of the room to the other.
7   During the silent reading time you notice a student passing a note to her neighbour.
8   The classroom is too cold. You think the reason could be the radiator.
9   The desks need rearranging into groups of four.
10 You notice a student doodling, rather than working.
11 The desks and chairs are very untidy and the class is about to end.

12 You see a number of students standing and talking together at the far end of the classroom.
13 There is a sudden thunderstorm and some of the students look disturbed.
14 Students shout answers out making it hard to monitor the discussion.
15 A student is quickly copying the homework answers from his neighbour's book.
16 You are not sure that the students have understood the instructions properly.
17 You've decided that you'll go round and check the students' work.
18 A student stands up to give his presentation but doesn't come to the front of the class.
19 At the end of an information sharing exercise the students need to return to their desks.
20 One student has been staring out of the window for the last five minutes.
21 Instead of using the piano, you're going to use a CD to accompany the students' singing.
22 The sunlight is reflecting on the board and the students can't read what it says.
23 The class have worked extremely well this lesson.
24 One of the electric lights keeps flickering on and off.
25 Although deep in conversation, a student is drumming on his desk.
26 At the end of the lesson the desks need to go back to their original places.
27 The class are talking too loudly.
28 A student receives a text message during a lesson.
29 A bag is blocking the way as a student rushes to show you his work.
30 The students are standing up and talking excitedly at the start of a lesson.

4 Bingo

For this exercise you need a game leader and up to eight players. The game leader uses the list of situations in the previous exercise. Each player has one of the eight players' cards overleaf. The leader chooses a situation at random and reads it out. The players try to find a phrase on their cards that is suitable for the situation. If they think they have a suitable phrase, they can mark it in some way. The first player to find phrases for six situations is the winner. The other players should then decide whether the phrases really do match the situations.

5 Describing

Imagine that you have a visitor coming to your class. Can you give precise instructions to help your guest find the way in your school?

1 From the car park to the main entrance.
2 From the entrance hall to the secretary's office.
3 From the secretary's office to your classroom.
4 From your classroom to the head teacher's office.
5 From your classroom to the staffroom.
6 From your classroom to the staff toilets.

1

How about opening the window?	Put the desks in groups of four, would you?	Please come to the front of the class.
Don't keep tapping the desk, please.	Perhaps you could just step outside for a moment.	Remember to straighten the desks and chairs before you go.
You may go back to your own seats.	Return your desks to their original places, please.	Make sure you pick up any rubbish near to you and put it in the bin.
OK, calm down everyone.	Keep your attention on your work, please.	Mind the bag!

2

Can I have your attention, please?	Return to your work, please.	Please come to the front of the class.
Return your desks to their original places, please.	Please arrange the chairs in a horseshoe shape.	Remember to straighten the desks and chairs before you go.
Keep your attention on your work, please.	Could you make sure your phones are switched off?	Could someone give me a hand?
Please raise your hand if you have something to say.	Would you mind if I pulled the blinds down?	Everyone sit down and stop talking now.

3

Perhaps you could just step outside for a moment.	Remember to straighten the desks and chairs before you go.	Go back to your own seats, please.
Quieten down now, could you?	Make sure you pick up any rubbish near to you and put it in the bin.	OK, calm down everyone.
Keep your attention on your work, please.	Mind the bag!	Don't disturb your neighbour, please.
Please raise your hand if you have something to say.	I'm very pleased with the way you've worked today.	Can I have your attention, please?

4

Please arrange the chairs in a horseshoe shape.	What's happening on that side of the class?	Keep your attention on your work, would you, please.
Make sure your phones are switched off!	Could someone give me a hand?	Please raise your hand if you have something to say.
Let's pull the blinds down.	Everyone sit down and stop talking now.	Let's check to see if the radiator is on.
Were the instructions clear for everyone?	Shall we turn that light off?	Can I have your attention, please?

5

Would you be good enough to pick up any rubbish near to you and put it in the bin?	OK, calm down everyone.	We'll use the recording as an accompaniment today.
Mind the bag!	Don't disturb your neighbour, please.	No copying, thank you.
I'm very pleased with the way you've worked today.	Do you think you could open the window?	Please put the desks in groups of four.
I'll come round during the lesson and mark your work.	Don't keep tapping the desk, please.	Perhaps you could just step outside for a moment.

6

Could someone give me a hand?	OK, calm down everyone.	Let's pull the blinds down.
I want everyone to sit down and stop talking now.	Don't disturb your neighbour, please.	Does everyone know what they have to do?
Shall we turn that light off?	Can I have your attention, please?	Do you mind returning your desks to their original places, please?
Return to your work please.	Please come to the front of the class.	Please arrange the chairs in a horseshoe shape.

7

Don't disturb your neighbour, please.	Do you mind? No copying, please.	I'm very pleased with the way you've worked today.
How about opening the window?	I'd like you to put the desks in groups of four.	I'll come round during the lesson and mark your work.
Don't keep tapping the desk, please.	Perhaps you could just step outside for a moment.	Remember to straighten the desks and chairs before you go.
I'd like you to go back to your own seats, please.	Quieten down now, if you could, please.	Make sure you pick up any rubbish near to you and put it in the bin.

8

Let's check to see if the radiator is on.	Were the instructions clear for everyone?	Shall we turn that light off?
Can I have your attention, please?	Return to your work, could you, please?	Please come out to the front of the class, if you don't mind.
Return your desks to their original places, please.	Please arrange the chairs in a horseshoe shape.	What's happening on that side of the class?
Keep your attention on your work, please.	Make sure your phones are switched off!	I wonder if someone could give me a hand?

Photocopiable © Oxford University Press

6 Explaining a game

This activity works best in groups. Each person in the group chooses a language teaching game they know or would like to try out. There is a list of some useful sources in the Useful reading and resources section, on page 171. The idea is simply to play the chosen game with the other group members. This will involve giving precise instructions in English before the game starts, and then making sure that the game runs smoothly and fairly. After the game, you and the players can discuss any problems you had with making the instructions clear and managing the game. One useful tip: it is always worth inventing a memorable name for a complicated game. It makes it much easier to play the second time. It may also be useful to have a trial run of the game with just one or two students before you try it with the whole class.

7 Photomontage

This is an activity for groups. Each person brings a photograph of a small family gathering or of a group of friends. The other people in the group must not see the photograph before the exercise. The idea is to get the other members of the group to stand in exactly the same way as the people in the photograph (for example, their position, gestures, facial expression). This will mean giving lots of precise and polite instructions. When *the photomontage* is ready, show the original photograph to the group.

8 Drama

Choose one of the following English proverbs and work out a short dramatic sketch that illustrates the proverb. Then get your fellow students to perform your sketch. They will need to rehearse and you will have to direct them in English.

Two's company, three's a crowd.
Strike while the iron is hot.
It's no use crying over spilt milk.
Don't cross your bridges before you come to them.

Audio practice

1 Classroom intonation

🎧 **3.1** Use the list of simple instructions below to make polite requests beginning with *could you* or *would you*. Remember to use a rising intonation. Then repeat them, adding *please* at the end. Listen to the recording for a model.

1 Sit down.
2 Stand up.
3 Come here.
4 Try it again.
5 Close the blinds.
6 Turn your desk round.

🎧 **3.2** Say the following instructions aloud using a tag form (*could you, would you, can you, will you?*) after the simple command. Then repeat them and add *please* at the beginning, in the middle, or at the end.

1 Stop working.
2 Stand in a line.
3 Go back to your seat.
4 Stop talking.
5 Repeat the words after me.
6 Join in.

🎧 **3.3** Use the instructions in 3.1 again, but this time address them to particular students. You can use the list of names below or choose your own. Remember to use the tag form, *please* and the name of the student (for example, *Join in, Harumi, please, would you?*). There are six different word orders possible, so try to vary your choice. Sample answers are given on the recording.

1 Kim
2 You two
3 Everybody
4 Song-wen
5 Mr Schmidt
6 Rashid

2 Key sounds

🎧 **3.4** Read the following sentences aloud and pay attention to the sounds /p t k/ and /b d g/. Listen to the recording for a model.

1 Push your desks together, please.
2 Be careful you don't trip on the cable.
3 The idea is to design and produce a colour poster.
4 Don't drop your backpack on the ground.
5 This is a tricky grammar problem.
6 The key is at the top of the page on the right-hand side.
7 I'll play a tune on my guitar and you try to guess the title.
8 Dramatize the text and pretend to be the people in it.

3 Word stress

🔑 🎧 **3.5** Say the following words aloud and mark the stressed syllable.
There are three types:

1 words stressed on the first syllable (for example, *'schedule*);
2 words stressed on the second syllable (*re'lax*); and
3 words stressed on the third syllable (*elec'tricity*).

Use the recording to listen and repeat.

1 radiator
2 narrator
3 melody
4 display
5 applause
6 accompaniment
7 circulate
8 original
9 reference
10 certificate
11 furniture
12 equipment
13 record (noun)
14 problem
15 comfortable
16 mobile
17 distract
18 definition
19 guitar
20 piano

4 Live lessons

You will hear some short extracts from different classroom
situations. Listen to each extract and then answer the questions.
Live lesson transcripts can be found on page 166.

🔑 🎧 **3.6** Arranging seating

1 Which of the following 'business' does the teacher take care of
before the actual lesson begins?
a She greets the students.
b She checks whether there is full attendance.
c She gets some of the students to rearrange their desks.
d She checks the students have done their homework
e She checks whether everybody is ready to begin.
2 Which student doesn't have to move?
a Mattias,
b Samuel,
c Alu.
3 The teacher gives the same warning in two different ways
using *if*. What is the warning?
4 Why does the teacher say *That's fair, isn't it?*

🔑 🎧 **3.7** Starting a game

1 What is the name of the game the students will play later?
2 How does the teacher make sure she won't forget the game?
3 What is the idea of the first game that the students play?
4 Do you think this is a good game to start with?

🔑 🎧 **3.8** Giving instructions for a game

1 Why does the teacher want to play the game at this point?
2 Explain the idea of the game briefly.
3 How does the teacher *not* want the game to be played?
4 Why does the teacher say that the ball is *hot*? How will that
affect the game?
5 What extra rules does the teacher add at the end?

3.9 Using a drawing

1 What do you think the teacher first draws on the blackboard?
2 Which of the following answers are *not* offered?
   a the earth
   b an orange
   c a ring
   d a ball
   e the moon
   f a cycle
3 What structures are being practised?
4 How does the teacher deal with guesses in Spanish?
5 What does the teacher add to the original drawing to make it clear?

3.10 Using the classroom

1 What are the basic rules of this activity?
2 Why does the teacher want to do this activity with her students?
3 Why does the teacher mention the Iron Curtain?
4 What do you think might be the next stage of the activity?

Working with the textbook

4

SECTION A

The textbook is still very much at the heart of school-based language learning, and much of traditional language practice originates in the dialogues, reading passages, exercises, ,and activities in the textbook. Both teachers and students are used to the textbook and accept it as an important way of structuring and supporting learning. In fact, some students are motivated by the simple fact of progressing through the textbook. As a natural element of classroom work, the textbook also gives you an opportunity to work with some important exponents of functional language; for example, using numbers, describing position (*up, down, top, bottom*), and direction (*left, right*).

1 Distributing
Give out the books, please.
Pass these handouts to the back.
You can keep these handouts.
One between two.

2 Checking
Has everybody got a copy?
You will have to share today.
Don't forget it next time.

3 Opening the textbook
Take out your books, please.
Open your books at page 49.

4 Turning pages
Turn over the page.
Turn to page 57 in your workbooks.

5 Finding the place
Have you found the place?
We're on page 27.
We're on line 24.
Have a look at section 3, line 2.

6 Closing and collecting
Close your books.
Put your books away now.
Collect the books in.
Hand in your work as you leave.

Using the textbook

Points to think and talk about

1 Do you remember the textbooks that you used at school? What sorts of things do you remember about them? Did you enjoy the characters and stories that were in them?
2 What is a good language teaching textbook like?
3 Have textbooks changed since you were at school? How? Are the changes only superficial?
4 What other materials do you offer your students in addition to the textbook—handouts, readers, authentic documents, websites? What sort of extra materials might suit your own students? Think of ways of getting hold of such materials.
5 Some textbook series have separate workbooks or activity books. What is the purpose of these?
6 Could you and your students manage without a textbook (or a photocopier)? How would it affect the way you teach?
7 When announcing a page number or exercise, do you also write the number up on the board? Think about the positive and negative sides of this.
8 In a class there may be students with learning difficulties. How could you help them to understand your instructions? Try to think of a set of simple hand signals to accompany some routine textbook phrases.

Language to think about

1 How would you give out a new set of textbooks (or handouts) quickly and efficiently?
2 What would you say if there were not enough copies for everybody?
3 What does PTO stand for? How many ways can you think of saying the same thing?
4 How many different ways are there of saying the number *142*?
5 Can you help your students find the place in a textbook?
6 Are you clear about the difference between *lend* and *borrow*?
7 If there are ten lines in a text, where is the ninth line?
8 Which is correct: *at page 20, on page 20,* or *in page 20*?

Classroom English vocabulary to collect

1 The names of the different sorts of published teaching materials. (For example, *textbook, reader, dictionary*)
2 Different types of paper and personal folders. (For example, *photocopy, notebook, file*)

Key to symbols:
ⓘ Idiomatic phrase   ⇨ Pedagogical pointer
Ⓢ Student reply   ⓧ Cross-reference
ⓧ Typical mistake   ⌒ Listen to the CD
Ⓛ Language comment   **RECORD** Record yourself

Distributing

1 Give out the books, please.
Get the textbooks out of the cupboard, and give them out.
Bring the workbooks off the shelf, and pass them out.
Fetch the dictionaries from the staff room, and hand them out.
Take the readers out of the bookcase, and distribute them.

2 Pass these handouts to the back.
*Pass these handouts **round/along**, please.*
Pass these to the back.
*Take one and pass **them/the rest** on.*
One each, please.
Pass them on so that everyone has a copy.

3 You can keep these handouts.
They're for you to keep.
You may have them to keep.
You can write on them.
*You don't need to **return them/hand them in**.*

4 One between two.
One book between two, please.
Could you share one worksheet between two?
(It'll have to be) Three students to one copy.
Four of you will have to make do with one book.
There's only one dictionary for each group.
Three copies for each table.
***I haven't/There aren't** enough copies **for everyone/to go round**.*

---

1 ⌊ The various paper copies that teachers give out are called
handouts, worksheets, copies, photocopies, sheets, papers.
*I have some papers to **give out/hand round**.*
Who wants to give out the handouts?
Pass out the exercise sheets.
Could you help give these out, please?

---

2 ⌊ Invite students to help themselves:
Help yourself to a copy.
Come out and pick up a copy of the exercise.
Grab a handout and start working!

⇒ Giving out papers is a simple opportunity to practice *here you are* and *thank you*. See Unit 2, B3.

---

3 ⌊ If the students have to return the material, say:
I'm afraid you can't keep them.
I want these back, please.
I want them back at the end of the lesson.
*You must **give them in/return them**.*
Please don't write on them.

Checking

1 Has everybody got a copy?
Have you all got a copy of the exercise?
Who hasn't got a copy?
Anybody without?
Who can't see a copy?

2 You will have to share today.
Share with Mats this time.
Could you share your book with Sara?
Is it alright if Jacques shares with you, Marc?
Can anybody lend Alain a copy of the book?
Would someone give Tim a copy of the text?
*You can **use/borrow** my copy this time.*
*Luckily I have some **extra/spare** copies.*

3 Don't forget it next time.
Don't leave it at home next time.
Remember it (for) next time.
Try not to forget it next time.
Make sure you bring it on Friday.
Be sure to remember it next Monday.

---

1 ⌊ Notice the typical double question that teachers often use:
Has everybody got a copy?	*Is there anybody who hasn't got a copy?*
Do you all have a worksheet?	*Is there anyone without a worksheet?*
Did you all remember your textbook?	*Is there anybody who didn't remember their textbook?*

---

2 ⌊ To check that the students have all the relevant handouts, you can say:
You should have three sheets.
Check (that) you all have two pages each.
Make sure you've got all four pages.
I can make extra copies for you two.

⌊ Notice:
to borrow something *from somebody: Can I borrow your pen?*
to lend something to somebody: *Could you lend me your pen?*

---

3 Ⓢ *Can I share with you, please?*
Have you got an extra copy?
Can I take one for Mats, please?

Ⓧ *I forgot my book at home.* ✗   *I left my book at home.* ✓

Opening the textbook

1 Take out your books, please.
Could you get out your notebooks?
Books out, please!
Out with your books, please.
You (will) need your workbooks for today's lesson.
Not that book. The other one, the blue textbook.

2 Open your books at page 49.
Open your books, please.
*Take out your books and open them at **page 209/lesson 15**.*
You'll find the exercise on page 145.
***Turn to/Look at** page 29.*
Look at exercise 5A on page 46.
***Take/Have** a look at the diagram on page 25.*

2   Notice the prepositions with *page*:
*Open your book **at** page 27. (In AE, also: **on**)*
*Turn **to** page 43.*
*It's **on** page 29.*

Also use **on** with *handout, photocopy, sheet,* and *paper*:
*Do the exercise **on** page 45.*
*Write the answers down **on** your handout.*
*Copy down the words **on** the sheet.*

  Page numbers can be said in various ways:
Numbers between 1 and 99 are read in their full form: for
    example, 89 = *eighty-nine*.
Numbers greater than 100 can be read in different ways:
142 = *one hundred and forty-two   one four two   one forty-two*
206 = *two hundred and six   two O /əʊ/ six*
206 = *two hundred six (AE)*

⇒   For the sake of clarity (for example, the number 119 is easily
confused with 190), it is good to repeat the number as
separate digits:
Open your books at page one hundred and ninety, page one nine o.

⇒   Understanding numbers is such an important part of everyday
communication (times, dates and years, prices, addresses,
telephone numbers, etc.) that you need to give your students
lots of practice. Announcing page numbers (rather than writing
them up directly on the board) helps your students to feel
comfortable with spoken numbers.

  It is sometimes useful to add:
You only need your textbooks out, nothing else.
You just want your workbooks on the desk.
You can put all your other books away (for the moment).
*You don't need to write anything; I'll give you some notes
    at the end.*

Turning pages

1 Turn over the page.
Turn (over) to the next page.
Turn over the page.
Over the page.
Turn to the next page.
Next page, please.
Let's move on to the next page.

2 Now turn to page 57 in your workbooks.
I want you to turn on to page 134.
*Turn **on/forward** three pages.*
Turn back to page 35.
Turn back to the previous page.

2   A very frequent mistake is to use the definite article *the* in front
of an identifying number or letter:
Turn the page. ✓   *Turn to ~~the~~ page 15.* ✗
Start the exercise now. ✓   *Let's try ~~the~~ exercise 14C.* ✗
Read the chapter at home. ✓   *So, read ~~the~~ Chapter 6 at home.* ✗
Prepare the unit on your own. ✓   *Prepare ~~the~~ Unit 5 for next time.* ✗
Can you read the number? ✓   *Try ~~the~~ number 6.* ✗

  Use *look* and *refer* when moving to earlier or later pages or
sections:
Now look back at the last chapter.
You can refer (back) to page 216.
Please refer to the grammar section.
Refer (forward) to the wordlist.
Keep one finger in this section and refer back to it when necessary.

  Approximate page references can be given like this:
*It's somewhere near the **front/back/middle** of the book.*
*It's **about in/around** the middle of the book.*
*It's **something like/about** halfway through.*

You only need your textbooks out - nothing else

Finding the place

1 Have you found the place?
Have you all found the place?
Is there anybody who (still) hasn't found the place?
Show Juan the place.
Help Alicia find the place.
Do you know where we are?
Show him where we are.

2 We're on page 27.
Page 96, everybody.
We're looking at the exercise on page 45.
*You're **looking at/on** the wrong page.*

3 We're on line 24.
*Not that line. The **next/previous** one.*
*Not line 6. The one **after/before**.*
Not the next line, but the one after that.
Not the previous line, but the one before that.
A few lines further on.
*Five lines further **down/up**.*
*The **first/next/last** five lines.*

4 Have a look at section 3, line 2.
*(The) third section, (the) second **line/sentence**.*
*The paragraph **beginning/starting/ending** (with) in 1999.*
The third word from the end of line 6.
Line 10, fourth word along.

1 ⌊ Sometimes it's useful to refer to the previous lesson:
Where did we stop last time?
How far did we get in the last lesson?
What were we talking about last time?
Let me refresh your memory.
Last time we got as far as exercise 5.
If I remember correctly, we were on page 29.

⌊ Describing the precise location of a line or word in a textbook can be quite difficult. The following phrases are useful:
Top/bottom
*at the (very) **bottom/top/end** of the page*
in the (very) middle
*somewhere **towards/near** the **top/bottom/end** of the page*
*about **halfway/three-quarters of the way** down the page*
left/right
*on the **left/right***
*on the **left-hand/right-hand** side*
*in the **left**(-hand)/**right**(-hand) **margin/column***
*the second **section/picture** from the right*
*in the **top/bottom left**(-hand)/**right**(-hand) corner*

Ⓢ Students could learn to ask:
***What/Which** line are we on?*
***What/Which** number are we on?*
Where are we up to?
How far have we got?

3 ⌊ The following phrases are useful when referring to lines:
*The **top/bottom/middle** line.*
The tenth line from the top.
The tenth line down.
Ten lines down.
The fourth line from the bottom.
The fourth line up.
Four lines up.
The last but one line.
*The **next/second/third** to last line*

⌊ Notice the prepositions with *line*:
*We are **on** line 5.*
*Start reading **at/from** line 5.*
*Let's move **on to** line 6.*
*Have a look **at** line 5.*

⊗ *The ~~two first~~ lines.* **X**
Notice the word order with *first, next, following,* and *last*: the number follows the adjective.

4 ⌊ Notice that the article can be left out in short instructions before *first, next, last* and ordinal numbers:
Look at the last line of the first paragraph.
OR: *First paragraph, last line.*
Read the last but one line in paragraph 2.
OR: *Paragraph 2, last but one line.*
Think about the seventh word on line 5.
OR: *Line 5, seventh word.*

Other examples:
Next sentence, please.
Next one.
Last line in the second paragraph.

Closing and collecting

1 Close your books
Shut your books.
All books closed, please.

2 Put your books away now.
Put your books in your desk.
*I don't want to see any books **open/on your desks**.*

3 Collect the books in.
Collect the homework (in).
Collect the sheets (up).
*Collect the readers **in/up** and put them away.*
Could the first person in each row collect the books, please?
One person in each group can collect the sheets.
Pile the books up on my desk, please.

4 Hand your work in as you leave.
Leave your work in my tray.
Make sure all the books are put away before you leave.
***Leave/Put** your **homework/sheets/essays** on my desk on your*
way out.
Have you all handed in your tests?
Make sure you put your test in the right pile.

Pile the books on my desk, please

---

1 ⌐ An alternative to putting books away is:
Turn your books over.
Put your books face down.

---

3 ⌐ You don't have to collect the material in from every student:
*Pass the sheets (up) to the **front/end** (of each row).*
Pass them to the front and the first person in each row can bring
them to me.

---

4 ⌐ In the case of important work (essays, tests), it is a good idea to
say:
*Don't forget to put your name(s) on **it/them**.*

Both *it* and *them* are possible. It depends whether you think you
are addressing all the students as individuals (*put your name on
it*) or as a single group (*put your names on them*).

⌐ You may have special arrangements for returning homework
and assignments:
Leave your work in my tray outside the staff room.
You can put your essays in my pigeon hole.

⌐ Other useful phrases include:

Make sure		you hand in all your papers.
Please see (to it)	(that)	you return all the papers.
Be sure		you write your name on it.
Remember	to	put your name on it.
Don't forget		hand in your answer sheet.
Try	not to	forget it next time.

⌐ Having collected in the books or test, you may have to say:
I'm one short.
I'm missing one.
*I have one too **many/few**.*
I've got an extra one.

SECTION B

The basic text, whether a reading passage in a textbook, a newspaper article, or a recorded dialogue, is still the backbone of most language teaching. Although it is usually supplemented by a rich variety of other exercises and activities, either ready-made or prepared by the teacher, the basic text is very often the starting point and context for practice. The routines of introducing the basic text to students, helping them to understand it, and then thoroughly exploiting it are the foundations of effective language teaching. They also lay the basis for more communicative and creative work. This section suggests some straightforward routines for working with the basic text.

1 Introducing a text
Today's text is about …
Let me tell you about the writer.
What kind of text is this?

2 Basic reading
Read the text to yourselves.
Check the new vocabulary.
Try to answer these questions.
Try to get the main idea.
What will happen next?

3 Checking understanding
Do you understand everything?
What's it about?

4 Reading aloud
Let's read the passage aloud.
Who would like to begin?
Another sentence, please.
Stop there, please.
Go on reading, please.

5 Looking at details
Let's talk about this chapter.
We'll look at some difficult points.
Look at line 15 for a moment.
What's the Finnish for this?
What's another way of saying this?

6 Checking vocabulary
Do you know the meaning of this word?
Are there any questions on this text?

Using the basic text

Points to think and talk about

1 A very important question for students is why they are reading a text. How would you answer them? Will your answer affect the way they read the text? How would you make students interested in the basic text before they even start working with it?
2 When linguistically preparing a basic text for presentation to a class, what sort of things would you pay attention to? What problems can you anticipate?
3 Is there usually a Teacher's guide to accompany the textbook you use? What sort of things does it contain? Does it have answers for all possible problems?
4 What is the role of the students' mother tongue in dealing with the basic text?
5 Is it important for the students to read the text aloud?
6 How and when do you teach the new vocabulary in a text?
7 How can you check that the students have got the gist or main ideas of a text?
8 A very common way of dealing with the basic text is to ask *Wh*-questions. Is it possible for a student to answer a *Wh*-question without really understanding the text?
9 What is a good *Wh*-question like? Think about the following: a) Should the question be formed with different vocabulary from that used in the text? b) Should it refer to information from different parts of the text? c) Should it ask the student to infer?
10 How do you deal with a misprint in the textbook?
11 What criteria would you use for choosing a set of class readers? What for you is an interesting reading passage?
12 Are you familiar with any monolingual English dictionaries? What are the advantages of using monolingual dictionaries? When would you use a bilingual dictionary?

Language to think about

1 How would you get your students to read aloud?
2 How do you ask for the translation of a word or phrase?
3 What is the difference between *skimming* and *scanning* a text?
4 What other ways do you know of saying: *in turns*?
5 Can you rephrase the question – *Where is she going?* – using *do you think*?
6 How else could you say: *This is a new word*?
7 What sort of comments could you write in English at the bottom of a student's written work?
8 Can you correct these phrases? a) *We handled this last week.* b) *It's the same than in French.* c) *Take the turns for reading.*

English vocabulary to collect

1 Words connected with vocabulary and describing vocabulary. (For example, *idiom, syllable, antonym*)
2 Words related to types of written material. (For example, *leaflet, application form, blog*)

Introducing a text

1 Today's text is about rain forests.
*The **topic/subject** of today's text is football.*
*Today we'll read about **a famous writer/an important event**.*

2 Let me tell you about the writer.
*I'll give you **a little/some** background information on this text.*
What do you know about the writer?

3 What kind of text is this?
How would you describe this type of text?
Where might you find this kind of text?

---

1 ⇒ Introducing a text doesn't only include the presentation of new vocabulary. You should also try to arouse interest in the text and relate it to the students' own experiences and expectations. There are many pre-reading strategies (see Useful reading and resources, page 171). Their idea is to give readers a way into the text without requiring them to understand everything immediately:
What could this be about?
*Look at the **cover/picture/title** and tell me what you think it will be about.*
On the basis of the title, what do think this text is about?
So, does anybody know anything about Australia?

⌐ A good way to introduce a text is to look at some features of its layout and appearance. Useful vocabulary:
title, subtitle, heading, subheading, picture, diagram, caption, column.

2 ⌐ Additional questions:
Have you read anything by this writer before?
Have you read any similar pieces of writing?
Does this text remind you of anything else you've read?

3 ⌐ Follow up with questions like:
Would you expect to find this kind of text in a newspaper?
What strikes you about this text?
What do you first notice about this text?
What kind of style do you think this text will use?

⇒ It is often useful to let students predict the words used in the text:
What key vocabulary would you expect to find in a text about cloning?
What words or phrases might you come across in a text called 'Asteroids'?
Write (down) a list of words you might expect to find in this text.

⌐ Typical written styles include:
journalistic, scientific, academic, fiction, factual, biographical, autobiographical.

Basic reading

1 Read the text to yourselves.
Read the passage silently.
Prepare the next three paragraphs.
Familiarize yourselves with the text.
Read through the conversation on your own.
Study the chapter by yourself.
Have a look at the next section in your own time.

2 Check the new vocabulary.
Use the wordlist.
Check the new vocabulary from the list at the back.
If there are any words you don't know, please ask.
Look up any new words in the dictionary.

3 Try to answer these questions.
While reading, try to answer these questions.
As you read, try to find answers to the following questions.

4 Try to get the main idea.
Read it through quickly to get the main ideas.
It doesn't matter if you don't understand every word.
Just try to get the gist. /dʒɪst/
Jot down some key ideas.
Skim the text (through).

5 What will happen next?
*Can anyone **guess/predict/suggest** what will happen next?*
Before you read the next section, can you guess how the story will end?
*How might the story **go on/continue**?*

---

1 ⌐ Add any special instructions:
Read what it says at the top of the page first.
Make sure you read the footnotes carefully.

2 ⌐ Notice the following phrases:

Refer to	*the wordlist*	*to find the word.*
Check	*the vocabulary list*	*to make sure.*
Use	*the alphabetical list*	*to speed things up.*
Consult	*the index*	*if you're having trouble.*

⌐ Encourage students to use reference tools:

	the index.
Look it up in	*the grammar section.*
Check it in	*the bibliography.*
	the appendix.
	the footnotes.
	an encyclopedia.
	a thesaurus.
Look it up on	*Google.*
	the Internet.
Why don't you	*Google it?*

Checking understanding

3 ⌊ It is useful for students to make their own questions before reading a text:
*What questions do you have **on/for** this text?*
What questions would you like this text to answer?
What questions do you think this text will raise?
What (kind of) opinion do you think will be presented in the text?
Write down three questions you would like the text to answer.

⇨ Giving students questions about a text before they read it will help guide their reading. Allowing them to come up with their own questions will help them develop a greater interest in the text. If you ask your students to prepare questions in this way, it is important to give them time to readdress these questions after they have read the text:
Did you get the answers you wanted?
Do you still have outstanding questions?
What new questions do you have?

4 ⌊ *Skim* = to read for the main ideas.
Scan = to read something and look for specific information.

1 Do you understand everything?
*Is there anything you **don't/didn't** understand?*
Is/Was everything clear?
Anything not clear (to you)?
Let's see if you've understood.
I'll just check how well you've understood.
*Let me ask you some questions **about/on** this passage.*

2 What's it about?
*What's this **story/article/extract/passage/text** (all) about?*
Can you briefly summarize the main ideas?
*Did you get the **main/general** idea of the passage?*
Did you get the gist of the text?

1 ⇨ Wh-questions are generally used for dealing with detailed comprehension of a text. In other words, they are used to check that students really have understood all the important points, and to highlight grammatical structures. These types of questions are examined in detail in Unit 6. Remember, however, that you can leave this task to the students:
*You had the **job/task** of preparing two questions each on this unit.*
*Who is going to ask the questions **about/on** this chapter?*

2 ⇨ Asking a student to give a brief summary of a text in the L1 is an authentic and motivating way of focusing on overall understanding. It will also encourage student discussion and participation:
(In a nutshell) What is this passage about?
*Tell me briefly in **Spanish/French/**... what happens.*

⌊ In advanced classes, you may want students to attempt a summary in their own words:
Use your own words, to describe what happened.
Using your own words, tell us what the text is about.
Explain the main message of the text in your own words.

⇨ Questions using the word *happen* (for example, *What happened? What is happening?*) encourage students to give more than a one-word answer and to explain the situation. Another technique is to ask about the role of individual words:
Why is the word 'carrot' important in the story?
What part does the word 'gold' play in the text?

⌊ If students are working from memory, you can ask:
Let's see if you remember what happened.
How much do you remember (of the story)?

Reading aloud

1 Let's read the passage aloud.
*Now we'll read the **text/dialogue/conversation** aloud.*
Read it out loud.
Let's read out what it says here.

2 Who would like to begin?
Lars will begin.
You start (reading), Sonja.
Any volunteers to begin?

3 Another sentence, please.
One more sentence.
Finish the sentence (off).
*Read to the end of the **line/sentence/paragraph**.*
Don't stop in the middle of the sentence.
Go on. I'll tell you when to stop.

4 Stop there, please.
*That's **enough/fine**, thank you.*
*That will do **fine/nicely**, thank you.*

5 Go on reading, Elli.
Someone else, please.
You go on, Sara.
(It's) your turn, Vera.
Now you, Juan.
Would you carry on (from there), Tino?
Michaela, go on from where Pablo left off.
Heidi, carry on from where Felix stopped.

---

1 ⌊ If you want to assign reading parts, use the following:
Who would like to be Romeo?
Elias, you can be Mr Jones.
Anne, you read the part of Watson this time.
***These two rows/the boys** can read this part, and the **back row/
girls** the other part.*
*Let's read the conversation, with Knut reading (the part of)
Mr Wilson.*
Let's try it again, but this time with Beatriz as the stranger.
*Let's try it again, but for a change with Leon **in/playing** the part of
Lord Cumnor.*

⌊ If you decide to provide a model, use:
I'll read it to you first.
First of all, I'll read it to you.
*Let's listen to it on the **tape/cassette/recording/CD** first.*

⇨ It is important to remember that reading aloud in a foreign
language practises and develops very different skills from silent
reading. Always give your students time to prepare any reading
aloud. As a teacher, you will need to practise reading aloud
clearly and expressively.

⊗ Some typical errors:
~~At~~ first I'll read it. ✗   First (of all), I'll read it. ✔
First I ~~read~~ it. ✗   First, I'll read it. ✔

2 ⌊ More specific instructions include:
Read just one sentence.
Read the first ten lines.
Start reading from line 6
*Read **as far as/down to/up to t**he end of the chapter.*
*Emilia, could you read the **next bit/section/paragraph**?*

⌊ In many cases, you can allocate reading as follows:
I want you to read in turns.
One after the other, please.
Round the class, starting here.
Three sentences for each of you.
*Three lines each, please, starting **here/with Ana**.*

⊗ See Unit 2, A2 for more on turn-taking.

4 ⇨ Remember to thank the student and acknowledge his/her
contribution. For other phrases of encouragement, see Unit 2, C2.
That was nicely read.
You read that very well.

5 ⌊ If the order of reading is already clear, you can simply say:
Next, please.
(And the) Next one, please.
Let's have a new round.
Let's keep to the order we decided on.

⊛ Encourage your students to ask:
*How do you **say/pronounce** the next word?*
I'm not sure how to say this word.
*Where's the **stress/accent** in this word?*

Read it out loud

Looking at details

1 Let's talk about this chapter.
Let's take a closer look at the text.
Let's look at the passage in more detail.
Perhaps we should have a detailed look at this again.

2 We'll look at some difficult points in the text.
Let's have a look at some of the difficult points.
Let's start with a look at the difficulties in this text.
There are one or two difficult points we should look at.
I'd like to point out some interesting words.

3 Look at line 15 for a moment.
Look at the last line of the first paragraph.
Look at the end of the very first line.
A little further down, about two lines from the bottom.

4 What's the Finnish for this?
What's 'conscious' in Japanese?
What's the German word for 'conscious'?
What is this sentence in Portuguese?
*How **do/would** you say that in Spanish?*
What does this sentence mean in Korean?
*How would you translate this **word/phrase** into Cantonese?*
What do you call this thing in English?

5 What's another way of saying this?
How else can you say the same thing?
*What's a **better/shorter** way of saying this?*
Can you say the same thing, using different words?

---

2 ⇨ To take a look at all the difficult points in a text might well overwhelm students, at least if you try to deal with them all at once. Decide beforehand what aspects of the text you will focus on first; for example, grammar, vocabulary. In more advanced classes, the focus may be on the presentation of the argument or opinion, on the structure of the text, or the style of the writer's language.

3 ⊗ For phrases connected with finding the line or the place in the text, see also Unit 4, A5.

  ⌊ These phrases are intended for a close analysis of the text, perhaps more useful in advanced classes:
Second paragraph, first line, the word 'content'.
In line 4 you can see the word 'luxury'.
If you look at line 15, you will notice the word 'happy'.

  ⌊ Notice these useful phrases:

Notice	the spelling of the word 'center'.
I'd like to draw your attention to	the word 'seeming' in line 26.
Pay attention to	the word 'ragged' in the last sentence.
Look out for	examples of the past tense.
Notice how the writer	presents his arguments.
Look at the way the author	uses the passive in paragraph 3.

4 ⇨ Translation provides a quick way of checking understanding of individual words and phrases. Where cultural differences make precise translation difficult, you can ask:
What is the (nearest) English equivalent of … ?
What corresponds to English Christmas pudding in Finland?

  ⇨ Translation of longer sections is also useful, but your focus should be on overall understanding:
Please translate.
*Translate **this/that** into Turkish.*
Could you put that into Spanish for us?
Translate from Japanese into English.
Don't translate word for word.
*Give me **a rough/an approximate** translation.*

---

5 ⌊ Notice the following questions:
What's another word that means the same (thing)?
Can you give me one phrase for the same idea?
Can you think of an alternative expression meaning the same (as this)?
What are two words with the same meaning?
What words mean more or less the same?

  ⊗ *The same ~~than~~ this.* ✗   *The same as this.* ✓

Checking vocabulary

1 Do you know the meaning of this word?
I want to make sure you know the meaning of the
  new words.
Let's begin by checking the meaning of one or two words.
I'll begin by teaching you some words we'll need later on.
*Let's have a look at the new **words/vocabulary**.*
I don't think you know this word.
This is probably a new word for you.

2 Are there any questions on this text?
Has anybody got anything to ask (about this text)?
Is there anything else you would like to ask about?
*Are there any points you're not **sure of/clear about**?*
*Would you like anything **explained/explaining**?*

---

1 🔔 Encourage students to ask about new vocabulary:
  Can I help you with any words or phrases?

Are there any	strange words new phrases expressions	you don't know the Finnish for? you don't know the meaning of? you are unfamiliar with? you haven't heard?
Who knows	what this word means? when you use this word?	

🔔 Sometimes it's useful to remind students if they have come
  across a new word before:

We	had met ran into came across	this word this phrase this expression this term	in your last lesson. last time. in unit 3. on Wednesday.

🔔 Encourage students to guess or try:
  It's almost the same in English.
  The English word is almost the same.
  The English for this is very similar.
  Have a guess! What could it be?

🔔 You can also explain the meaning of a new word through
  contextualized examples and descriptions of typical use,
  location, and so on:
  This means (more or less) the same as 'he left'.
  The meaning of this sentence is (something like) 'he didn't
    understand'.
  It has something to do with electricity.
  *It's another word **for/meaning the same as** 'huge'.*
  You use it for opening a door.
  You can find it on a computer keyboard.
  If I keep trying and don't give up, then I'm 'persistent'.

ⓧ Typical mistakes:
  We ~~handled~~ this word last time. ✗   *We dealt with … ✓*
  Let's pick ~~up~~ the new words. ✗   *Let's **pick out/look at** the*
                    new words. ✓

2 Ⓢ Encourage your students to ask when they come across a new
    word:
    *Excuse me, what does '**famous'/this word** mean?*
    I'm not sure of the meaning of this word here.
    Can you explain 'absolute' to me?
    *I've never **met/seen/heard** this word before.*
    What's the German for this word?

ⓧ *Are there any questions ~~of~~ this text?* ✗
    *Are there any questions **on/about** this text?* ✓

Would you like
anything explained?

$$E\psi(x) = -\frac{\hbar^2}{2m}\frac{d^2\psi(x)}{dx^2} + V(x)\psi(x)$$

4

SECTION C

Exercise management (setting an exercise and going through it) is a well-established part of teaching, a pedagogical ritual that allows for great variation and improvisation. It is certainly one of the most interesting events in the classroom if we think about the opportunities for language use, interaction, and negotiated meaning. It is the perfect context for expanding students' receptive vocabulary and getting them used to the various forms of asking questions and giving instructions. In fact, checking an exercise is the kind of task that can occasionally be given to students. For once they will be the person giving directions in English rather than merely responding to the teacher's commands and questions. Exercise management should be both practical and efficient, but it can also be an enriching and empowering part of the lesson.

1 Setting an exercise
Try exercise 6.
This is the way we'll do it.
The idea of this exercise is to practise ...

2 Writing and copying
Do the exercise in your notebooks.
Copy this down in your notebooks.
Rewrite it at home.

3 Starting to check an exercise
I think you have had long enough on this.
Let's see how you did.
Let's go though this exercise.

4 Going through the answers
What's the answer to number 1?
Can anybody help?
Let her try it on her own.
Let's have a look at it together.
The correct answer is A.

5 Giving corrective feedback
Is that right?
Is there another way of saying it?
That's also possible.
That wasn't quite right.
Did anyone notice the mistake?

6 Evaluating
How did you get on?
Anybody with one mistake?
Come and see me after the lesson.

Managing exercises

Points to think and talk about

1 Are there any types of textbook exercise that you particularly like to use in your teaching? Why do you think you like them?
2 Do you think it is important to mention the aims of an exercise to your students?
3 What are all the factors that influence the type of feedback you give?
4 A student answers your question in English. The answer is right, but there are grammatical mistakes. What would you say? Would you correct the mistakes? If so, how? What if it was a pronunciation mistake? When should you overlook errors?
5 At what point in an oral exercise or activity should you correct a student's errors? Should you interrupt immediately or wait? Do you think you should give the feedback personally to the student or in a general way to the whole class?
6 How could you make use of the other students in correcting mistakes?
7 What could you do when a student gives no answer at all? Or when a student comes to a stop in the middle of a sentence?
8 Should students be allowed to see or hear incorrect English? Do students remember incorrect material more easily than correct material? How would you deal with misprints or typing errors in written material? And what about errors made by native speakers?
9 Do you think it is important for students to receive a mark or score for the work they do?
10 Do you think it is a good idea to occasionally allow a student to act as the teacher when checking the answers to an exercise? What benefits would this give? What other 'teacher' tasks could the students sometimes take over?

Language to think about

1 Can you set an exercise and explain what you want the students to do?
2 Can you tell the students where you want them to write their answers?
3 How many ways do you know for asking *What's the answer to number 1*?
4 Do you know how to help students find their own mistakes?
5 How many ways do you know of saying *That was right* and *That was wrong*?
6 What's wrong with the following? *Let's go the answers over*; *How do you answer to the question 3*?
7 When could you say: *That was a piece of cake*?
8 Do you use *do* or *make*? *I want you to ... exercise 3. Who can ... question 4*?

Classroom English vocabulary to collect

Equipment that students use during a lesson. (For example, *ruler, paper clip, pen*)

Setting an exercise

1 Try exercise 6.
I want you to do exercise 7A.
Try the next exercise as well.
Let's go on to exercise number 3.
I'd like you to write the answers to exercise 5.

2 This is the way we'll do it.
This is how we shall do it.
What we shall do is this.
Watch me first.

3 The idea of this exercise is to practise asking questions.
*The **aim/goal/purpose/point** of this exercise is (for you) to ask each other questions.*
What this exercise is trying to do is to help you practise the past tense.

1 ⌊ Use these phrases when students don't do the whole of an exercise:
*Do **the whole/part/some** of the exercise.*
Answer the first four questions.
Answer every other question.
You can leave the last one out.
There's no need to do the last five.
Just do the first half of the exercise.
Don't bother with the second part.
We'll skip the first two.

⌊ You can warn the students about possible difficulties:
If you get stuck, skip the question.
If you get stuck on one, leave it and come back to it later.

⊗ *I want you to ~~make~~ exercise 7.* **✗**

2 ⌊ If you are going to give a longer series of instructions, the following phrases are a good way to begin:
Before you begin, let me tell you how I want you to do it.
I would like you to do it (in) the following way.
*Could you do it **this way/like this**?*
Listen now while I explain what I want you to do.

If the students are familiar with the exercise type, you can say:
Do it the same way as last time.
Let's do it the way we did it last time.

Mention any changes in working routines:
This time let's do it without looking.
For a change let's try it in English.
To add some variety, let's listen to some music.

⌊ Notice the use of *with + -ing* to describe a working method:
This time we'll do it with Julie reading.
Let's try it with six of you working in each group.

3 ⇨ It is always useful to tell your students what the goal of an exercise is or why they are doing it. Often the goal is clear, but it's worth mentioning it so that the students focus on the important points in achieving the goal.

Writing and copying

1 Do the exercise in your notebooks.
Use your exercise book for this.
Do the exercise in writing.

2 Copy this down in your notebooks.
***Take/put/get/write/copy** this down in your exercise books.*
*Make a note of this **in your books/on a slip of paper/somewhere**.*
*Copy this down **from/off** the board.*

3 Rewrite it at home.
***Write/copy** it out **neatly/tidily/legibly** at home.*
Try not to scribble.

1 ⌊ For oral exercises, use:
We'll do this exercise orally.
Let's try it aloud before we write it down.

⌊ Younger students may need more precise instructions:
***Do/write** the exercise **in pencil/ ink/ ballpoint/Biro**.*
*Use **a pen/a pencil/ink** to do the exercise.*

⇨ You may have to find solutions to unexpected problems, but such situations can produce a lot of real communication.
No pencil? Did you leave it at home?
*Has anybody got **an extra/a spare** pencil?*
Go and get one from my desk.
Have you got a spare pen on you?
Luckily I've got a spare one on me.
Come out and sharpen your pencil.

2 ⓘ To jot something down = make a quick note
Jot this down somewhere so that you don't forget it.

⌊ If you want the students to write in a particular place, say:
*Write it **in the margin**.*
*Write it **in the empty space** **at the top**.*
*Make a note of this **at** the back.*
Write the sentence up on the board.

⌊ For highlighting important words and structures, you can say:
Underline the new words.
Highlight this structure.
Use your highlighter (pen) to mark this.

⌊ Notice the prepositions:
in a textbook   *on a sheet of paper*
in an exercise book   *on a transparency/ an overhead/ an OHP*
on a page   *on the Internet*

ⓢ Students may ask:
Shall we do this in our exercise books?
Are we supposed to hand this in?

3 ⌊ If unclear handwriting is a problem, you can say:
I can't read your handwriting.
What is this word supposed to be?
I can't make out what you've written. Your handwriting is illegible.

⌊ If you want to be sure of understanding the students' writing, say:
*Write it in **block letters/capitals**.*
Print it.

⌊ Other typical fonts in textbooks and word-processed documents:
Read the words in italics.
*Say the words in **bold**.*
Repeat the <u>underlined</u> words.

Starting to check an exercise

1 I think you have had long enough on this.
It looks as if you are all more or less ready.
You all seem to have finished, so ...
You've probably had enough time on this.

2 Let's see how you did.
*Let's see how you **went/got** on.*
*I wonder how you **managed/did**.*

3 Let's go through this exercise.
Let's check the answers.
Let's run through the answers quickly.
Let's go over the exercise together.
Let's go through the sentences on the board.

---

1 📖 If an exercise has been given as homework, you can begin by checking that everybody has done it:
This was your homework from last time.
You were supposed to do this for homework.
*Did you all (manage to) **do exercise 12/prepare this chapter**?*
Did everybody finish off this exercise at home?
Have any of you not made a list of questions?

📖 When returning students' work, such as tests, or exercises, begin by saying:
I'll return your tests now and we can run through them together.
I'll give you your tests back and we can go over them.

⇨ Students should be encouraged to check their own work. This allows you to give individual help:
Check your answers on page 123.
The right answers are on page 123.
***Change/Exchange/Swap/Switch** papers with **someone/your neighbour/your partner**.*
Mark your own.

3 ⊗ *Let's go the answers ~~over~~. ✗   Let's go over the answers. ✓*

Don't fall into the trap...

Going through the answers

1 What's the answer to number 1?
*What have you **put/written/marked/got/answered** for question 2?*
What do you have for the next one?
How have you answered number 4?
How does the first one go?

2 Can anybody help?
Help Luisa, could you?
Who would like to help (out)?
Can anybody give her a hand?
Has anybody got any (other) suggestions?
Any other ideas?
Did anybody have anything (else) for this one?
Did anybody have a different answer?
Let's hear a few more answers.

3 Let her try it on her own.
Don't help him.
Don't whisper the answer.
I'm sure she can manage on her own.
*Don't keep **prompting/interrupting**.*
Please don't shout out.
Put your hand up if you want to answer.

4 Let's have a look at it together.
We can try this one together.

5 The correct answer is A.
*'Never' is the **correct/right** answer.*
The answer you're looking for is 'wise'.

---

1 ⇨ You can address questions to the whole class:
Let's go on to number 2.
Has anybody got anything for the last one?
Could somebody read out what they put for number 2?

But it is often better to address them to individual students:
And the next one, please. OK, you try that one, Tara.
What about the last one? Yes, Carmen, please.
Ragnar, I want you to try the first one, please.
I think it's Juan's turn next.

Ⓢ *What number are we on?*
Where are we (up to)?
Can you read out the answer to number 2 again?

⊗ *Please answer ~~to~~ question 3. ✗*
What is your answer to question 3? ✓

📖 Sometimes it helps to tell students how difficult the next task is:
*The next one is **fairly/pretty** easy.*
This is very straightforward.
*This one shouldn't cause you any **trouble/difficulty**.*
Think about this one carefully.
There's a catch in it.
It's a trick question.
Don't fall into the trap.

1 ⓘ Notice these idiomatic expressions as well:
This was a cinch! (BE = very easy)
This was a piece of cake. (= very easy)
Easy-peasy.
*This was a real **stinker/teaser**! (= very hard)*
Question 7 was a nasty one.
This one beats me!

Ⴑ If you are returning homework or a test, you could also say:
*You found this one very **hard/easy**.*
The last one didn't give you any trouble at all.
*Everybody got this one **right/wrong**.*

2 ⇨ It is important to use English in one-to-one situations with students. If you are circulating in the class, you could say:
Can I help (you)?
Would you like some help?
Shall I give you a hand (with it)?

Giving corrective feedback

1 Is that right?
Is/Was that the correct answer?
Can you say that?
Can you say it like that?
Are you sure about that?
Have another think about what you said.

2 Is there another way of saying it?
What else could you say?
How else could you say it?
What's a better way of saying it?
Try to put it in other words.
Could you phrase it slightly differently?
What other word could you use here?

3 That's also possible.
That's another possibility.
That's an alternative answer.

4 That wasn't quite right.
That was almost right.
You made a small mistake.
Just one little slip.
*You made a **small/little/slight** slip on this.*
*It was just a minor **mistake/error**.*
Think about what you said. Is it English?

5 Did anyone notice the mistake?
What's wrong with this sentence?
*Is there anything **to correct/that needs correcting**?*
*(Is there) anything wrong **with/in** sentence 3?*

1 ⇨ Your role as a teacher is first and foremost to encourage students to use the language, and not to point out and correct their mistakes. Nevertheless, especially when you are practising a new structure, for example, it is good to give helpful corrective feedback:
How should you say it?
What should you say?
How should you answer?
What would you say, Mischa?

2 Ⴑ It is useful to encourage students to think about alternative answers rather than just accept a single correct one:
*Is there a **better/shorter** way of saying the same thing?*
*Can anyone improve on **that/what Aila said**?*
*That is **very good/fine/OK/all right**, but is there another way?*
(Does) anybody have any alternative suggestions for number 6?
Can anyone say it another way?

3 ⇨ Students can often surprise you with original answers:
I hadn't thought of it that way.
That's an interesting suggestion.
That possibility has never struck me.
That's one way of looking at it that I hadn't thought of.
I don't see why not.
That seems fine to me.
I'll have to think about that.
I'll have to check that.

4 ⌞ The student's answer may be very good, but still need some small changes:

What you said isn't wrong,	but maybe it sounds better to say it like this.
That's not wrong,	but perhaps it would be better to say:
There's nothing wrong with that,	but I think it might be better to say:
That sounds OK to me,	but maybe you could think of another way.

4 ⌞ You can give detailed feedback to more advanced students who are used to grammatical terminology:
There's something missing.
*You've **missed/left** the verb out.*
*You've **forgotten/omitted** the preposition.*
*You used the wrong **word/tense/preposition**.*
What tense should you have used?

4 ⊗ For more phrases connected with giving feedback, see Unit 2, C.

Evaluating

1 How did you get on?
*How many did you get **right/wrong**?*
Did anybody get them all right?

2 Anybody with one mistake? Two mistakes?
Hands up if you made more than three mistakes.
Put your hand up if you scored more than 7.

3 Come and see me after the lesson.
Come and see me after the class if you have any more questions.

1 ⇒ You have to decide yourself whether it is a good idea to score exercises and to announce students' scores. Students themselves are generally keen to find out how well they did:
What was your score?
How many points did you score?
Count up your points.
One point for every one right.
Give yourself one point for every correct answer.
Take off a point for every one (you got) wrong.

🗩 Encourage advanced students to ask:
Why can't I say this?
*Is it **wrong/a mistake** to say ...?*
What's wrong with saying ...?
Why did you mark this wrong?

2 ⌞ You may have to explain how you awarded points:
I didn't count it as a mistake if you put 'big'.
I didn't take any points off if you forgot the question mark.

⌞ General class feedback can be very useful and motivating, but it is important to encourage all your students equally:
If you scored more than 8, you did very well.
Anybody who scored over 9 did really well.
If your score was under 5, then you need to work harder.

⌞ Personal written feedback—a small comment on a test or exercise—can be surprisingly motivating. Here are some of the commonest:
***Excellent/Nice/Good** work.*
(Very) Well done.
A pleasure to read.
***Good/Great** stuff!*
Keep it up.
Getting better.
Much better.
Great improvement.
Good effort.
Satisfactory.
Could do better.
Too many careless slips.
*Careful with your **spelling/vocabulary**.*
See me about this.

3 ⌞ It is always possible to give individual feedback:
I'd like to speak to you for a moment at the end of class, Sara.
Maya, could I have a word with you about your test?
Anybody who scored a C, could you stay behind at the end?

Classroom essentials

ASKING QUESTIONS (2)

Or and *Wh-* questions

1 *Or* questions

- *Or* questions (sometimes called alternative questions) offer students a clear choice between two or more alternative answers. The reply can consist simply of one of the alternatives offered in the question. In this sense, *Or* questions are straightforward, useful, and efficient.

  Is the answer A or B? — A.
  Would you like to work with Matt's group or Leta's group? — Matt's.
  Do you prefer blue, red, or green? — Red.

Four forms

- *Or* questions can take one of four forms:

1 Basic form — the alternatives are adjacent.

   Is he leaving today or tomorrow?
   Does she live in Toronto or Vancouver?
   Do you finish your homework or watch TV in the evenings?
   Did Liverpool or Chelsea win the game?

2 Postponed form—the second alternative is at the end.

   Do you finish your homework in the evenings or watch TV?

3 Expanded form—the second alternative is in its own verb phrase.

   Is he leaving today or is he leaving tomorrow?
   Does she live in Toronto or does she live in Vancouver?
   Do you finish your homework in the evenings or do you watch TV?
   Did Liverpool win the game or did Chelsea win it?

4 *Wh-* form—a normal *Wh-* question with both alternatives at the end.

   When is he leaving, today or tomorrow?
   Where does she live, in Toronto or in Vancouver?
   What do you do in the evening, finish your homework or watch TV?
   Who won the game, Liverpool or Chelsea?

   The last-mentioned *Wh-* form is very useful since it practises the understanding of normal *Wh-* questions. Students can answer by simply choosing one of the alternatives offered.

Intonation

- In a list of alternatives, the first item(s) are spoken on a high-rising intonation, but the final item is on a falling intonation:
  Are the children on the ⤴red line or the ⤵blue line?
  Are the reasons ⤴political or ⤵economic?
  Who is at the station, ⤴Jerry, ⤴Chip, or ⤵Kate?
  Which alternative is correct, ⤴A, ⤴B, ⤴C, or ⤵D?

» See 🎧 4.1

Questions as clues

- Where the items in the list are not real alternatives but are meant as clues to help students get the correct answer, a rising intonation is used on the final item as well. This type of *Or* question typically follows an unanswered *Wh-* question. Often the original *Wh-* question is then repeated.

  Teacher: Where are the tourists going?
  Students: (Silence)
  Teacher: Well, are they going to a ⁊museum or a ⁊cinema, or a ⁊library ... (or where are the going)?

- Where you don't want to mention a particular alternative, but nevertheless help the student towards the correct answer, the second alternative can be **or something**. A rising intonation is required:

  Teacher: Why did the family emigrate?
  Students: (Silence)
  Teacher: Well, did they want a better life or something?

- ⑧ See 🎧 4.2 for more practice.

- Notice that **Yes/no** questions can be turned into *Or* questions by adding **or not?**

  Have you done it or not?
  Do you know which page we're on or not?

2 *Wh-* questions
Wh- words

- As the name suggests, *Wh-* questions are questions beginning with *Wh-* words, namely:

Who	*Who would like to clean the blackboard?*
Who(m)	*Who(m) shall we ask to do the next one?*
Whose	*Whose turn is it to act as secretary?*
What	*What is the answer to number 9?*
Which	*Which group would you like to join?*
When	*When will you hand your essay in?*
Where	*Where did we stop last time?*
Why	*Why don't you come and sit at the front?*

- *How* also belongs to the group:

How	*How would you translate this into English?*
	How many of you are there in this group?

- Notice:
  a *Who's = Who is, who has.* *Who's away today?*
  Who's finished already?
  b *Whom* is the object form of *who*. It is still used, but is nowadays considered formal.
  To whom shall I address the letter?
  c *What ... for = Why* *What did you say that for?*
  d Normally, *Wh-* questions are spoken on a falling intonation. A high-rising intonation is used in so-called echo questions:
  Teacher: What ⟍time is it?
  Student: Five to ten.
  Teacher: (surprised or not catching): ⁊What time is it?

- ⑧ See 🎧 4.3

Problems

When using *Wh-* questions effectively and accurately in the language classroom, there are four problem areas: a) word order; b) word order in indirect questions; c) special grammatical difficulties, and d) special types of question. This unit deals with the first two problems and Unit 6 with the others.

A Word order

- Word order in *Wh-* questions is always a problem for students, and occasionally for non-native teachers. The basic word order is:

Question word	Auxiliary verb	Subject	Main verb	Object
Who	are	you?		
Who(m)	are	you	waiting for?	
What	is	the matter?		
What	are	you	doing?	
Where	are	they?		
Where	did	they	find	the book?

- Most problems occur when the *Wh-* question word is the subject of the sentence:

Wh- word as subject	Typical error	*Wh-* word as object
Who began last time?	*Who ~~did begin~~ last time? ✗	Who did I begin with last time?
What helped you most?	*What ~~did help~~ you the most? ✗	What did I help you most with?
Which word rhymes?	*Which word ~~does rhyme~~? ✗	Which word does it rhyme with?
How many watch it?	*How many ~~do watch~~ it? ✗	How many do you watch?

- Notice that the incorrect sentences in the *Typical error* column are possible, but only with a different intonation and meaning:
  I didn't begin, and you didn't, so who did *begin last time?*

Prepositions

- Modern usage tends to avoid the use of a preposition + *whom* at the start of the question (*At whom are you staring?*), and prefers starting with *who* and placing the preposition at the end (*Who are you staring at?*). In some languages the idea of the preposition may be already contained in the question word. Because the preposition comes at the end of the sentence in English, it is very easy to forget it, especially in longer sentences:
  Which particular word were you thinking of?
  What word did you finish the last sentence with?
  Which example did you want me to take another look at?

B Word order in indirect questions

- Indirect *Wh-* questions are very frequent and useful in the classroom situation. There are two types of indirect *Wh-* questions, easily remembered as *do you know ... ?* and *... do you think ... ?* types.

Do you know...?

Direct *Wh-* question	Indirect *Wh-* question	
Why is this answer better?	Do you know	why this answer is better?
What does this word mean?	Does anybody remember	what this word means?
When did the film start?	Have you any idea	when the film started?
Who invented the transistor?	Can you tell me	who invented the transistor?
Why is this answer better?	Let me ask you	why this answer is better.
What does this word mean?	Let's see who knows	what this word means.

Other similar questions are:
Can anybody explain ... ?
Can you guess ... ?
Has anybody thought ... ?

... do you think ...?

Direct Wh- question	Indirect Wh- question
Why is this answer better?	*Why do you think this answer is better?*
What does this word mean?	*What do you imagine this word means?*
When did the film start?	*When do you reckon the film started?*
Who invented the transistor?	*Who do you suppose invented the transistor?*

- In the case of the verb *to be* and *who* or *what* as the subject, there are two word orders possible:

Who is the king of Spain?

What was the answer to number 4?

Who do you think	the king of Spain is? is the king of Spain?
What do you think	the answer to number 4 was? was the answer to number 4?

- Typical mistakes:
  What do you think ~~means this word?~~ ✗
  Who do you think ~~did invent the transistor?~~ ✗
  What do you think ~~where does she live?~~ ✗
  What do you think ~~how old is he?~~ ✗

Practice

👤 1 The four different types of *Or* question are summarized below:

1	Basic form:	Does group 1 or group 2 want this topic?
2	Postponed form:	Does group 1 want this topic or (does) group 2?
3	Expanded form:	Does group 1 want this topic or does group 2 want it?
4	*Wh-* form:	Which group wants this topic, group 1 or group 2?

Ask *Or* questions using the clues below. Try to ask two different *Or* questions for each item.

1 Mrs Jones (a secretary/a researcher)?
2 This (a book/a pencil)?
3 The correct answer (A/B)?
4 Like to answer the next one (Mia/Sally)?
5 The correct preposition (in/at/on)?
6 Shakespeare was born (16th century/17th century)?
7 Capital of Peru (La Paz/Lima/Santiago)?
8 Mari spends her summer holidays (travelling around Europe/relaxing at her summer cottage)?
9 Won the Nobel prize for their work on DNA (Crick and Watson/Best and Banting)?
10 Michael's age (11/12/13)?

⊗ See 🎧 4.1

2 Ask questions about the subjects and objects in the following sentences.

EXAMPLE:
The teacher [subject] watched the student [object].
Who did the teacher watch? [*Who* = object]
Who watched the student? [*Who* = subject]

1 The teacher knows the student.
2 The teacher handed out the textbooks.
3 The student beat the teacher in the race.
4 The student wanted to see the teacher after class.
5 The teacher helped the student check her homework.
6 The student saw the teacher arriving late.
7 The teacher marked the student's test.
8 The teacher stared at the student in amazement.
9 Her success depended on hard work.
10 The dangerous road conditions led to several accidents.

3 Ask a question about the highlighted words in the sentences below. Then make it into an indirect question, using a variety of both '*do you know?*' and '*do you think?*' forms from the list of examples above.

EXAMPLE:
The train arrived **at 7 o'clock**.
When did the train arrive?
Do you know when the train arrived?
When *do you think* the train arrived?

1 **Ottawa** is the capital of Canada.
2 You can leave it out **because it's unnecessary.**
3 The word *mansikka* means strawberry in Finnish.
4 You can say *Bless you!* **when somebody sneezes.**
5 The adverb of time usually comes **at the end.**
6 Insulin was discovered **by two Canadian scientists.**
7 The word is pronounced **exactly the same.**
8 You must put the stress **on the second syllable.**
9 The student spent the whole night thinking **about his English test.**
10 **A terrible accident** happened late last night.

Exercises and activities

1 Vocabulary and structure

See the OUP website http://www.oup.com/elt/teacher/pce.

2 Prepositions

at	in	on	to
at the **top/ bottom**	in an exercise book	on page 20	turn to page 3
at the **beginning/ end**	in the textbook	on a sheet	refer to the list
	in ink, ballpoint	on line 13	listen to a story
at the **back/front**	in the middle	on the **left/right**	an answer to a question
open … at page 10	in the margin	questions on a text	go on to the next page
look at page 3	in the (top) corner	spend time on this	
	in your own words	on the board	get down to work
	in English	on the Internet	
	in pairs	on the screen	
	in detail		

Use the list above to revise the use of *at*, *in*, *on,* and *to*. Then complete the following text, using these four prepositions.

Let's start, then. Group 1 I want you to open your books … (1) page 29. Have you found it? Now, … (2) the left you can see three pictures. Look at the picture with the detective. The picture … (3) the top of the page, not the one … (4) the middle. Everybody got it? Right. Now turn … (5) page 67. OK? … (6) the top right-hand corner you can see another picture with a detective in it. I want you to compare these two pictures … (7) detail. How are they the same, how are they different? Work … (8) pairs and please try to speak … (9) English. You'll find some ideas … (10) your workbooks … (11) page 43. It might also be a good idea to refer … (12) the wordlist … (13) the back … (14) page 176. Look … (15) the words … (16) the margin.

Just before you begin, could you turn for a moment … (17) Chapter 9? Do you remember all those useful adjectives we practised last time? Perhaps you could keep one finger … (18) this section, and then you can refer back … (19) it if you want some more ideas. When you finally get down to writing your comparison, write it … (20) your exercise books, please, and … (21) ink, not pencil. You can spend twenty minutes … (22) this.

And now, Group 2. Take out your readers and open them … (23) page 13. First of all, finish off the work from last time. Remember? Harry arrives at Hogwarts School. Then go on … (24) Chapter 7, 'The Sorting Hat'. First read the text and make a summary … (25) your own words. Then try the exercise I've written … (26) the blackboard. Try to find answers … (27) all these questions. Write them out … (28) the sheet of paper I'm going to give you, and this time please remember to write your name … (29) it!

Right, everybody. Are there any questions? OK, let's get down … (30) work!

3 Moving around in the textbook

Revise the phrases in sections A1–6 of this unit. Work in pairs or small groups. Make sure everyone in the group has a copy of the same textbook (or use this one). Take it in turns to act as the teacher. Give a series of five instructions to do with the textbook; for example, distributing, taking out, opening at a certain page, turning over, referring to another unit, closing, handing in. All the time check that everyone is following.

4 Finding a word

Work in pairs or small groups. Revise the phrases in Unit 4, A4. Each person then underlines five separate words, one on five different pages of this book. Now take it in turns to give instructions to help your partner(s) find the words you have underlined. For example: *Open your books at page 23. Have a look at section 5. My word is on the third line, six words from the beginning.*

5 Working with a text

Find a passage of some 15–20 lines from a textbook, newspaper, or magazine. Make enough copies for your fellow students. Then:

1 Go through the text and pick out five words that you would like to pre-teach. Think of appropriate ways of presenting the words.
2 Think of five general questions related to the topic of the text that you would ask students beforehand in order to orientate them to the text and arouse interest in it.
3 Think of three general questions that you could use after reading the text to check that students have understood the main points of the text.
4 Think of an additional five *Wh-* questions that would check whether students have understood specific sentences and ideas. Try to use some *do you know?* and *do you think?* questions.
5 Pick out and talk about five words or structures that you would like students to notice, perhaps underline, and think about.

RECORD 6 Now try out your text and questions on your fellow students. You may want them to read the text aloud at some point, so check the phrases in Unit 4, B3. If you have a recorder, you may want to tape yourself.

If several groups work on the same text, you can discuss the questions afterwards and try to pick out the best ones.

6 Explaining vocabulary

For this exercise, work with a partner. You and your partner have different lists of some everyday and some more unusual words in English. One of you will use the list below and the other one will use the list on page 157. Don't look at each other's lists in advance! You may want to check the meaning of some of the words in a dictionary.

Without actually using the word, take it in turns to explain, define or talk about one of the words on your list until your partner is able to say the word, or its translation.

> **Student A**
> Nouns: soap, flag, key ring, eagle, paper clip, library, peace, bully, etiquette, mirror.
> Adjectives: enormous, guilty, innocent, calm.
> Verbs: to prevent, to stumble, to hiccup.

7 Classroom scenario

Passages A–B below describe different situations of an English lesson. At the places numbered, try to think what the teacher could say in the situation. You are free to invent other information where necessary. Remember to use different forms of commands and requests in your instructions (you can revise them in the Classroom essentials section of Units 1 and 3). If you are working in a group, try to think of several alternative phrases for each situation.

A   You plan to get through a lot of work in this lesson. The first task is on page 65 in the textbook, so you ask the students to find the place (1). Some of them look rather puzzled, so you check whether they have their books with them (2). You're not too pleased that some of them have left their books at home again (3). Håkan and Stine only have one book between them. You suggest a solution (4). You're looking at a text on British pop music in the 1990s. You introduce the text (5) and then let them read it through (6). You check their general understanding (7) and ask for a summary (8). There seem to be a few tricky points in the text so you decide to deal with them (9). You make sure they all have the right place (10), which is three paragraphs down (11), and the second to last word on line 4 (12), *innovative*. You explain the word in English (13) and then check by asking for a translation (14). You go through the other difficulties and then ask everybody to read some lines of the text, one after another (15).

B   After this you decide to take a look at the new grammar in the textbook. The students' job is to make notes and write down the examples (16). It's been some time since you checked their notebooks, so you ask Henning to collect them up and bring them to your desk (17). The next task is in the workbook, on page 76 (18). Before they begin, you explain what you want them to do (19). They have to do the first half of exercise 10B (20). There's no need to do question 3, which is too difficult (21). When everybody seems to have more or less finished (22), you ask them to stop (23) and go through the exercise (24). You ask Stig to answer the first question (25). Stig's answer is not wrong, but you ask for other suggestions (26). Leif comes up with an idea you didn't expect (27). You give the last question to Marie. Her answer's good, but not perfect (28). You ask for help correcting it (29). You give the students one more exercise. You plan to go through the exercise orally first (30), but you are short of time so you ask the students to write out their answers in their notebooks at home (31).

8   Recasting

Look at the student answers below. Each one contains a small grammatical slip or vocabulary problem. Reply to the student by recasting the reply in a natural way and adding something to what the student said.

EXAMPLE:
Student: ... and later he breaked the world record ...
Teacher: Yes, you're right. He broke the world record in 1996 and then went on to win two Olympic medals.

1   There will be no lesson on Wednesday because the ... err ... *Fotograf* will be coming to the school.
2   In 1945 the Allies beat the Nazis and wanted to throw out them.
3   Nobody knew exactly how many people did die in the crash.
4   In the Highlands many sheeps and cattles are raised.
5   The ships could sail up the River Clyde until Glasgow.
6   Gaelic is still spoken in the west Scotland.
7   This book is not the same kind than the other one.
8   He wanted that his friends would come to the party.

Audio practice

1 Classroom intonation

4.1 Make *Or* questions using the following clues. Then listen and repeat.

1 This idea – a success or a failure?
2 Tom arriving – 23rd, 24th, or 25th?
3 Marianne's opinion – agree or disagree?
4 Stop last time – page 56 or 57?
5 Prefer working – on your own or in groups?
6 Correct form – *depend on* or *depend from*?
7 Found the reference – in a dictionary or on the Web?
8 Go first – group 1, group 2, or group 3?

4.2 In the following sentences, the teacher is trying to prompt the students. This is signalled by the rising intonation at the end. Read out the sentences and then listen and repeat.

1 Where did they meet? Well, did they meet at the station or at the cinema or … ?
2 Why did they stop? Was it because of money or something?
3 OK, they agreed to postpone the talks. And?
4 Who would you say this to? I mean, would you say it to a friend or a stranger, or … ?
5 What were his motives? What do you think? Was he looking for revenge or something?
6 OK, you say that they failed to agree. So?

4.3 Listen to each sentence on the CD and then react to it by reading out the question. Decide whether it is an echo question (you are surprised or didn't hear correctly) or a normal *Wh-* question. Then listen and repeat.

1 What was the name of the film you saw?
2 What size is the screen?
3 When was she born?
4 How many times has he been absent?
5 What was the name of film you saw?
6 What size is the screen?
7 When was she born?
8 How many times has he been absent?

2 Key sounds

4.4 The sentences below contain examples of the sounds /f/, /v/, and /w/. Identify the sounds and read the sentences aloud. Then listen and repeat.

1 You all read very well.
2 Turn over and find five verbs.
3 What I want is for everyone to work individually.
4 Refer forward to the vocabulary list on page 74.
5 Every one of these words starts with a vowel.
6 On the way out would everyone please leave their workbook on my desk.

3 Word stress

4.5 Say the following words aloud and mark the stressed syllable. There are three types:

1 words stressed on the first syllable, (for example, '*schedule*);
2 words stressed on the second syllable, (*re'lax*);
3 words stressed on the third syllable, (*elec'tricity*).

Use the recording to listen and repeat.

1	effort	11	describe
2	dictionary	12	scientific
3	diagram	13	omit
4	academic	14	error
5	appendix	15	alternative
6	reference	16	correspond
7	detail	17	refer
8	equivalent	18	satisfactory
9	illegible	19	familiar
10	predict	20	variety

4 Live lessons

You will hear some short extracts from different classroom situations. Listen to each extract and then answer the questions. Transcripts can be found on page 171.

4.6 Using the textbook
1 How does the teacher solve the problem with the textbook?
2 What does she warn the student not to do?
3 The students have their textbooks open. Are they allowed to look at them?
4 Why do you think the teacher chooses to work like this?

4.7 Checking understanding
1 What three words or expressions does the teacher check by asking for a translation?
2 What were the other two new words or phrases? How does the teacher make them clear to her students?
3 Even though the explanation is clear, why does she ask for a translation?
4 Why does the teacher say 'That is nice'?

4.8 Practising a structure. The class are using the textbook page shown overleaf.
1 What structures is the teacher practising?
2 Fill in the missing four words:
Imagine — _____ this _____ _____ _____ — imagine that you are waiting for a friend.
What does *this* probably refer to?
3 How does the teacher contextualize the structures in a memorable way?
4 How would you describe the dialogue between the teacher and students?

4.9 Checking an exercise
1 What do you think the instruction for this exercise was?
2 Why is the teacher going to use the mother tongue in the lesson?

3 The teacher says: *We already know which rucksack it is.* How does this reinforce the correct use of articles in English?

4 How many times does the teacher use *please*?

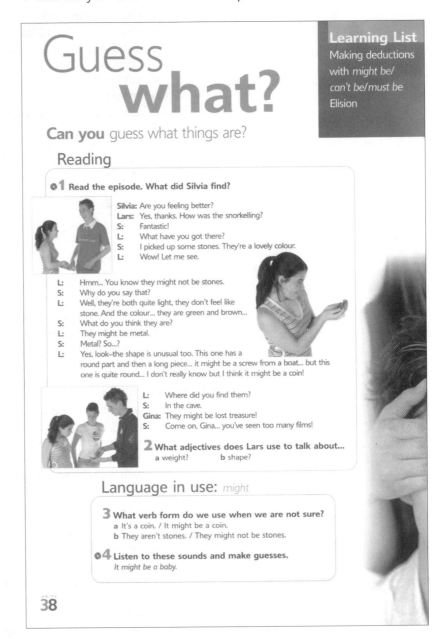

2 **What adjectives does Lars use to talk about...**
   a weight?   b shape?

4.10 Giving corrective feedback

1 What structure is the teacher practising?
2 What pronunciation mistake does the teacher correct?
3 How does the teacher try to make the exercise more communicative?
4 What grammatical error does the student make?
5 How does the teacher draw the student's attention to the mistake? Can the student correct it?
6 One small detail gets changed in the question. What was it?

Using technology **5**

5

The visual presentation of information has long been a central part of teaching. Nowadays information technology has brought a whole new range of communication tools to the classroom—tools that students are often already familiar with through home use. In addition to traditional classroom presentation media—the board, overhead projector, slide projector, television, and video—the digital revolution has brought CDs, DVDs, beamers, document cameras, interactive whiteboards, and the Internet, not to mention webcasts and real-time communication via cable and satellite connections. While it is difficult to predict what the pedagogical impact of these developments will be, it is clear that they will ultimately enhance learning opportunities in the classroom. Working with technology also enriches the language of the classroom.

1 Using the board
Please look at the board.
Come and write the answer on the board.
Step aside so that everyone can see.
Is the sentence on the board right?
Remember to copy down the homework.
It's in the top left-hand corner.

2 Managing the board
Would someone clean the board, please?
The board eraser is here.
I need to add some information.
Can you change the homework page to 126?
Please don't wipe the date off.
You'll need a whiteboard marker.

3 Preparations and problems
I'll just plug the projector in.
Can everyone read the transparency OK?
The writing needs focusing.
I'll move the projector.

4 Presenting with projected visuals
To begin with, there'll be a short presentation.
It's important that you follow carefully.
You don't need to take down notes.
I'll give you copies later.

5 Discussing visuals
I have a poster here.
I'll reveal it slowly.
What can you see in the picture?
Any ideas?

Displaying information

Points to think and talk about

1 What are the advantages and disadvantages of using visual displays to present information? Do visuals have a different role at different stages of a lesson?
2 How can you use visuals to capture the interest and imagination of students? Consider the use of traditional pictures, overhead transparencies, and slides as well as modern equipment.
3 Alongside the overhead projector, the board is probably the most used presentation tool in teaching. What advantages and disadvantages does the board have? Can you remember any situations where the board has been used very effectively?
4 Research suggests that the board has three functions: 1) to show 'permanent' information that is referred to at different stages of the lesson; 2) to record the contents and progress of the lesson; and 3) to serve as a notepad. How do you use the board? Can you think of any other uses? Do your students also use the board?
5 What is your attitude towards teaching technology? What plans do you have for developing your own technical skills?
6 What is the attitude of your students to using technology in the classroom? Do you think they see it only as a benefit and an added bonus?
7 Even a well-prepared teacher is likely to face unforeseen difficulties in using technical equipment. Suggest some possible problems.
8 Do you think it is a good idea to have a display board of students' work in the classroom?

Language to think about

1 How would you check that all of the students have a clear view of the projector screen?
2 What would you say to a student who is blocking the other students' view of the board?
3 How would you 'warn' students if you are using a piece of equipment for the first time?
4 How would you get the students to assist you in setting up a piece of equipment?
5 How would you apologize for the poor quality of an old transparency?
6 What is a *board monitor*?
7 What guidelines would you give to a group of students preparing a transparency to present to the rest of the class?
8 What is a *flipchart, a fuse, a sponge*? What is the opposite of *background*?
9 What would you say to your students if the projection equipment you were using suddenly lost power?
10 You usually distribute lecture notes at the beginning of the class, or you ask the students to take notes. Today you plan to hand out the notes at the end. Can you explain this to your students?

Classroom English vocabulary to collect

1 Words connected with using the board. (For example, *whiteboard, permanent marker, board rubber*)
2 Visual aids and their parts. (For example, *projector, lens, in focus*)

Key to symbols:		
ℚ Idiomatic phrase	⇨	Pedagogical pointer
ⓢ Student reply	⊗	Cross-reference
ⓧ Typical mistake	ℚ	Listen to the CD
Ⅼ Language comment	**RECORD**	Record yourself

Using the board

1 Please look at the board.
*On the board you will find today's **exercise/questions/task**.*
***Answer/Read** the questions on the **board/screen**.*
Let's all read the sentences from the board.
*Follow the **instructions/guidelines** on the board.*
***Do /Finish/Complete** the exercises written on the board.*
Let's go over the answers on the board (together).
Copy (down) the instructions from the board.

2 Come and write the answer on the board.
Come (out) to the board, please.
Please come and add the labels to the diagram.
Please add some more ideas to the mind map on the board.
*Come and **underline/ring/tick** the correct **answer/option**.*
Use a red marker to highlight the words.
*Look at the map and point **to/out** London.*
Use my pointer and show us where the Rockies are.
Come and put your transparency on the OHP for everyone to see.

3 Step aside so that everyone can see.
Move out of the way so that the class can see what you've written.
Move to one side so we can all see the board.
You're standing in the way.
You're blocking everybody's view (of the board).

4 Is the sentence on the board right?
Are there any mistakes in the sentences on the board?
Can anyone see anything wrong with the sentence?
(Is there) anything wrong with sentence 2?
Can you see anything to correct in the last sentence?
Correct the spelling mistake on the board, please.

5 Remember to copy down the homework.
Note down the homework instructions, please.
Copy this straight down in your notebooks.
Make a note of what you have to do for homework.
Has everyone seen the homework note?
*Have you all **noted/written** down the homework exercise?*

6 It's in the top left-hand corner.
*Look **at/in** the bottom right-hand corner.*
The reminder is in the top right corner.
*Look at the **left/left-hand** side of the board.*
*In the **centre/middle** of the board you'll see the homework.*
*On the **right/right-hand** side of the board you'll find the homework.*

1 The traditional *blackboard* or *whiteboard* can also be referred to simply as a *board*. This also applies to interactive whiteboards.

If you are using a beamer, overhead projector, or TV, you can use *screen* instead of *board*:
*If you look at the screen, you'll see the **topic/instructions** for today.*
Turn this way and look at the TV screen.

1 ⇨ The walls of the classroom offer excellent opportunities to display students' own work. See also Unit 3, C4.
Come and put your picture on the wall.
*Have a look at the **diagram/chart/illustration** on the **wall/notice board**.*

2 Other useful phrases include:
Take a piece of coloured chalk.
Use a whiteboard marker.
Don't use a permanent pen!
Try to write clearly.
Keep your writing straight.
Make sure your writing is big enough (so that everyone can read it).

The following phrases might also be useful, but be careful of the common errors:
You've already been out to the board. ✓   *You have been ~~on~~ the board.* ✗
You've already had a turn. ✓   *You ~~were already~~.* ✗
Whose turn is it to write the sentence up?

3 Notice the prepositions:

to write **on**	*the board.*
	*a **transparency/slide/overhead**.*
	*a **page/sheet of paper**.*
	a computer.
to write **in**	*a **book/notebook**.*
	pencil/ink/ballpoint.

⊗ You're standing ~~on~~ the way.

4 Use the following instructions when helping a student to correct mistakes on the board:

Rub	out	*the first letter.*
Wipe	off	*this word.*
Cross		*the full stop.*

» For more on correcting written mistakes, see Unit 4, C5 and 6, B5.

You may want to use these phrases if a student spots an error that you have made on the board:
Oh, dear I've spelt it wrong.
Thanks for spotting that mistake.
I was just checking that you were all awake.
So what should it be (then)?

6 These phrases are useful for students to practise following simple instructions involving adverbials of place:

Take	a piece of some	chalk		(over) here.	
				(just) there.	
			and write it	next to	this word.
Use	this	marker pen		below above	

Managing the board

1 Would someone clean the board, please?
Is there/Can I have a volunteer to clean the board?
I'd like someone to wipe the board for me, please.
Who is the board monitor this week?
I'll just give the board a wipe.

2 The board eraser is here.
*You'll find the board **rubber/duster** at the side of the board.*
*The **cloth/rag** is on my desk.*
The sponge /spʌndʒ/ *is by the sink.*
*You'll need to **wet/dampen/moisten** the sponge (under the tap).*

3 I need to add some information.
*We need to **change/update/correct** the date.*
*I need some **space/room** for a **diagram/some new instructions**.*

4 Can you change the homework page to 126?
Instead of/ Rather than pages 6 and 7, write 10 and 11.
Alter the instructions to say 'questions 9 and 10 are optional'.
It should say 'April the second' and not 'April the third'.

5 Please don't wipe the date off.
*Don't **remove/get rid of/wipe off** the homework (yet).*
Leave the instructions for the next lesson.
You can leave this sentence up.
You don't need to clean the left-hand side.

6 You'll need a whiteboard marker.
Use the whiteboard pens, please.
Make sure it's the right type of pen.
*Don't use the **permanent/magic** marker by mistake!*

---

1 ⌊ If you are using a flipchart or other paper display, the following may be useful:
*Could someone **rip/tear** off that page from the flipchart?*
*Please **find/turn to** a clean page on the flipchart.*
Flip over to the next page.

Ⓢ *Is there a mistake on the board?*
Haven't you made a mistake on the board?

---

5 ⌊ Notice how *out, off,* and *away* are used:
***Rub/Wipe** this letter* off/out.
***Turn/Switch** the lights* off/out.
Take your books out.
Put your books away.

Ⓧ *Rub this letter* ~~away.~~ **X**

---

6 ⌊ Other useful equipment includes:
The magnets are in the corner.
*The **drawing pins/thumbtacks** (AE) are in the **tub/tin/container/tray**.*
*I'll need some **sticky tape/Sellotape/Blu-tack**.*

6 ⌊ There may be problems even with more traditional technology:
I've run out of chalk.
That was my last piece of chalk.
My marker pen has dried up.
*Go and look for **some chalk/a board rubber** for me.*
Go and see if there's any more.
Go and fetch some more from the office.
Please find another pen from next door.
Go and ask Mr Jiménez for some more chalk.

Please don't wipe off the homework yet!

Preparations and problems

1 I'll just plug the projector in.
Put the plug in the socket.
The plug socket is on the back wall.
This plugs into the extension lead.
*I'll just make sure everything is **connected/plugged in**.*
Everything seems to be connected up.
Now I'll switch it on.
***Switch/Turn/Put** the projector on.*

2 Can everyone read the transparency OK?
Can you all read the text on the slide?
*Is the **picture/writing** clear enough?*
*Is the screen too **high/low**?*
Is the screen at the right height for everyone?
*Has everyone got a **good/clear** view of the screen?*

3 The writing needs focusing.
It's out of focus.
*The writing is **out of focus/too fuzzy/unclear**.*
*The **text/writing** is too small.*
The text doesn't all fit on the screen.
The colour makes it difficult to read.
*I'll use another **pen/colour**.*
There's nothing on the screen!

4 I'll move the projector.
*I'll adjust the **focus/mirror**.*
Let's see if I can get this in focus.
I'll try to sharpen the picture.
*Perhaps if I move the projector **forwards/backwards** it will help.*
*I'll have a go at **raising/lowering** the projector.*

1 Your preparations may include the following:
Close the blinds.
***Draw/Pull** the curtains (across).*
Pull down the screen.
***Turn/Switch/Put** the lights off.*
***Lower/Dim** the lights.*
Lights out, please.

If you want to use student volunteers, say:
*Who would like to be **the projectionist/operate the projector**?*
Can you set the beamer up for me?
Could you switch on the TV and find the AV channel?

Notice the verbs used with the words *button, switch* and *knob* /nɒb/:
*To **press/push/click** a button.*
*To **press/flick/flip** a switch.*
*To **pull/push/turn** a knob.*

When the equipment is no longer needed, the following phrases might be useful:
Unplug the equipment.
*Pull the plug out of the **socket/wall**.*
***Switch/Turn/Put** everything off.*
***Switch/Turn/Put** the lights back on.*
Don't forget to power off the equipment. (AE)

1 Mistakes to avoid:
~~Open~~ the projector. ✗
~~Close~~ the projector. ✗
Pull the plug ~~off~~. ✗
~~Plug out~~ the recorder. ✗

2 Notice also:
Don't sit so close to the screen.
It's not good for your eyes to sit too close.

3 One common problem is with showing slides the right way round:

The transparency		upside down.
The slide	is	back to front.
The overhead		the wrong way round.

The transparency should be the other way round.
I'll turn the slide round.

4 Video tapes and CDs can also be problematic:
I can't find the place.
*I'll just **rewind/fast forward** to the beginning.*
*What number is the **AV/video** channel?*
I can't find the remote control.

Technical problems will occur even with the most careful preparations:
Maybe I should try taking the lens cap off!
I hadn't plugged the right cable in.
The lead is too short!
*I'll get **a longer/an extension** lead.*
*The bulb **has gone/will have to be changed**.*
The glass needs to be cleaned.
The projector has overheated.
*The magazine is **stuck/jammed**.*
*The fuse has **gone/blown**.*
The batteries are dead.
*There must be a power **cut/failure/outage** (AE).*

Use the following excuses for recurring problems:
The same old trouble, I'm afraid.
Typical! Why does it always happen to me?
Just my luck to get a broken one!
This is the third time this week.
It worked perfectly on Monday.
Does anybody believe in Murphy's Law?
These things are sent to try us!

The verb *seem* is often used in difficult situations:
The fuse seems to have gone.
There seems to be something wrong with the projector.
I don't seem to be able to find the right section.

Presenting with projected visuals

1 To begin with, there'll be a short presentation.
We'll start with an introduction to the subject.
Let's begin with a PowerPoint presentation.

2 It's important that you follow carefully.
There are some important points to highlight today.
Pay particular attention to the highlighted points.
Try to concentrate on the key points.
Watch carefully.

3 You don't need to take down notes.
There's no need to copy down the information today.
Just watch and listen now.
You don't need to bother making your own notes for this.

4 I'll give you copies later.
There'll be printed notes passed round in a minute.
You can collect copies at the end of the lesson.
I'll talk you through the information and then I'll distribute the notes.
*I'll send the notes to you **by email/in electronic format**.*

1 　It is often good to introduce the topic of the presentation:
Today's topic is immigration.
What I'd like to talk about today is …
The subject of my lecture today is …
Our theme today is …
What we're going to have a look at this time is …

⇒ You may want to take a more thought-provoking approach:
What comes to mind when you hear the word 'desert'?
What is the connection between these three pictures?
Three famous people. What do they have in common?
It's called 'Ice and Fire'. What do you think it will be about?

　A brief visual presentation is often a good introduction or accompaniment to a lecture or talk:
I'll start by showing you a video clip about Wales.
Let's begin with an excerpt from a music video.
Perhaps we might start by watching a short film about Vancouver.
By way of introduction, let's look at a series of slides about child labour.
I'll use the document camera to project some interesting statistics on …
*The results of a recent **survey/opinion poll** show that …*
Let's see what the official government website has to say about the topic.

　The soundtrack on films, videos, and TV shows can be:
subtitled — the translation is displayed at the bottom of the screen; or
dubbed— the original soundtrack is re-recorded in the foreign language.

Discussing visuals

1 I have a poster here.
I have something to show you today.
This is a photograph of a famous place.
*Here is a **picture/illustration/diagram/chart/table**.*

2 I'll reveal it slowly.
I'm going to unroll it slowly.
*I'll reveal it **gradually/bit by bit**.*
I won't give you the complete picture at once.
It's out of focus, but do you know what it could be?
I'll zoom in on the people drinking coffee.
*I'll show you one **picture/card** at a time.*

3 What can you see in the picture?
What is happening in the picture?
*What different **things/objects/people** can you see?*
Describe some of the people in the picture.
What does it remind you of?

4 Any ideas?
Does anyone have any suggestions?
Shout out your ideas.
Say the first thing that comes into your head.
Try to guess what this is.
*Are there any other **alternatives/interpretations**?*
Let's see what more ideas there are.

1 　Introduce the visual with a short comment:

The first	picture photo clip	I want	to show you you to look at	is of a famous castle. was taken in Wales. will give you some idea of what London is like.
In the (first) picture		you can see		some typically Canadian scenery. a view from the Empire State Building.

⇒ You may want to pass material round for students to have a closer look:
*I'll pass this round for **everyone/you all** to see.*
*I'll let this book **go round/circulate**.*
Have a look and then pass it on.

⊗ Unit 3, C5 deals with using realia and objects in the classroom.

⊗ Mistakes to avoid:
This picture is taken in Scotland. ✗   *This picture was taken in Scotland.* ✓

A picture from a castle. ✗   *A picture of a castle.* ✓
I'll let this pass. ✗   *I'll let this circulate.* ✓

3 ⇨ Help your students to see the details by drawing their attention to particular parts of the picture:
*It's in the **foreground/background**.*
It's at the edge of the picture.
It's right at the front.
It's on the very left.

⇨ Visual material provides excellent opportunities for students to use language creatively, for example:
See if you can guess what the correct sequence is.
What would be the correct order of events in this procedure?
When was this picture taken? How can you tell?
Can you tell me the story behind the picture?
*Do you notice anything **unusual/odd/strange** about this picture?*
*Now give your own commentary on the film **sequence/clip**.*
*You'll have thirty seconds to **look at/study** the picture.*
*Now I'm going to **hide it/cover it up**.*
Can you remember anything about the picture?
What was happening in the picture?

⇨ Visuals are also useful for introducing background cultural information:
What is interesting about this picture is …
Of particular interest in this picture is …
***Take/Have** a **good/close** look at the costumes.*
*Does anybody know what this **thing/person** is called?*

4 ⇨ Visuals provide a handy transition to conversational questions drawing on the students' own experiences:
Talking of mountains, how many of you have been climbing?
While we're on the subject of music, which is your favourite rock group?

5

SECTION B

Technological progress has turned traditional language laboratories into multimedia learning centres or studios. These allow access to a wide range of authentic audio and visual material. More importantly, they encourage self-directed learning. Despite this progress, however, the majority of schools have to manage with much simpler tools: a CD player, or even a basic cassette player.

Even in the high-tech classroom, your actual role as teacher fundamentally remains the same: to offer meaningful and structured learning opportunities, to motivate students, and to act as a model of the target language. The language learning studio is just one more context where you can use English genuinely and naturally. You can, for example, help your students to become familiar with specialized terminology by 'thinking aloud' when handling technical equipment.

1 Getting to know the equipment

Today we will use the language laboratory.
Check that your equipment is working.
Look at the control panel in front of you.
There are a number of buttons.
Use the buttons to move through the recording.
Press the 'call teacher' button if you need help.
Please remember to rewind your tape.

2 Working independently

Today we have a short dialogue to listen to.
I'll record the dialogue onto your machines.
You'll be able to work independently.
Then there'll be a task to complete.
I'll be monitoring you as you work.

3 Technical problems (1)

Is there a problem?
Please be patient.
Maybe I could try this.
Is that any better?
Good, everything's working now.

Working in the language laboratory

Points to think and talk about

1 In what ways do your students come into contact with modern spoken English outside school? How can you make use of this?
2 Think about the classroom environment you usually work in. What teaching equipment is permanently available?
3 What other teaching aids can be brought into the classroom? How demanding is it to set up and use the equipment?
4 Do you have any personal experience of working in a language laboratory, either as a teacher or student? Share your experiences with others in the group.
5 What additional dimensions can the use of a language laboratory bring to language learning?
6 How can you ensure that each student benefits from this experience?
7 What kind of exercises and activities work best in a language laboratory?
8 What kind of technological developments do you predict in the field of language teaching?

Language to think about

1 What words for the audio equipment in a language lab do you already know?
2 Can you name the parts of a DVD player? A CD player? A language laboratory console?
3 How would you apologize for a delay in getting the lesson started?
4 You have set up all the equipment before the lesson, but when the class arrives the video player doesn't work. What would you say to the students?
5 What would you say to encourage the students to become familiar with the equipment in the language lab?
6 What would you say if you wanted to do a trial run before starting an actual listening exercise?
7 Think of classroom phrases using the following verbs: *to monitor, to recap, to rewind, to fast forward.*
8 What possible technical problems could you have in a language lab?
9 How could you enlist the expertise of the students when dealing with technical problems?
10 What would you say to ensure the students leave the language lab tidy and with the equipment properly turned off?

Classroom English vocabulary to collect

The technical equipment found in a language lab. (For example, *headset, control panel*)

Getting to know the equipment

1 Today we will use the language laboratory.
For this lesson we can make use of (the facilities in) the language lab.
Today you'll be able to use the video camera in the language lab.
This lesson we have the chance to use the recording equipment.

2 Check that your equipment is working.
Make sure your equipment is in working order.
*Make certain you have **headphones/a headset**.*
Please check your headset is plugged in and working.
*Ensure that there are no loose **leads/cables**.*
*Double-check that the **monitor/console/TV** is switched on.*
I'll just do a voice check. Testing. One, two. Can everyone hear?
*Adjust the **volume/tone** if you need to.*
*Turn up the volume **up/down** on the teacher's track.*
*I'll **increase/turn up/decrease/turn down** the volume.*
Set the counter to zero.

3 Look at the control panel in front of you.
Have a good look at the control panel.
Take a careful look at the screen in front of you.
*Familiarize yourself with (the layout of) the **console/display panel**.*
Take a few minutes to become familiar with the control buttons.

4 There are a number of buttons.
*You'll see a number of **icons/symbols**.*
There should be a selection of buttons in front of you.
*It should remind you of a **video/CD** player.*
*It's **almost like/very similar to** a cassette recorder.*

5 Use the buttons to move through the recording.
*The buttons are to **move/go** through the recording.*
*Use the **buttons/icons** to navigate through the text.*
*To listen to the extract again, **press/select** the **repeat/recap** button.*
Fast-forward the tape until you find the part you want.
Remember to use the fast-forward and rewind buttons.
It is possible to skip forwards and backwards through the tape.
To find a particular section, use the fast-forward button.

6 Press the 'call teacher' button if you need help.
Press the help button if you need assistance.
*You can **call me/get my attention** by pressing the 'call teacher' button.*
*Carry on working and I'll **contact/come to** you as soon as I can.*

7 Please remember to rewind your tape.
Do remember to rewind the recording at the end of the class.
Make sure the tape is rewound at the end of the lesson.
Hang up your headset properly.

Let me know about any problems you had with the equipment.
I'll pass on your comments to the technician.

---

1   The language laboratory goes under many names, including:
language lab, language studio, language learning laboratory, audio laboratory, listening centre.

  The following phrases can be used to guide students to their places:
*Find an empty **seat/booth/workstation/console**.*
Go to your usual places.

---

2   Check that everything is in working order:
Say if something doesn't work.
*Let me know if you can't **see/hear** anything.*
Put up your hand if you can't hear.
*Raise your hand if there's **a problem/something wrong**.*
Now's the time to say if you have a problem.

⇒ Sometimes it's a good idea to try out a small part of an exercise to see that the equipment is working and that the students understand what they have to do:
*We'll **do/have** a **trial/practice** run first.*
*Before we begin, we'll just **do/have** a quick test run.*
*Let's **see/check** that everything **works/is working** first.*
I hope I've set everything up properly.

I'll	just play	a short	extract clip snippet sample	to check	you can all	hear.
	only use	a brief		to make sure		see.

---

3 ⇒ Your instructions will, of course, depend on the type of equipment available in your lab, for example, digital recorders, computer display, mouse interface.

---

7 ⇒ Unlike older analogue systems, modern digital language labs don't use tape and so recordings don't need to be rewound.

Working independently

1 Today we have a short dialogue to listen to.
*You will listen to a **job interview/radio programme/news bulletin**.*
This is an extract from an interview with the president.

2 I'll record the dialogue onto your machines.
*You'll find a **copy/recording** of the dialogue on your machine.*
*The **interview/extract/programme** will be **copied/recorded** onto your own machine.*
*You can **listen to/view** the interview through your own **console/control panel**.*

3 You'll be able to work independently.
*You'll be able to go over the dialogue **by yourself/on your own**.*
*It'll be possible to **repeat/recap** the dialogue independently.*
*You can re-listen to the **dialogue/story/review** at your **own pace/speed**.*
You'll be able to go over the text in your own time.
*You can listen to the **recording/interview** in short sections.*
Listen to it as many times as you like.

4 Then there'll be a task to complete.
*You'll then participate in **a role-play/an information sharing** activity.*
*We'll have a **negotiation/discussion** task to do.*
This should give you the chance to work in small groups.
*This will help you to focus on **listening/speaking/pronunciation** skills.*

5 I'll be monitoring you as you work.
I'll be able to follow your progress from my console.
I'll see how you're getting on from my console.
Don't be surprised to hear me speak to you over the intercom.

---

1 Video and digital equipment means the possibility of both watching and listening to recordings:
*You'll have the chance to watch **an extract/a scene** on video.*
We'll watch a short clip of a documentary on New Zealand.

---

3 ⇨ In an ordinary classroom with a cassette or CD playing to the whole class at the same time, you can control playback and check students' understanding of the content:
Did everyone understand that?
Did you all catch that?
*Did you manage to get **the gist/main idea** of what was said?*
*How did you get on with the **beginning/middle/end** section?*
*We'll listen to it **once more/one more time**.*
We'll go over that section again.
*I'll repeat **that/the end section/the individual sections**.*

4 ⇨ Modern computer-controlled language labs allow several different types of practice activities:
Pair and group discussions; *I'll pair you up and give you a task to work on.*
Listening and note-taking or transcription; *Listen and transcribe the dialogue.*
Simultaneous translation; *Listen and translate.*
Voice recordings; *Watch the video clip and record your own commentary.*
Pronunciation exercises; *Repeat and compare your version with the model.*
Video recording; *Let's film the dialogue and then analyse it.*

5 ⊗ Unit 6, A2 also includes phrases that are suitable for listening work in the language lab.

⇨ The language lab offers an often rare opportunity for you to give private and personal feedback. Try to use this opportunity to motivate and encourage.

Technical problems (1)

1 Is there a problem?
Are you having difficulties?
*What seems to be the **trouble/matter/problem**?*
We seem to have run into a problem.
There's something wrong with the equipment.
It isn't working properly.
*I can't **make it/get it to** work.*

2 Please be patient.
This'll take a few moments, I'm afraid.
This hopefully won't take very long.
Thank you for your patience.
***Do/Try to** bear with me.*

3 Maybe I could try this.
*I'll just try **pressing this button/adjusting the settings**.*
*Let's try **changing the/a new** tape.*
Check that everything is plugged in (properly).
*What about **swapping/changing desks/headphones**.*
*This has got me **puzzled/confused**.*
Does anyone have any suggestions?
Do any of you know anything about camcorders?

4 Is that any better?
Has that made any difference?
How about now?
Is that an improvement?

5 Good, everything's working now.
*OK, we can **carry on/continue** now.*
All solved!
That's fixed it.
Problem over.
There we are (at last). It's OK again.
Thank goodness (for that)!
That's a relief.
*I'm glad that's **fixed/sorted out**.*
Well, that was a bit of a mystery.

---

1 ⌊ Notice *snag, hitch,* and *glitch*:
*We seem to have **hit/run into** a snag.*
There seems to be a slight (technical) hitch.
There seems to be a glitch in the system.

---

2 ⌊ No matter how advanced or user-friendly the equipment is, problems can still arise, whether through human error or a technical fault. Prepare yourself for the following:

Headsets:
*The headphones are **missing/unplugged/the wrong way round/ broken/damaged**.*

Buttons:
*The button was **switched off/in the off position**.*
The volume was turned down.
The button wasn't pressed.
I may have pressed the wrong button.

Control panel:
The controls are locked.
The controls have been incorrectly set.
The settings have been changed.

Display:
*The monitor is **off/flickering**.*

Even older technology is not problem-free.

Cassettes:
*The tape is **jammed/stuck/snarled up/chewed up**.*
*The tape is **too old/of poor quality/too fuzzy/too quiet**.*
*There's too much **interference/hiss** on the tape.*
The tape is missing.
I've brought the wrong tape.

⌊ Suitably mild expressions to express your frustration and/or disappointment when equipment doesn't work:
Oh dear!
Dear oh dear!
Dear me!

Stronger language includes:
Damn (it)!
Curse it.
Oh hell!

---

3 ⌊ When it is only a question of finding the right place, you can say:
*I just need to find the correct place on the **tape/disc**.*
Let's check the tape is in the right place.
Wait a second. I'll just rewind the tape.
Look at the questions while I find the place.

---

5 ⇨ Always apologize when things are not working properly:
*I'm sorry about **that/the mix-up/the delay**.*
I'm sorry this isn't working.
Sorry to have to disappoint you.
I do apologize for this.

---

6 ⌊ When the problem cannot be solved you can say:
It's a shame we can't (seem to) fix that now.
It's a pity this won't work now.
There's nothing we can do about it.
There's nothing to be done.
That's life.
That's the way it goes.
We'll have to do something else.

SECTION C

Information technology has made huge resources available for individualized and autonomous learning. The most important perhaps are those offered by the Internet via online publications, dictionaries, search engines, and specialized websites on almost any subject. Mobile phone technology will also have a huge impact on the way we communicate and access information. For the teacher, the computer revolution has brought all of the above, but also specialized computer-assisted language learning (CALL) software and practical tools for preparing, implementing, and managing lessons. Despite these great changes, we should remember that the online teaching environment can be as rich in language as the normal classroom. In fact, it will only further underline the importance of the teacher as an interactive model of language use.

1 Getting up and running
Please turn your computer on.
Wait for it to boot up.
Enter your username and password.
Click OK.

2 Basic word processing
Open the word-processing application.
Get familiar with the screen and keyboard.
Use the mouse to navigate around the screen.
Set the spellchecker.
Remember to save your work.
Print out your work.

3 Going online
You can check your email first.
We'll be using the Internet today.
Enter a search engine address into the address bar.
Type an appropriate keyword into the search field.
Select one of the titles in the list.

4 Technical problems (2)
Oh dear, the document won't print.
Let's check the connection.
Everything looks OK.
I'm not really sure where the problem is.
Let's ask the technician.

Using a computer

Points to think and talk about

1 What experiences do you have of using computers, both to deal with everyday tasks and particularly to develop your English skills?
2 Have you ever seen computers being used in language teaching? If so, describe what you saw. If not, imagine how a computer-based lesson might differ from a normal lesson.
3 How does technology in the classroom change the dynamics of the classroom? How does this affect your role as a teacher?
4 How do the reading skills needed for online research differ from those required in a traditional library? What kind of support do students need when doing this kind of reading?
5 Besides editing, saving, and printing, what other useful features do word-processing programs have? How familiar are you with these features? How can word-processing tools be used to support the development of student writing skills, rather than to replace them?
6 The temptation to copy and paste text directly from the Internet can be very difficult to resist. How can students be encouraged not to do this? And how can you identify when this has happened? Is plagiarism (copying work without giving credit to the source) considered unacceptable in your educational culture?
7 The Internet is a gateway to a wealth of information, but not all of it is reliable, impartial, or healthy to access. How can you monitor your students as they carry out online research? How do you yourself check the validity of information you find on the Internet?
8 Your students probably use email to communicate amongst themselves and with friends in other classes and schools. How could you make email sessions a regular part of your English lessons? What would be the benefits of this? And the possible problems?

Language to think about

1 Make a list of instructions you would need to give to a class that is using a computer network for the first time.
2 Think of classroom phrases that use the following words: *log on, boot up, right click, drag and drop, toolbar, printout.*
3 What would you say to get students to stop checking their email and to open a new Word document?
4 What instructions would you give if your students wanted to print out their work?
5 How would you say the following email and Internet addresses? *jbc2ed@tec. suv.fi* and *www.bbc.co.uk/webwise/*
6 Can you name all the 'extra' keys on a keyboard (for example, backspace, shift)?
7 How would you explain a search engine to your students? What instructions would you give to help them use a search engine?
8 Think of four things you could you say to your class if nothing that you've tried has managed to get the printer to work.

Classroom English vocabulary to collect

1 Computing terms connected with writing. (For example, *printer, scroll bar, cursor*)
2 The world of the Internet. (For example, *password, download, browser*)

Getting up and running

1 Please turn your computer on.
*Press the **on/power** button on your computer.*
*Please **turn/switch** on your **monitor/printer**.*
All of the computers should already be on.
Press any key to reactivate the computer.

2 Wait for it to boot up.
Let the computer boot up.
*Don't **press/do** anything while the computer boots up.*
*Wait for the **operating system/Linux/Windows** to load.*

3 Enter your username and password.
***Type in/Give** your username and password.*
*Log in to the **computer/network**.*
*Log on with **your username and password/your user ID**.*
It might be necessary to use a password.

4 Click OK.
***Press/Hit return/enter**.*
The desktop will now come up on screen.
*The desktop is now **in front of you/on screen**.*

---

1 ⊗ ~~Open~~ *your computer.* ✗   *Open a program.* ✔

3 ⌊ Use the same phrases when going online and using the Internet or accessing email.

⌊ At the end of the computer session you can say:
Close your session and switch off.
*(Remember to) log **off/out**.*
*Shut down **the computer/Windows** properly.*

4 ⌊ Software manuals are full of useful computer instructions. The following are just a sample:
*Click the **left/right** mouse button.*
*Click (on) the **menu bar/icon**.*
Click on the window to make it active.
Open the menu.
*Click **on the option/in the field** you want.*
*Select the option you want by **left clicking/double clicking**.*
Keep the left mouse button pressed down.
Right click on the icon.
*Select **the location/where you want** to save the document.*
Highlight the text.
Drag and drop the icon.
*Use the **mouse cursor/scroll bars** to navigate through the document.*
Click the cross in the top right-hand corner to close the document.
To close the program, double-click the program icon in the top left-hand corner.
Tick the check box.
*Select 'Close' from the File menu to close the **document/program**.*

Basic word processing

1 Open the word-processing application.
*Click on the word-processing program **on your desktop/from the Start menu**.*
*Double-click the **Word/Word Perfect/Word Pro** icon on the desktop.*
Right click on the Word icon and choose 'Open' from the pop-up menu.
***Left click/Select** the Word icon and then press return.*
Open a new document.
To create a new document, select 'New' from the File menu.

2 Get familiar with the screen and keyboard.
***Take/Spend** a little time familiarizing yourself with the screen.*
Have a good look at the different features on the screen.
Take a few minutes to explore the screen.
What buttons can you identify on the toolbar?
What menus can you find?

3 Use the mouse to navigate around the screen.
*Use the scroll **bar/wheel** to move up and down through the document.*
Use the keyboard shortcuts as well as the mouse.
*Use the arrow keys to navigate **through the text/around the screen**.*

4 Set the spellchecker.
Open the Tools menu and set the language.
Please select British or American English to help you with your spelling.
Remember to spell check what you write.
Run the spellchecker before you print out your work.

5 Remember to save your work.
Press Control-S to save your work.
Left click the save icon on the toolbar to save your work.
Select 'Save' from the drop-down menu to save your work.
Make sure you save your work regularly.
Save your files onto the hard disk.
*Back everything up on a **disk/USB drive/memory stick**.*
Make a back-up (copy) of your work (on your diskette).
*Save it as a **Word file/text file**.*

6 Print out your work.
Make a printout of what you've written.
Don't forget to make a hard copy of your work.
Print it double-sided and save paper.

---

1 ⌊ These instructions apply to most computer programs.

4 ⌊ Other useful language support tools include:
Have a look in the thesaurus.
Use the online dictionary.
***Do/Carry out** a word count.*

⇒ Students can very often check their grammar and usage by entering phrases into Google:
Check your grammar by doing a Google search.
See which phrase gets most hits in Google.

Going online

1 You can check your email first.
I'll give you a few minutes to read your email.

2 We'll be using the Internet today.
*Let's browse the **Web/Net/Internet**.*
You have the opportunity today to do some research using the Internet.
We need to access the Internet.
Today we're going to research Edinburgh on the Internet.
*Let's see what the **BBC/Guardian** website **has on/says about** Nepal.*
*Open **Explorer/Navigator/Firefox/Opera/your Internet browser**.*
See what Wikipedia has to say on the topic.
Let's have a go at doing a webquest.
I want you to collect information on threatened species.

3 Enter a search engine address into the address bar.
*Please **write/type** the following address in the address bar.*
Type www.google.com into the address bar.
Click the down arrow at the end of the address bar.
Select an address from the drop-down menu.
*Use your list of **bookmarks/favourites**.*

4 Type an appropriate keyword into the search field.
Add a suitable search word in the search field.
Enter one or two key subject-related terms into the search engine.
Do a keyword search.
Do a search on national parks.

5 Select one of the titles in the list.
Click on the address provided by the search engine.
Choose the closest match from the given list.
Decide which link seems to be the most promising.
*It's just **luck/pot luck** if you find a really useful site.*
If none of the titles seem appropriate, enter a new search word.
You can refine your search.
Bookmark the address.
This is a password-protected site.

1 ⌊ Often students immediately open their email when they sit down at a computer. If you want to get on with your lesson, say:
Please close your email now.
Please check your email after the lesson.
I don't want to see anyone checking their email now, please.

⌊ The following are useful if you are in email contact with your students:
I'll email you about this.
*I'll let you know **via/by** email.*
Send me an email.
Send me your essay as an (email) attachment.
You can forward your stories to each other (by email).
Remember to check your email.

This assumes they have email access:
Do you have email?
Do you have an email address?
*Can I **contact/reach** you via email?*
*Are you **contactable/reachable** by email?*
Do you have access to the Net?
Do you have a broadband connection from home?

⌊ Some email functions have been taken over by mobile phones (AE: cellphone, cellular phone):
*I'll send you a **text message/an SMS** about this.*
*Remember to **text/SMS** me if you have a problem.*

⇨ Sending and receiving short email messages is more like casual conversation. Students enjoy this kind of communication in English and, more importantly, it increases their confidence to use the language. Time set aside for emailing or regular email sessions is not wasted.

2 ⌊ Prepositions:
*on *the Internet, on *screen*, on *a disk*, on *a USB*.

3 ⌊ Pronunciation:
WWW = /ˈdʌbəlju: ˈdʌbəlju: ˈdʌbəlju:/

4 ⇨ Guided or structured search exercises are often more effective than random web-surfing. It can be a valuable exercise for students to brainstorm search criteria together in a group. It encourages them to find subject-related vocabulary before they begin their search. The search itself is then more effective as the students have a clearer idea of what kind of information they are looking for. This type of exercise helps students to become autonomous learners.

5 ⌊ The following phrases are useful if students want to download information:
Download the file to the Temp(orary) directory.
Save it to your personal directory.
Delete the file at the end of the session.
Don't download anything onto your computer if the virus protection isn't activated.
Make sure you scan the file for viruses.

Technical problems (2)

1 Oh dear, the document won't print.
Oh no, there's no paper in the printer.
The ink cartridge is empty.

2 Let's check the connection.
Have you checked the connection?
Is the connection tight?

3 Everything looks OK.
*Everything seems to be **fine/correct/as it should be**.*
*It's **on/plugged in**.*
There's no loose connection.
The button was definitely clicked.

4 I'm not really sure where the problem is.
*I'm not entirely clear **what/where** the problem is.*
*I can't really **see/say** what the problem is.*
*It isn't very **clear/obvious** what's wrong.*
*It's difficult to **say/identify** what the fault is.*

5 Let's ask the technician.
We'll have to ask someone who knows.
We need an expert to help us.
I'll ask for some technical help.
We'll have to wait until this is fixed.
*We can't do anything until someone has **fixed/solved/seen to** the problem.*

---

1   It can be frustrating, but not entirely unpredictable, when equipment may not work as we expect. If catastrophe strikes, the following list of phrases may prove useful:

Central processing unit (CPU):
*The computer has **frozen/stalled/crashed**.*
The server is down.
The system keeps crashing.
Try switching off and rebooting.

Leads:
The lead isn't plugged in.
The leads are connected incorrectly.
*There seems to be a **loose connection/missing lead**.*

Disk:
The disk is stuck.
*It says the disk is **empty/full**.*
The disk needs formatting.
*The disk **won't open/won't run/isn't recognized**.*

Screen:
There's no picture.
*The screen **has frozen/keeps flickering**.*

Mouse:
The mouse isn't responding.
The mouse cursor has disappeared.

Printer:
*The printer won't **print/stop printing**.*
The printer has run out of ink.
*The **printer/paper** is jammed.*
*The printed text **is the wrong size/doesn't fit within the margins**.*
The paper's out.
The printer's out of paper.

---

3   If you can't remember the correct technical word, useful 'filler' words include: *thingy, thingummy, thingamabob, thingamajig, whatchamacallit* (BE), and *whatsit* (BE):
The thingummy on the mouse has broken. You know, the scroller.
It needs a new thingamabob.
I've lost the thingy for the speakers.
Switch the whatchamacallit on.
Make sure you've turned the whatsit off. Yes, that's it. The monitor.

---

4   Sometimes you will just have to admit defeat in the face of technical problems:
I give up.
*It's got me **beaten/stumped**.*
Your guess is as good as mine.
It could be anything.

I'll ask for some technical help

Classroom essentials

GIVING INSTRUCTIONS (3)

Suggestions and advice

The teacher holds a position of authority in the classroom. For this reason, all of the instructions given, whether commands, requests or suggestions, will carry the force of a command. In normal social situations, though, if we suggest something, it means that we are offering the other person an opportunity to accept or reject it, or at least to talk about it. Suggestions are an essential part of a discussing and democratic community.

Even though suggestions in the classroom do not carry all of the implications of real suggestions, they are nevertheless a stimulus and encouragement to communication. This is one reason for giving some of your instructions in the form of suggestions. Another reason is simply to enrich classroom language and expose your students to the many forms of suggestions in English. The following section introduces some different ways of making suggestions and giving advice.

1 Suggesting

Let's

- This is a very common way of expressing a suggestion:

  Let's go through the new words.   *Let's ask the technician.*
  Let's finish this next time.   *Let's listen to it once again.*

- Notice that the formal *let us* is seldom used in everyday speech. *Let's* also exists in a negative form, *let's not*. There is an alternative form, *don't let's*, sometimes used in BE:

  Let's not spend too long on this   *Don't let's waste any more time.*

- The question tag *shall we?* is often added to suggestions beginning with *let's* and *let's not*. In both cases the tag is the same. *OK?, Yes?* and *Alright?* function in the same way:

  Let's finish off what we're doing, shall we?
  Let's settle down to work, OK?
  Let's not take too long over this, shall we?
  Let's not bother with number 6, alright?

- ⊗ See 🎧 5.1

about

- You can also make suggestions with *how about* and *what about*, followed by a noun or an *-ing* form. Once again, *OK?, Yes?* and *Alright?* are often added:

  How about trying to use the spellchecker?
  What about saving it under a new name? OK?
  How about another song? Yes?
  What about a printout?

- Notice how you can refer to a specific student or group:

  How about Sam operating the projector?
  What about this group starting? OK?

- *How about* and *What about* are also useful when you want to nominate and involve students:

  How about you, Laura? Any ideas?
  What about the last one, then? Sergio?

⊗ See 🎧 5.2

What if

- A similar expression is *What if* followed by a verb phrase, usually in the present tense:

  What if we speed things up a little bit?
  What if we try a Google search?

- Notice that *What if* followed by a negative is not a suggestion, but a real question:

  What if we can't open the file?
  What if we don't have enough seats?

- Notice that in colloquial speech you will hear *What/How about if*:

  How about if you work in pairs?
  What about if you try rebooting the machine?

Why not

- Questions using *Why not*, *Why don't we,* and *Why don't you* are very common in making suggestions:

  Why not put your poster here?
  Why don't we look at some overheads?
  Why don't you come and sit here?
  Why can't you try copying and pasting the text?

- Typical mistakes: *Why not ~~to~~ try again? ✗ Why ~~to~~ bother? ✗*

suggest

- There are also phrases that use the verb *suggest* and the noun *suggestion*. Notice the various forms of complementation (*-ing* form, *that*+ verb, and *to* + infinitive):

I suggest	*saving* your work every few minutes.
I'd suggest	*rechecking* all the cable connections.
I would suggest	not *working* in groups of more than three.
Can I suggest	not *spending* too much time on this.
I suggest (*that*)	you make a printout of your work.
I'd suggest (*that*)	we keep in touch by email.
May I suggest (*that*)	you make a back-up copy.
My suggestion is (*that*)	you work two to each computer.
My suggestion is	for you *to finish* this exercise before the bell.

- An informal way of introducing a suggestion is to say:

  If I can make a (small) suggestion, why don't you ...?

- Typical mistakes:
  I suggest ~~to make~~ a copy. ✗
  I suggest ~~you to make~~ a copy. ✗
  Can you ~~suggest me~~ a good dictionary? ✗

2 Advising

- Advising somebody is very similar to making a suggestion, but usually you add a reason or justification. Advice can seem more acceptable when it is expressed as a suggestion only. Similarly, a command or piece of advice can be softened by using *I think*, *don't you think?* and *perhaps*:

  I think everyone should copy these sentences down.
  The headsets could be put back in their places, don't you think?
  You can return to your own seat now, perhaps.

idea

- Phrases using the word *idea* are often used to give advice. Note the different forms of complementation:

It	might would mightn't wouldn't	be	an idea a good idea a better idea a bad idea	for	you everyone this group you	to work alone. to save their work. to have a look at the screen. to read the instructions.

You can also use an *if* clause with the past tense:

It	might would mightn't wouldn't	be	an idea a good idea a better idea a bad idea	if	you everyone this group you	worked alone. saved your work. looked it up. read the instructions.

... as well

- Notice the following sets of phrases that use the modal auxiliaries *can*, *could*, *may*, *might*, and *would*, followed by *as well* or *just as well*:

You	can	just as well	delete the file.
We	could	just as well	leave this word out.
We	may	(just) as well	wait until everyone is quiet
You	might	(just) as well	rewind and try again.

It	would be might be	just as well	to save your work every few minutes. to check it's a water-soluble pen.

Second conditional

- Advice used to persuade often takes the form of a second conditional:

It would be	better quicker more effective	if you worked in small groups. if you underlined just the new words. if you left number 6 out.

- Notice the following:

  If I was you, I would try Control + Alt + Del.
  If I were you, I'd make a note of the address.

had better

- Be careful with this useful structure. A typical mistake is to include *to*:

  *You had better ~~to~~ stop. ✗
  You'd better concentrate now.
  You had better stop now.
  We'd better start, hadn't we?
  We had better listen to it again.

would rather

- This basically means the same as *I would prefer*. Notice the past tense:

  I would rather (that) you tried.
  I'd rather (that) you didn't print it all out.

Advice

- More formally, the verb *advise* and the noun *advice* can be used:

  I advise you to make detailed notes.
  My advice (to you) is to rewrite it
  You would be well advised to make a backup.

- Notice also the more informal:

  Take my advice and save your work.
  *Let me give you a **word/piece** of advice.*

Practice

1 In each pair of sentences below, the second one has some of its words mixed up. Rearrange the words to complete the second sentence so that it means more or less the same as the first one.

EXAMPLE:
Let's check the connection.
It might be … connected to idea see properly if it's an
It might be an idea to see if it's connected properly.

1 Turn to me and look at the TV.
  I suggest … facing screen turning way this and the
2 Can we go faster?
  What if we … try speed up to bit things a ?
3 I think you should write these words down.
  You might as … down words in notebooks well these copy your
4 I'll give you five minutes for this and no more.
  I'd rather you … minutes spend more this didn't than five on
5 You should get your files organized.
  Take my … organize advice files and your.
6 Why not use the dictionary and make sure ?
  It wouldn't be … check a bad to this in dictionary idea the
7 We've spent long enough on this.
  You had better … spend on any this not time more
8 Come out here and show everybody else.
  What about … the others out front and the to coming showing ?
9 How about working in threes or fours?
  My suggestion … four that you of is work three in groups or
10 I think you should write it in capitals.
  If I were … capital this use letters I'd you for

2 Working in groups, try to re-express the following suggestions in as many different ways as possible. Each participant in turn gives an alternative. These clue words may help:

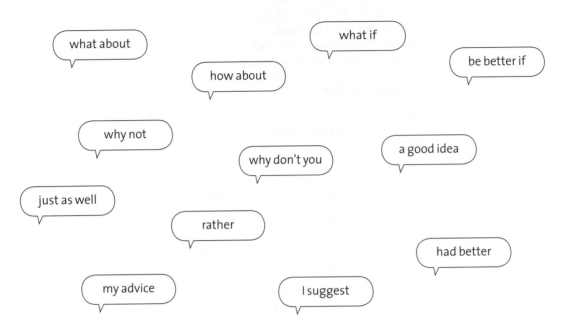

1 Let's rewind and try it again.
2 Let's read the instructions.
3 Let's not do this work in pairs.
4 Let's tidy the classroom before we go.
5 Let's call the technician.
6 Let's open the window if it's hot.
7 Let's not leave this work until next time.
8 Let's settle down, everyone.
9 Let's close the blinds.
10 Let's work around the computer.
11 Let's not argue about this.
12 Let's rearrange the desks.

3 As a group, make suggestions for an educational visit or excursion with your class. Think of all the practical problems involved and come up with ideas for solving them. Alternatively, you can plan a special day at school, devoted to sports, culture, or the environment.

Exercises and activities

5

1 Prepositions and vocabulary

See the OUP website http://www.oup.com/elt/teacher/pce.

2 Situations

In each of the following situations, you can read the teacher's thoughts. What did the teacher actually say in English in each situation?

1 I think I'll ask Heidi to come and show us where Los Angeles is on the map.
2 Wow, that's the third time Kim has volunteered today. Better try someone else, though.
3 Kris is standing right in front of what he's written. How can the rest see?
4 I wonder if any of them have noticed Ken's spelling mistake in sentence 4 on the board.
5 I think it's about time I had the board cleaned.
6 It's probably worth keeping this exercise up on the board for the next class.
7 Oh dear, the marker pen has dried up! I suppose there might be one next door.
8 No wonder they can't read the OHP. It's terribly unclear.
9 Of course, this is the classroom with only one socket. And this is the projector with the short lead.
10 I suppose I'd better find someone to operate the projector.
11 Ah, so that's what the Eiffel Tower looks like upside down!
12 This is the wrong video! I must have put it in the wrong box.
13 I like this part of the DVD. This is the way I imagine Scottish scenery to be.
14 This book has some nice pictures of castles. I'll let them all see it.
15 Silly me! Of course the CD player won't work if it's not plugged in.
16 Was the song before this unit or after it? Ah well, keep hunting!
17 Better safe than sorry! I'll just use a short extract to check everything's working.
18 Phew! I thought I'd never sort out that problem. Now we can get on.
19 I mean, the spellchecker would find most of her spelling mistakes!
20 I wonder how much they'll find on the Web about butterflies.
21 I'd better remind them about saving their work and making back-ups.
22 Panic! I've tried everything! I've absolutely no idea what to do!
23 There's a good idea. Why don't I ask them to send me their work via email?

3 Using pictures

RECORD Work in small groups. Each member needs a visual, such as a picture from a magazine, a poster. Take it in turns to introduce your visual. You have two aims: firstly, to get the other members of the group to interact with the visual and each other as much as possible, and secondly, to generate as much vocabulary based on the visual as possible. Finally, try to work out a story that makes use of all the pictures in the group.

4 Using a video recording or presentation

RECORD Find a five-minute clip from a film or TV programme. Prepare a short lesson based on the clip. Present it to the rest of the group. Alternatively, you might want to produce some PowerPoint slides as part of a presentation.

5 Equipment

Label the different parts of the following diagrams and try to explain their function. What could go wrong with each piece of equipment? How would you explain the problem?

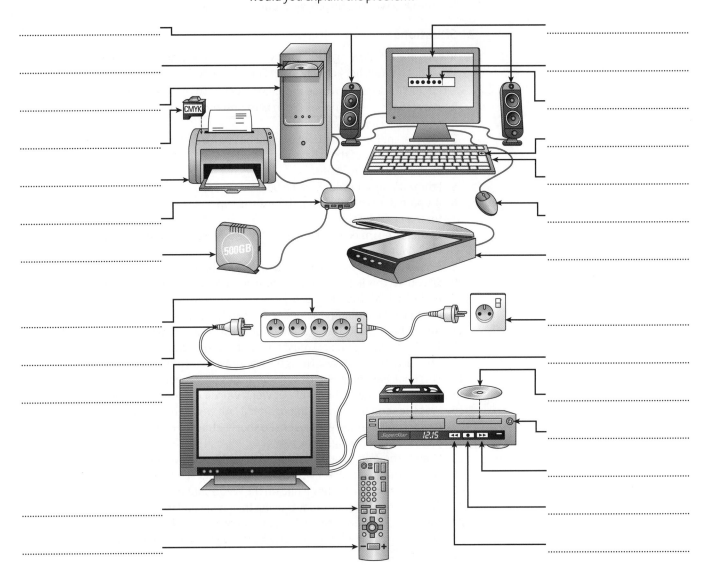

6 Future visions

Begin by designing and drawing your vision of either 1) the ultimate all-in-one classroom teaching aid for the 21st century, with all the necessary buttons, leads, displays, and so on, or 2) the ideal language teaching classroom, with furniture, equipment, and so on. Then work in pairs or small groups. Without showing the others your drawing or plan, describe your invention or classroom so that they can draw it and label it. At the end you can compare your drawings and develop an even better teaching aid or classroom.

7 Browsing the Web

Either: Search for ten good websites offering useful English teaching and learning resources. *Or*: You and a partner should each make a list of ten rather difficult general knowledge questions; for example, the longest place name in the world. Exchange lists and browse the Web for the answers. Afterwards explain your search strategies to each other.

Audio practice

1 Classroom intonation

🎧 **5.1** Use the following clue sentences to practise making suggestions beginning with *let's* or *let's not*. At the end add the tag *shall we?* or another suitable question word; for example, *OK?, Alright?, Yes?* Notice the rising intonation on the tag or final word. Listen and check.

1 I want you to concentrate on the key ideas.
2 Rewind your tape and try again.
3 We're standing in the way and blocking everybody's view.
4 There's no need to bother with the last task.
5 Why don't we close the blinds?
6 Don't spend more than five minutes on this.
7 Close your eyes and listen to the music.
8 We won't print it out until it's finished.

🎧 **5.2** Practise asking particular students to answer or contribute. Use *how about?* or *what about?* and remember the rising intonation in the second part of the question. Then listen and repeat.

EXAMPLES:
Question 6 – Markus
How about question 6? Markus?
Salman? – any opinion?
What about you, Salman? Any opinion?

1 The first one – Giulia?
2 Beatriz – any idea?
3 Number 2 – Ralf?
4 Miguel – any suggestions?
5 The meaning of the first sentence – Carmen?
6 Jeanne – Anything to add?

2 Key sounds

🎧 **5.3** English pronunciation problems are often caused by the irregular correspondences between spelling and sound. There may be silent letters (for example, *comb*), unexpected sound changes (*south — southern*) and deceptive spellings (*cello*). Personal and place names seem to cause particular difficulty. Have a try at pronouncing the following names. Then listen and repeat.

1	Brussels	11	The Danube
2	Cologne	12	Geoffrey
3	Cyprus	13	Graham
4	Edinburgh	14	Hugh
5	Egypt	15	Ian
6	The Mediterranean	16	Keith
7	Prague	17	Leonard
8	Warsaw	18	Nigel
9	The Rhine	19	Roger
10	The Thames	20	Sean

3 Word stress

🎧 **5.4** The majority of compound nouns in English have the main stress on the first word (for example, *tape* recorder, *pho*tocopier), but there are exceptions (apple *pie*, electric *train*). Notice also that abbreviations are stressed on the final syllable (BB*C*, U*N*). Go though the following list of words and decide where the main stress is located. Then listen and check.

1 a video camera
2 a fax machine
3 a DVD player
4 a data projector
5 a digital camera
6 a satellite dish
7 a keyboard
8 a USB connection
9 a plastic bag
10 a mouse button
11 a remote control
12 an extension cable
13 a headset
14 a web browser
15 an overhead transparency
16 a CD player
17 an ink cartridge
18   an operating system

🎧 **5.5** Very many compounds in English consist of a noun or verb, and a particle (for example, *worn out, outbreak*). There are some simple—but not watertight—rules to remember where to put the main stress:

If the compound is a **noun**, the main stress is on the first word: an *out*break, a *come*back.

If the compound is a **verb**, the stress is on the verb: to over*take*, to under*rate*.

If the compound is an **adjective**, the stress is on the first word: a *worn*-out engine, an *up*hill struggle.

If the verb is a **phrasal verb** (verb + particle), the stress is on the particle:
to log *on*, to break *down*.

Try and apply these rules to the following sentences. Then listen and repeat.

1 You'll find the command in one of the pull-down menus.
2 This online dictionary is really handy.
3 Don't forget to make a back-up.
4 Have you installed the latest updates?
5 Don't forget to log off when you've finished.
6 It has two built-in speakers.
7 Let's go online and link up with the other class.
8 This is a phrase that you'll have to look up.
9 We should buy the upgrade as soon as possible.
10 I've forgotten my log-on name.

4 Live lessons

You will hear some short extracts from different classroom situations. Listen to each extract and then answer the questions. Transcripts can be found on page 166.

🎧 **5.6** Using a recording
1 Is this the first time the students have listened to the recording?
2 Why does the teacher say 'Keep your books closed'?
3 What is the phrase the teacher uses when she starts the recording?

🔑 🎧 **5.7** Using an overhead

1 The student Phillip mispronounces a word. What is it?
2 The name of a former Communist country is also mispronounced. What is it?
3 What was the grammatical mistake in the student's last question about the Warsaw Pact?
4 The teacher corrects none of the above mistakes, but she does correct another? What is it and why do you think she corrects it?

🔑 🎧 **5.8** Doing an oral drill

1 The teacher is doing a substitution drill based on a recording. Why does she explain it in Japanese?
2 What does the teacher do while her students are repeating?
3 What possible problem with substitution drills does this extract show?

🔑 🎧 **5.9** Comparing pictures

This is a continuation of the lesson on political ideologies that you heard part of in Unit 3. The teacher refers to the illustrations above.

1 The class is going to look at and talk about two statues. Why?
2 How do you think the activity will actually take place?
3 Why does the teacher ask what the students already know about the statues?
4 What is the piece of information that the students seem to disagree on?
5 The teacher stumbles on the word *anniversary*. What word did she confuse it with?
6 The teacher's next words at the end of this extract were *Now this*. What does *this* probably refer to?

Developing skills **6**

6

SECTION A

This section focuses on speaking and listening skills. The phrases illustrate a range of approaches to the teaching of these skills, beginning with simpler, more teacher-centred techniques and moving towards increased learner independence. In building up your students' confidence to speak and take part, it is particularly important to ask for their opinions, even on the material and activities you use in the class. This will make them feel that they are active and valued contributors to the lesson. Pair and group work are also motivating ways to develop your students' confidence and speaking skills.

1 **Listening activities**
Now we'll do a listening exercise.
Before you listen, ...
Now listen again and this time ...
Let's finish off with a dictation.
Listen and take notes.

2 **Listening and repeating**
Let's listen to the conversation.
Listen and repeat.
All together now, please.
Again, please.
Louder, please.
Now just this group.

3 **Helping with pronunciation**
How is this word pronounced?
Let's check your pronunciation.

4 **Introducing speaking activities**
We'll do it like this.
First I'll say it and then you can try.
Would you rather work in pairs?

5 **Moving towards free conversation**
Let's talk about this picture.
Can you explain how it works?
Did you enjoy that activity?
Which activity did you like best?

6 **Running a class discussion**
Let's talk about the problem of ...
What do you think?
Why?
Do you really think so?
I'm not sure what you mean.
Has anybody else anything to say on this?

Working with the spoken language

Points to think and talk about

1 In what situations outside school do you imagine that your students listen to and speak English? What sort of English do they listen to? What do you think they enjoy talking about in their own language?
2 What differences are there between listening in a multiple-choice comprehension test and normal listening in an everyday situation outside school?
3 How many different listening activities can you think of? Do you have some favourites?
4 Language teaching experts talk about recycling language in the classroom. What do you think this means? Why do you think it is important?
5 What do you think of repetition as a form of pronunciation practice? How does it usually take place in the classroom? How can it be made more effective?
6 Is it important that students can read phonetic symbols? What about actually using them? How can you help them to learn them and use them?
7 Why do you think information gap or communication exercises (where students have different sets of information which they have to communicate) are motivating and rewarding?
8 How can you make sure that all the students are active in a discussion activity? Is it important that everybody says something? What is your role during a group discussion?
9 How do you react to language errors made during an informal class discussion? Would it be useful to keep a written record of frequent errors? How?
10 Do you ever ask your students for their comments on a particular text or exercise that they have done, even in their native language? Is this a good idea? Would it work in your school system?

Language to think about

1 What would you say to a student who is speaking too softly?
2 What do *listen here* and *look here* mean?
3 Can you describe the position of your mouth when you say the /θ/ in *think*, the /v/ in *valley* and the /ʃ/ in *shape*?
4 Is there any difference between these two questions: *How did you like the book?* and *What did you like about the book?*
5 Can you think of other ways of saying *Copy me*?
6 In a conversation, when can you say *I see*? What other phrases carry the same meaning?
7 Do you know any other phrases that mean the same as *By the way...*?
8 Can you explain the words *gist*, *paraphrase*, and *summarize*?
9 Do these questions have the same meaning? *Was that fun?* and *Was that funny?*
10 Use the following words in classroom phrases: *expand*, *sidetracked*, *whisper*.

Classroom English vocabulary to collect

1 Verbs for oral communication skills (For example, *to explain*, *to describe*)
2 A list of different types of comprehension activities (For example, *multiple choice*, *gap-fill*)

Key to symbols:

(i)	Idiomatic phrase	⇨	Pedagogical pointer
(S)	Student reply	(»)	Cross-reference
(x)	Typical mistake	(CD)	Listen to the CD
L	Language comment	RECORD	Record yourself

Listening activities

1 Now we'll do a listening exercise.
I want you to listen to (a) part of a conversation.
Now we'll listen to an extract from a news bulletin.
Your job is to listen to a section of a dialogue.

2 Before you listen, ...
What could this dialogue/conversation be about?
What do you think this recording will be about?

3 Now listen again and this time ...
Fill in the missing words.
Make a list of all the words to do with colour.
Listen and choose the most suitable answer.
Decide what will happen next.

4 Let's finish off with a dictation.
First of all, listen to the whole text.
Now I'll re-read the text in small sections.
I'll read each section twice, with a short pause.
Now I'll read the whole text once more at normal speed.
Listen and make any small corrections.
Now you have five minutes to check it through.
Now check your version against the original.

5 Listen and take notes.
Write a summary of the lecture.
Write a one-page summary on the basis of your notes.
Give an oral report on what happened in the meeting.

---

1 Before the listening exercise you can say:
You cannot expect to understand everything.
I don't expect you to catch every word.
There are lots of words you won't understand.
Just try to get the main ideas.
Don't worry about (understanding) the details.
*This time just listen (out) for the **general idea/gist/key points**.*

Success at listening gives students a powerful motivational boost. It requires extensive exposure to the spoken language to develop good listening skills. If you run your class in English, you are really helping your students to learn to listen. You should make this point clear to your students.

After the first listening, you can say:
So, that was it.
*Right, now you've **heard/listened to** it once.*

---

2 Many of the pre-reading strategies mentioned in Unit 4, B1 can also be used to help students prepare for a listening activity. Just as with a reading activity, it is important for students to know why they are listening. You can, for example, direct the students to listen for just the main idea:
*What is the **main/central/key idea/message**?*

Or to listen out for specific information:
I want you to listen out for the following information:
Where is this conversation taking place?
*How many people are **speaking/involved**?*
*What **time of day/day of the week** is it?*

The following may also be useful:
Listen, but don't write anything.
Listen carefully to the instructions.

Before listening, read through the questions.
Familiarize yourself with the questions before we start.
Listen, and at the same time answer the questions.
As you listen, do exercise 2B.
Fill in the missing words while you listen.
While you are listening, answer question 2.

The first time through, direct the students just to listen. You could then ask a few questions (in the L1 or English), to get an overview of the topic:
So, briefly, what was it about?
Now, in your own words, what happened?
OK, in one or two sentences, how did it end?

---

3 The following is a list of typical listening activities:

a Listen and complete.
*Listen and fill in the information on the **chart/table/diagram/map**.*
Mark Columbus's route on the map as you listen.
Listen to the description and draw a picture.

b Listen and identify.
Is he saying 'chin' or 'gin'?
How many times do you hear the word 'never'?
Pick out the words which tell you how she felt.
Listen for the phrase that explains why he failed.
*What words does the speaker use when he **hesitates/pauses**?*

c Listen and match.
Listen and write the number under the correct picture.
Listen and choose the best description for each photograph.
Listen and find the person described in the picture.

d Listen and choose.
Mark the statements as true or false.
Tick the correct statements.
Listen and correct the mistakes on your worksheet.

e Listen and predict
What will happen next?
What's he going to say next?
How will it end?

f Listen and arrange.
Listen to five extracts from a story.
Rearrange the extracts in the correct order.
Arrange the following headlines to match the order of events on the recording.

---

4 In partial dictation, students fill in missing words, phrases, or sentences on a prepared sheet. Full dictation involves transcribing a passage read aloud. As well as the general format described here, some other useful instructions include:
I'll read it at normal speed.
If there is punctuation, I will say 'full stop', 'comma', etc.
If I say 'new paragraph', then begin a new paragraph.

---

5 Advanced students can listen to a talk or lecture and take notes, after which they can write or present a summary. With this type of more extensive listening exercises, it is useful to help students develop effective note-taking techniques and listening strategies. These include:

a learning to anticipate and decode the structure of the lecture;

b noting down the personal opinions of the speaker in a different way to facts;

c using examples and anecdotes given in a lecture more as a memory prompt than something to be recorded in detail;

d developing some simple shorthand and abbreviations.

Listening and repeating

1 Let's listen to the conversation.
Now you'll hear the conversation.
You will hear the sentences on the recording.

2 Listen and repeat.
All together, repeat after the CD.
***Everyone/everybody**, say it after me.*
***Say/Repeat** after me: 'Nice to meet you'.*
Listen again and say it after me.
*Listen to **how/the way** I say it.*
Listen again carefully and then you try.

3 All together now, please.
Let's say it all together.
All of you.
The whole class, please.
Not just this row.
Everybody join in.
Join in with the rest of us, Yoshio.
You, too, Rem.

4 Again, please.
One more time.
*(And) once **more/again**, please.*
*Say it **again/once more**.*
Let's try it again.

5 Louder, please.
Speak up.
*Say it **louder/in a loud voice**.*
Say it a bit louder, please.
Once again, but louder.
Say it so that everyone can hear you.
I can't hear you.

6 Now just this group.
Let's begin with the girls.
*Now **just/only the boys/this row/this group**.*
*The **boys/girls** on their own.*
This row on its own.
(The) next group.
(The) back row.

1 ⇨ *Recording* is a general word for the great range of audio media in use (for example, tape; cassette; CD; minidisk; MP3; podcast). See also Unit 5, B.

⇨ It's a good idea to have a final readiness check:
*Are you all ready? Right. **Here goes/Off we go/Here it comes**.*

⊗ ~~*Listen the conversation.*~~ ✗

Whenever the verb *listen* is followed by an object, the preposition *to* is required:

Listen.		Listen **to** the recording.
Listen carefully.		Listen **to** me carefully.
Listen again.	BUT	Listen **to** John saying it again.
Listen now.		Listen now **to** how I say it.

⊗ *Listen here* (like *Look here*) usually precedes an angry threat or piece of advice:
Listen here! I'm fed up with all this noise.

2 ⇨ You may want to read aloud with your students. This often helps to keep the rhythm and speed of the original:
Let's read in chorus. /ˈkɔːrəs/
Let's all say it together.
Say it (in time) with me.

⇨ If repetition is used—and it has an important place in language learning at all levels—then make sure it is effective.

3 ⇨ Make sure everybody is actively repeating. If possible, use a student to operate the equipment to allow you to circulate, listen, and encourage. Don't be afraid to act as a model yourself.

4 ⇨ Give the students more than one opportunity to repeat. Some students only wake up when the first repetition is over.

5 ⇨ Encourage the students to repeat loudly and confidently. You can also vary the volume and fluency of repetitions:
Once again, but more fluently.
***Speak/Say it** more clearly.*
***Shout/Whisper** it this time.*
***Softer/Not so loud**.*
There's no need to shout.
It doesn't have to be quite so loud.
I'm not deaf.

It helps if you ask them to imagine themselves in a real situation where they might say the phrase being practised. Repetition is also a good opportunity for simple role-playing:

Say it	like an old man.
	as if you are tired.
	proudly.
	in a whisper.
Pretend	you are surprised/angry/sad.
Imagine	you've just won a million euros.
Act as if	you are a tourist.

6 ⇨ Vary between individual, group, and class repetitions. This makes practice more dynamic and keeps the class focused.

⌐ Ask individual students:
Now you, Sami.
Just you, Olaf.
On your own, Rafael.
Your turn, Mario.

⊗ The verb *say* needs a direct object:
~~*Say so that we all hear.*~~ ✗ ~~*Say again.*~~ ✗ ~~*Say louder.*~~ ✗

A3
Helping with pronunciation

1 How is this word pronounced?
How do you say the next word?
*How do you say this **part/bit** of the word?*
How do you pronounce these letters?
What sound does this word start with?
These two words are spelt the same, but pronounced differently.
This word rhymes with 'age'.
Don't mix up this word with 'cheer'.
*Don't get 'cheer' and 'jeer' **confused/muddled/mixed up**.*
*Can you hear **any/the** difference?*

2 Let's check your pronunciation.
Again, please, but watch your pronunciation.
It wasn't pronounced correctly.
Be careful with the 'sh-' sound.
*Pay attention to the word **stress/accent**.*

---

1 ⇨ If you ask your students to read aloud, it is a good idea to practise the difficult words in advance or at least to remind them of the problems:
Everybody! Let's repeat the following words before you start reading.
Be careful with the word 'language' on line 3

⇨ Where appropriate, refer to the phonetic spelling:
Use the phonetic symbols.
The phonetic symbols are there to help you.
Check the correct pronunciation whenever you look up a word.
These marks show you where to stress the word.

---

2 ⇨ Precise guidance can often help students improve their pronunciation:
*Watch my **mouth/lips** closely.*
Let the tip of your tongue touch the back of your upper teeth.
Make sure your upper teeth make firm contact with your lower lip.
Shape your lips as if you are saying the /j/ in 'your'.
***Watch/notice** how my lips **stick out/are rounded**.*
Say 'sssss'. Now slowly pull your tongue back.

👆 More specific instructions include:
You are saying 'tree'. I'm saying 'three'.
You said 'chances'. Listen to the correct pronunciation: 'changes'.
The first sound is /θ/, as in 'think'.
*The word is **accented/stressed** on the second syllable.*
Where is the main stress in this word?
This is the American pronunciation of the word.
You can pronounce this word in two different ways.

👆 It helps if you …
***Use/Clap** your hands to **beat/keep** the rhythm.*
Nod your heads in time with the rhythm.
***Beat/Tap** the rhythm on your desks.*
Beat the rhythm with your fingers.
*Say it **aloud/out loud**.*
***Use/Look in** a mirror*

👆 If you are dealing with intonation, which is extremely difficult to teach, it helps to point out pitch changes:
Listen to the way my voice goes up.
The speaker on the recording lets his voice rise like this.
You must let your voice fall at the end of the sentence.
It's a 'Yes/no' question, so it has rising intonation.
Follow my hand movements as the pitch rises and falls.

A4
Introducing speaking activities

1 We'll do it like this.
*I'll show you **how/what** I mean.*
Listen to me saying it first.
I'll do it with one of you, so that you know what I mean.
I'll do the first one for you, so that you understand.
I'll give you an example to help you get started.
Let's do the first one as an example.
Now you know what to do, you can begin.

2 First I'll say it and then you can try.
*Now you **ask/make a sentence**.*
Now ask the person sitting next to you.
Now change the sentence. Begin 'Yesterday I …'
What would you say in this situation?

3 Would you rather work in pairs?
And now in pairs.
Try this in twos.
Here's a task for you to work on in pairs.
Here's a little problem for you to solve in pairs
You'll need to split into groups for this activity.
Discuss your choice with the person sitting next to you.
*Try to **persuade/convince** your neighbour that you're right.*

---

1 ⇨ With all oral activities, it is important to make clear to your students what is expected from them before they start, otherwise you will waste time explaining to individual students and interrupting the class. Demonstrate what you want them to do. This will also give them the appropriate examples of language use.

👆 If you are showing actions or movements (for example, for a game or acting), the following are useful:
*Do **it like this/it this way/what I'm doing**.*
Copy me.
Watch me (doing it) first.
I'll demonstrate.
Try to do it exactly the same way as I did it.

⊗ *Do ~~like this~~.* ✗

---

2 ⇨ Typical teacher-led whole-class oral activities often begin with listening and repeating (see A1). Other ask-and-answer activities include:

1 Chained questions and answers:
Now ask your neighbour the same thing.
I'll start and then we'll continue round the class.
Then you ask Kirsi, and she asks Ari, and so on round the class.

2 Exercises or drills based on manipulating a particular structure or pattern:
Listen to what I say and then reply 'Yes, I do' or 'No, I don't'.
*Listen to the **cue/prompt** and then use the **cue/prompt** word.*
Reply to my questions, using the pattern on the blackboard.
Keep to the same pattern.
Depending on my question, answer either in the past tense or the present perfect.
So, what would you do? Begin 'If I won a million euros, …'

3 Exercises based on a dialogue, picture, or a situation:
Answer my questions, based on the story.
I'll read the waiter's part. Look at the menu and then order a meal and a drink for yourself.
Look at the pictures and tell me something about each person's hobbies.
Make (up) a true sentence about the pictures.
What would you ask if you didn't know his address?
Supposing you needed a dentist, what would you say?

4 Exercises involving memory:
Now I'm going to rub some words off. Can you still say the sentence?
Turn round and face the back. How many sentences can you remember?
Without looking at the board, how many sentences can you say?

3 ⇒ Speaking activities in pairs and small groups help to develop students' communication skills (see also Unit 2, A4). You need to prepare your students carefully for such activities and then circulate and provide feedback as the students discuss. Typical examples are given below. See also Useful reading and resources, page 171.
Practise the conversation in pairs.
*In twos **make up/improvise** a short **dialogue/conversation** based on the picture.*
Ask each other, for example: 'Have you ever been to Spain?'
Say where you want to spend your holiday and why.
I want you to work in pairs and find out what each other's favourite programmes are.
Work in groups and decide on a list of equipment you will have to buy for your trip.

⇒ Communication or information-gap activities offer students a motivating and authentic opportunity to work together and solve problems. They work particularly well in a language lab or over a computer network. Each student has a different picture or set of information. Some typical instructions are:
You must work back to back.
Turn your seats round and face different ways.
Don't let the other person see your sheet.
You each have the same six pictures on your card. But they are not in the same order.
Describe one of your pictures until your partner knows which one it is.
Your partner has the timetable of trains to London. Talk to him and find out the answers to the questions on your sheet.
You and your partner have the same pictures, but there are ten small differences. Talk to each other and find out what the differences are.

A5

Moving towards free conversation

1 **Let's talk about this picture.**
Who is this man?
Where do you think he's going?
What's he thinking about at the moment?
Why does he look so happy?
What will happen to him?

2 **Can you explain how it works?**
Tell me where you live.
*Explain (to me) how to **get there/use it/do it**.*
Show me what to do.
Tell me what I have to do.

3 **Did you enjoy that activity?**
*Did you like that **exercise/activity/lesson/story**?*
*Was that **fun/interesting**?*
*Did you find that **challenging/boring**?*
Was it worth doing?

4 **Which activity did you like best?**
*Which activity type do you **prefer/like most/like least**?*
Which exercise did you enjoy most of all?
Do you prefer this book to the old one?
Which one (of these) would you choose?
Who is your favourite singer?
*Arrange them in order of **preference/importance**.*

1 ⇒ Pictures are excellent stimuli for your students to use their imagination. See also Unit 5, A5.

2 ⇒ Oral activities involving descriptions, explanations, and instructions can help students to produce longer sections of continuous speech. This helps them to develop their free conversation skills. Remember that these activities need careful preparation and frequent practice. A good place to start is with questions like:
*Did you have a good **weekend/holiday**?*
*Can you tell us **all/more** about it?*
What was it like?
How did it go?
What happened?

3 ⇒ Get your students used to being asked for their opinions. This shows that you value what they say and creates a more positive cooperative atmosphere in the class. It also underlines the fact that the classroom is a real social context for using language.

⊗ Some typical mistakes:
It was worth ~~of~~ doing. ✗
That was fun. (= enjoyable) is not the same as *That was funny. (= it made me laugh).*

4 ⇒ Allowing your students to make a choice and to express that choice, even in connection with classroom working methods, is an important stepping stone to confidence in speaking.

Running a class discussion

1 Let's talk about the problem of ...
Today we're going to have a discussion. The topic is ...
*There are four questions I want you to **concentrate/focus** on.*
I want you to discuss these questions in groups.
*Please **think/talk** about your ideas.*
Make a list of the pros and the cons.

2 What do you think?
What do you think about this question?
What did you think of the film?
*How do you feel about this **issue/problem**?*
*What's your opinion **on/of/about** this **subject/topic**?*
What opinions do you have on this topic?
Do you have anything to say on this?

3 Why?
Why do you think so?
How (exactly)?
In what way?
What reasons do you have for saying that?
Can you support what you say?
Is there any evidence to support what you say?

4 Do you really think so?
Is that your honest opinion?
Is that what you honestly think?
You're convinced of this, are you?

5 I'm not sure what you mean.
I'm not sure what you are getting at.
Could you explain what you mean (by 'too much')?
What exactly are you trying to say?
What do you mean exactly?
Be a little more precise.
Could you rephrase the question?
Could you give me an example?
Could you go into more detail?
Could you expand on that a little?

6 Has anybody else anything to say on this?
Have you got anything to add (to what Elli said?)
*Who **agrees/disagrees** with **Elli/what Elli said**?*
Hands up if you agree with Elli.
*Does anybody share Elli's **opinion/views**?*
Have you got any input on this?
Any other contributions?

1 ⊗ *Let's discuss ~~about~~ this.* ✗   *Let's discuss this.* ✓

⇨ It is often useful to carry out a small opinion survey on the topic (for example, a questionnaire) before beginning a classroom discussion.

2 👂 Discussion often involves taking sides:
   Are you in favour of raising the age limit or against it?
   Do you support the idea of private schools or oppose it?

⊗ *What did you like about ~~that~~?* ✗
   BUT: *What did you like about the **film/article/story**?* ✓

3 👂 These comments show that you are listening and are interested:
   I see.   *Yes, (that's) true!*
   Really?   *That's a very good point.*
   Is that so?   *That's exactly the point.*
   That's interesting.   *You can say that again!*
   What you said is very interesting. *Absolutely!*
   I didn't know that.   *I hadn't thought of that.*
   Good question!

4 ⇨ Encourage students to develop their ideas and keep talking:
   Keep going!
   Don't stop there.
   Do go on.
   Let's hear the rest of what you have to say.
   You can't make a comment like that and then just leave it.

👂 If you want to question a student's argument, you can say:
   Don't you think, though, that ...
   I'm not so sure about that.
   Well, that all depends, doesn't it?
   Honestly?
   Really?
   You can't be serious.
   *You must be **joking/kidding**.*
   That's a very original idea.

5 👂 Help your students to get their message across:
   Is this what you mean?
   Is this what you're trying to say?
   You mean, then, that ...
   Correct me if I'm wrong, but do you mean that ... ?

6 👂 You can refer back to earlier points:

Perhaps we could	come back to	what something	Vicki	said	earlier.
Let's	think about	a point a comment	Marco	made	a while ago

👂 Sometimes the class discussion may drift off the subject:
   *Let's try to keep the discussion **focused/moving/on track**.*
   *Try to **keep/stick** to the point.*
   Let's not get sidetracked.

You will then have to refocus it:
   Where were we?
   What were we talking about before (we were interrupted)?
   We got a bit sidetracked there.
   Let's get back to the topic.
   To pick up where I left off, ...
   To continue what I was saying, ...

You may also be suddenly reminded of important ideas:
   Incidentally, ...
   By the way, ...
   Before I forget, ...
   *While I **think of it/still remember**, ...*
   While we're on the subject, ...
   Now that you mention it, ...
   It's just occurred to me that ...
   Oh yes. That reminds me.

SECTION B

Although text messaging and email have perhaps given a new relevance to writing, there are few authentically communicative writing activities for the classroom. On the other hand, the classroom is perfect for exposing students to a wide range of written texts. A display of English notices, posters, advertisements, newspaper cuttings, and comic strips, for example, can help create an English atmosphere in the class and arouse interest in reading. One simple idea is to use English in your own written instructions and feedback.

1 Revisiting the basic text
Go through the text and underline the adverbs.
What does the word mean in this context?
Find a word meaning 'tired'.
What's the corresponding noun?
How do you understand this comment?

2 Reading activities
Answer the questions.
Let's look at the questions you prepared on this text.
Fill in the blanks.
Match the questions and answers.
Rearrange the text.
Use the text to complete the crossword.
Think of your own title for the story.

3 Basic writing activities
Have you all got something to write with?
Now we'll do a writing exercise.

4 Advanced writing
Write an essay on one of the following topics.
First of all, let's brainstorm this topic.
Think about who will be reading your work.
Try to make an outline.
Begin by drafting your essay.
Take time to review what you've written.
Check your spelling.
This essay will be graded.

5 Spelling, punctuation, and grammar
How do you spell 'giraffe?'
Spell it in English.
Have you spelt it right?
You need a comma here.
What's wrong with this sentence?

Working with the written language

Points to think and talk about

1 What sort of things do you read and write outside school? What sort of things do your students read in English outside school? What will they probably read in the future?
2 What sort of writing do they do outside school? And in the future?
3 Which skill in English will be more useful to your students, reading or writing? Why? Which do they find easier?
4 How does your school leaving examination affect the teaching of reading and writing?
5 Do your students have any particular writing problems in English? Think about spelling. What are the letter combinations and spelling conventions that your learners have difficulty with?
6 How many different types of writing activity can you think of? Do you have a favourite? What type of activity seems to motivate your students most?
7 Are you familiar with the idea of process writing? Process writing emphasizes the importance of pre-writing. What do you think this means?
8 What, in your opinion, is the best way to collect and learn vocabulary? What is the best way of testing that your students have learned vocabulary?
9 Do you think it is a good idea to spell out words using the English names for the letters?
10 Do you give your written instructions in English? What are the advantages and disadvantages of doing this?
11 Project work, where students deal with a particular topic in depth, offers a lot of benefits in terms of cooperative learning. What other benefits can you think of?
12 What do you understand by the term *mind-mapping*?

Language to think about

1 Can you explain the instructions for the following types of exercise clearly and logically? a) multiple choice, b) fill in the blanks, c) true–false, d) match the two halves.
2 Can you spell fluently?
3 Can you orally corect the spellng msitakes in this sentence?
4 Can you correctly use the verbs *to correspond, to refer,* and *to derive*?
5 Can you correctly use the words *connotation, equivalent,* and *synonym*?
6 What sort of language is *colloquial, figurative, slang,* or *a four-letter word*?
7 Do you know the names of these punctuation marks in English? ! ; / * ( )
8 Can you think of synonyms for *omit, insert,* and *jumble*?

Classroom English vocabulary to collect

The names of the letters and punctuation marks in English. (For example, *full stop, capital letter*)

Revisiting the basic text

1 Go through the text and underline the adverbs.
Highlight all the connectors in the text.
How many idiomatic expressions can you find?
How many references to colour are there?

2 What does the word mean in this context?
What does this word mean here?
What does it refer to here?
In what sense is the word (being) used here?
In/with what meaning does the writer use the word?

3 Find a word meaning 'tired'.
Find a phrase that means 'she was angry'.
Find a sentence which tells/shows you that …
Pick out the words that describe the countryside.
Which two words make it clear that …?

4 What's the corresponding noun?
What is a synonym of/for 'dear'?
What is the opposite of 'tall'?
What adjective is derived from 'nation'?
What noun comes from 'electric'?
Do you know the noun corresponding to the verb 'organize'?
Give me the adjective that corresponds to 'persuade'.

5 How do you understand this comment?
What is the author referring to when she/he says…?
What is this a reference to?
What could the author mean when she/he says…?

---

2 🔲 When a word is used in an unfamiliar or special way, you can say:
This word has several meanings.
The word is (being) used with a special meaning in this context.
This is a (rather) special/strange/unusual use of the word.
The writer isn't using the word in its everyday meaning.

4 🔲 When exploring vocabulary, you may find the following useful:
What's the equivalent British/American English word/expression?
What do they say in American English?
What's a person who works for a company called?
What do you call someone who moves to another country?
What do you say when someone sneezes?
What's the word for when you feel that your head is spinning?
What's the difference between a bat, a club and, a racket?

🔲 Advanced students can usefully learn to recognize the different parts of a word (for example, prefixes, suffixes) and their meanings. This will help them approach new vocabulary.
What is the meaning of the prefix 'anti-'?
What is the function of the suffix '-fy'?
What are the connotations of the word 'slow'?
What do you usually associate this word with?

🔲 You could also encourage advanced students to identify the style of a word:
This is a very formal/informal/colloquial word.
Only use this word if you're talking to friends.
Never say this unless you know the person very well.
This is a slang expression.
This word is being used figuratively.
This is a swear word/four-letter word.
This is impolite/rude.
That's what they use in American English.
This is typically American usage.

Reading activities

1 Answer the questions.
Read Chapter 3 and answer these questions.
Find answers to the following questions.
Answer the questions with reference to the text.

2 Let's look at the questions you prepared on this text.
You had the job/task of preparing two questions each on this unit.
Who is going to ask the questions about/on this chapter?
What answers did you find to your questions in the text?
Ask your partner three questions based on the text.
Summarize the text that you had to read for your partner.
Agree with your partner on the three main ideas presented in the text.

3 Fill in the blanks.
Find the right word for each blank/gap.
Fill each blank with a suitable word.
Complete the sentences with an appropriate word.
Complete the cloze passage on page 5.
Every seventh word has been left out/omitted. /əˈmɪtɪd/
Supply /səˈplaɪ/ the missing words.

4 Match the questions and answers.
Find a picture to match each word.
Match the sentences/words with/to the pictures.
Find the sentences that refer to this picture.
Which picture goes with this sentence?

5 Rearrange the text.
Arrange the lines of text so that the story makes sense.
Arrange the jumbled /dʒʌmbəld/ sentences/paragraphs.
Put the conversation in the correct order.
Number the sentences in the correct order.
Arrange the sentences into a (sensible) paragraph.
Match the jumbled halves of the sentences.
Classify/Sort the words into groups/families/sets.

6 Use the text to complete the crossword.
Label the diagram.
Fill in the chart/table on the basis of the text.
Read the text and fill in the missing information.
Read the story and mark the route on the map.
Reproduce the text as a mind map.

7 Think of your own title for the story.
Write another ending for the story.
How else could the story have ended?
What would you have done if you had been the hero?

---

2 ⊙ See also Unit 4, B2.

---

3 ⇨ Multiple-choice and true–false questions are a quick way to check understanding.
Ring the right alternative.
Mark/tick/circle the correct answer.
Put a ring/circle round the best alternative.

Choose the correct answer from a, b, c, and d.
Mark the statements (as) true or false.
Correct the untrue statements.
*Find the odd **man/one** out.*
Cross out the word that doesn't belong.

5 ⇨ Activities like this develop reading skills because they encourage students 1) to actively process what they have read, and 2) to work with texts they might not normally consider accessible. Anagrams, crosswords, and word puzzles are also useful.

7 ⇨ These more imaginative activities work well with narrative texts. Other examples:
*What questions would you like to ask the **main character/author**?*
What would have happened if she hadn't arrived in time?
In a group dramatize the climax of the story.
*Make a **living picture/freeze-frame photograph** of this scene.*
Now you are the hero. Take turns to sit in the hot seat and be interviewed.

Summarize the text for your partner

Basic writing activities

1 Have you all got something to write with?
For this next exercise you'll need your pens (out).
You'll need your pencils for this next activity.
*You need something to write **on/with**.*
Has anybody got a spare pencil?
Could you lend Erick something to write on?

2 Now we'll do a writing exercise.
Join the sentences together.
Copy out the true sentences.
Follow the example.
Use the pictures to tell the story.

1 ⊛ See Unit 4, C2 for other basic writing phrases.

2 ⇨ Where Roman script is strange to students, there will be huge problems, both in handwriting and in developing keyboard skills.
Trace the letters.
Use the right stroke order.
Place the letters correctly on the line.
Part of the letter extends below the line.

⇨ Writing exercises are usually of four types. The following list gives some typical examples.

a Combining and changing
Rewrite the story with the correct punctuation.
Write out the sentences to form a paragraph.
Put the sentences in order and build the story.
Connect these sentences using a relative pronoun.
*Use **linking words/connectors** to **join/combine** the sentences.*

b Matching and copying
Write a sentence to match each picture.
Write five true sentences, using the information given.
Use the table to write ten true sentences.
Match the questions and answers, and then write out the conversation in full.
Look at the pictures. Then copy out the true sentences and correct the false ones.

c Writing from a model
Write three sentences about yourself using the same pattern.
Look at this table of information and make up five sentences about Helsinki.
Write about your typical weekend. Follow the example.
Use the information below and the model sentences to write about your hometown.
Write your own 'For Sale' advertisement, following the model.
Write a paragraph about winter sports, using suitable words from the list below.

d Using a stimulus
As you listen, take notes.
Fill in the information on the basis of what you hear.
Expand the notes into a full letter.
Here is the first paragraph. Now write the rest of the essay.
Summarize the article in your own words.
Give me a brief summary of the contents.
Write a 150-word summary of the passage.

Advanced writing

1 Write an essay on one of the following topics.
Carefully read through the essay title to see what you are being asked to do.
Your task is to produce a report on a recent item in the news.
I want you to write a cover letter to your CV.

2 First of all, let's brainstorm this topic.
The first step is to decide what to include in your writing.
Use a pre-writing method to brainstorm the possible content of your writing.
We have to generate as many ideas as possible.
You should make a mind map first.
Read this first. It will give you some ideas for your own essay.
You should research the subject before you start writing.

3 Think about who will be reading your work.
Who is the intended reader?
What will the reader expect to see in your work?

4 Try to make an outline.
Have you got a (skeleton) **plan/outline/framework**?
Make a list of all the things you want to mention.
Group your ideas together.
Arrange/Organize *your main points into paragraphs.*
Put them in order of importance.
What is the best order for your points?
Arrange the points in the most effective order.

5 Begin by drafting your essay.
Make a first draft.
Develop your ideas in each paragraph.
Go into more detail on this topic.
Say a bit more about this problem.
What **examples/illustrations** *can you include?*

6 Take time to review what you've written.
Is your main argument **clear/logical**?
Is the structure of your essay clear?
Does this make sense?
Have you got an introduction and conclusion?
What other examples can you give to support your argument?
Is there any **unnecessary/irrelevant** *information?*
Is the style appropriate?

7 Check your spelling/punctuation/grammar.
Remember to proofread your essay (for spelling mistakes).
Use a spellchecker.
Give yourself time to **read/check/look** *through your work.*
Be careful with **tenses/subject–verb agreement/word order**.
Try and correct your own mistakes.
Try to think **of/up** *a good title.*
Don't forget the layout.
Begin a new paragraph with an indent.

8 This essay will be graded.
I shall mark this essay.
It will count towards your final **mark/grade**.

---

1 ⇨ Different types of written texts require different styles and organisational formats. Make sure your students work with a variety of written texts so that they become familiar with these differences.

» See Useful reading and resources (page 171) for more on strategies and techniques in advanced reading and writing (for example, SQR3; MURDER).

---

2 ⇨ Process writing is exactly that: students go through a process to produce a written text and each step has a different focus. Initially students need to generate ideas and to do the background research. Get your students to write these ideas down in English. That way they can start gathering key vocabulary from the very beginning, without having to worry about sentence structure or style.

---

4 ⇨ After the ideas have been generated, the next step is to introduce some order. Selecting what to include and what to exclude and deciding on the order of information will help students produce a well-structured piece of writing.

5 ⇨ It is only at this point that students should begin to focus on actual writing. In this phase they will spend a lot of time on drafting and redrafting text, but if the pre-writing phase has been done properly, then this second phase should also be a positive experience.

6 ⇨ The final phase is editing and polishing. If the text is well-prepared and well-structured, the writer can focus on the details of language and presentation. Feedback is important at this stage:
Let one of your fellow students read through your draft version.
Read your first draft aloud to your neighbour.
Circulate your draft and see what the others think.

7 ⇨ If you mark early drafts of students' written work, then it is useful to develop a simple system of abbreviations or symbols. This will help students to see their mistakes or difficulties, and encourage them to make corrections themselves. For example: Sp = spelling, WO = word order, ^ = something missing, T = tense, A = agreement. Don't forget to include encouraging comments like *good point, well argued, interesting idea*.

» See also Unit 4, C6 for comments and feedback on written work.

8 ⇨ Use the following if students are producing a portfolio of their work or a more extensive project:
I want you to produce a portfolio on the places you have studied in this chapter.
Include everything in your portfolio.
Collect, select, and reflect.
Select your best work for your portfolio
Include your rough /rʌf/ drafts and the final version.
Write your work up with an introduction and conclusion.
Reflect on what you have learned.
Keep a learning journal during the course.
Explain how you feel you have **progressed/developed**.

⇨ The finished products resulting from project work (a book, magazine, newspaper) can make excellent teaching material in other classes.

Spelling, punctuation, and grammar

1 How do you spell *giraffe***?**
Who knows how to spell it?
How is 'giraffe' **spelt/spelled***?*
What is the **correct/normal** *spelling of this word?*
The word is **spelt/spelled** *c-a-s-u-a-l.*

2 Spell it in English.
Use the English names for the letters.
Do you know how to say the alphabet in English?

3 Have you spelt it right?
Let's see/I wonder** if you've spelt it* **right/correctly.*
Watch your spelling.
Is there anything wrong with the spelling?
Can anybody correct the spelling?

4 You need a comma here.
Check your punctuation.
There should be a full stop.
Put a comma after this word
Can we leave this comma out?
Do we need a comma here?
You forgot the apostrophe at the end.
There is an apostrophe missing at the end.
You need to punctuate the sentence to make it clear.

5 What's wrong with this sentence?
Can you see anything wrong with this?

---

1 🔔 *Write/written can be also be used instead of spell/spelt.*

2 ⇨ Make sure your students can spell fluently in English, beginning with their name and their hometown. 'Difficult' letters vary for different groups of learners, but *A, E, G, H, I, J, Q, R, U, V, W* and *Y* seem to be common problems. Encourage them to spell in English and make sure you spell in English:

A	/eɪ/	G	/dʒiː/	M	/em/	S	/es/	Y	/waɪ/	
B	/biː/	H	/eɪtʃ/	N	/en/	T	/tiː/	Z	/zed/ (BE)	
C	/siː/	I	/aɪ/	O	/əʊ/	U	/juː/	Z	/ziː/ (AE)	
D	/diː/	J	/dʒeɪ/	P	/piː/	V	/viː/			
E	/iː/	K	/keɪ/	Q	/kjuː/	W	/dʌbəljuː/			
F	/ef/	L	/el/	R	/ɑː/	X	/eks/			

🔔 Remember the correct indefinite article:
a + B, C, D, G, J, K, P, Q, T, U, V, W, Y, Z
an + A, E, F, H, I, L, M, N, O, R, S, X

3 🔔 Where there are mistakes (for example, on the board), use the following:
I'm afraid this is spelt **wrong/incorrectly***.*
I'm sorry, you've made a spelling mistake.
There are two words you've spelt wrong.
You slipped up on two words.

3 🔔 Spelling mistakes typically involve:
  a Missing letters
  What letter is missing?
  (There's a) 'k' missing.
  It's spelt with two 'p's, not one.
  It's spelt with double 'k'.
  You need an **additional/extra** *letter here.*
  Add another 't'.

  b Extra letters
  There's one letter too many.   You only need one 's'.
  There should only be one 'n'.   You've got an extra letter.

  c Tricky spelling
  Spell it with an 'i' and then an 'e'.
  There should be an 'o' instead of a 'u'.
  It begins with a 'y'.
  These two letters are the wrong way round.

  d Writing conventions
  Write it with a capital 'I'.
  Use a capital letter for names of languages.
  Write it **with/in** *small letters.*
  Write it as **one word/two words***.*
  You can't divide the word here.
  This is the American spelling.

⊗ *One letter is too ~~much~~.* ✗
  You've got one letter too many. ✓

---

4 🔔 Notice the different ways of referring to a full stop.
  Sentence: *... the end.* = full stop (BE), period (AE).
  Decimals: *5.2* = *five point two.*
  Websites: *abc.com* = *abc dot com.*

5 🔔 In good intermediate and advanced classes, you can ask questions related to grammar and structure:
  What's the past (tense) of 'to go'?
  What tense should you have used?
  What are the three forms (infinitive/irregular past/past participle) of 'sing'?
  Is the word order right?
  Where do we usually put adverbs of frequency?
  Is a relative pronoun necessary here?
  Which tense do we use after 'if'?
  Which preposition comes after 'to concentrate'?
  What preposition does the verb 'depend' take?
  What's the rule about 'some' and 'any'?

🔔 You can also comment on the same things and help students to correct themselves:
  I'm afraid you can't leave the preposition out.
  The past tense of 'go' is 'went'.
  Put the adverb at the end.
  Remember that time adverbs come at the end.
  Once again, but **remember/watch** *the word order.*
  Watch out for the conditional tense this time.
  Mind the preposition.
  This time start with 'who'.

🔔 Notice the word stress:
  adjective /ˈædʒɪktɪv/ *but adjectival* /ædʒekˈtaɪvl/
  adverb /ˈædvɜːb/ *but adverbial* /ædˈvɜːbiəl/

⇨ Try to balance the focus on accuracy with more communicative activities. And remember to comment on correct usage as well as on mistakes.

SECTION C

Academic and thinking skills can be as much a part of the language classroom as the content classroom. The challenge for you as a language teacher is to find an approach that develops these skills as a natural part of language learning. Group work, discussion, and debate based on a theme or current issue provide one such meaningful context for students to practise thinking skills. They can, for example, be shown how to assess the accuracy and balance of the information they read. They can learn to respect and consider other viewpoints. They can get used to weighing up all the evidence before reaching a conclusion. This section includes material for advanced students that helps develop these skills. Notice that all the key phrases are in the form of questions.

1 Describing, classifying, and comparing
How would you describe 'national identity'?
How would you classify the different viewpoints?
What's the difference?
How do they compare?

2 Defining and exemplifying
How would you define 'identity'?
What is a good example of a pollutant?

3 Describing processes and effects
What happens first?
What was the result of this?

4 Using statistics
How many per cent?
What changes have taken place?
What can we conclude?

5 Explaining and hypothesizing
Why does this happen?
What's your hypothesis?
What if ...?

6 Thinking critically (1)
What does the text say?
How did you react?
What does the writer think?
Do you agree?

7 Thinking critically (2)
What other opinions are there?
What is the solution to this problem?
What's wrong with this theory?
How does this change your opinion?
What more do you need to know?

Developing academic and thinking skills

Points to think and talk about

1 What do you understand by academic skills? And by thinking skills?
2 Does your school system generally give students time to think carefully about the material they are working with, or is the emphasis more on learning facts and mastering processes?
3 How could you increase opportunities for your students to engage in critical and cooperative dialogue (discussing, enquiring, debating, assessing)? Is this possible in the normal language teaching classroom?
4 How could you deal with a controversial and sensitive issue in your class?
5 Do you allow your students to evaluate their own performance, for example, by asking them to say what they have learned after a series of lessons? Is this a good idea? What other questions could you ask them that would help their learning?
6 Do you think it is a good idea for students to write their own report or course certificate after a course?
7 How can a teacher model good critical thinking in the day-to-day running of classes?
8 Which is easier to assess, factual learning or critical thinking? Why?
9 What do you understand by the following: *fair-minded, open-minded, independent-minded*?
10 Do your students study other school subjects in English? In what ways can this so-called CLIL approach (Content and Language Integrated Learning) improve their language skills?

Language to think about

1 Are you familiar with some common ways of giving a definition? Try to define *psychology* and *linguistics*.
2 The words *classify, categorize,* and *assign* are all to do with grouping ideas. Can you use these words correctly?
3 Can you make sentences to show the correct usage of the words *consist, comprise,* and *compose*?
4 Can you describe a simple process clearly and logically? Try, for example, to explain how rain is formed.
5 Can you read out numerical information, including years, decimals, fractions and percentages, fluently? Try these: 7,967, 12,023, 1985, 2006, 625, 1004, 5½, 6¾, 1½%.
6 How else can you say: *The number of accidents has fallen*?
7 Can you explain the following words associated with critical thinking: *generalization, inference, premise, conclusion, bias, correlation, counter example*?
8 Can you use the words *effect* and *affect* correctly?
9 The words *result, amount,* and *total* are also verbs. How are they used?
10 Correct these sentences: *What mark of car do you drive? He has a 29-years-old son.*

Classroom English vocabulary to collect

Words related to presenting evidence and reaching conclusions. (For example, *infer, justify*)

Describing, classifying, and comparing

1 How would you describe *national identity*?
Who can describe the landscape of Britain?
What adjectives best describe the Finnish climate?
*What **adjectives/nouns/ideas** come to mind when you hear the **word/term** 'prejudice'?*
*What are the typical **features/characteristics** of a reality TV programme?*
What does this remind you of?

2 How would you classify the different viewpoints?
How can we categorize the various alternatives?
Is it possible to group these ideas under two or three headings?
*Which **group/category** would you assign this example to?*
Which heading would you place this piece of writing under?
Can we subdivide our examples into two groups?
*What **class/group** does this idea belong to?*
*What different **categories/subgroups** exist when we talk about wetlands?*

3 What's the difference?
*What are the **differences/similarities** between Spanish and Portuguese?*
*What are the points of **difference/similarity** between Australia and New Zealand?*
How does Art Deco differ from Art Nouveau?
*In what **way/respect** is this different from her earlier novels?*
To what extent is this similar to his other films?

4 How do they compare?
*How do these **two things/ideas** compare?*
*How does this **compare/contrast** with the earlier example?*
Are these two things comparable?
*What can you compare this **with/to**?*
What would be a good comparison?

1 ⇨ If you ask your students to give a physical description or explore complex ideas, it is helpful to ask them to use a graphic organizer, such as a concept or mind map:
Let's make a mind map for this task.
A concept map will help us see what we already know.
Write the main idea in the centre of the page.
Write related ideas on branches that radiate from the central idea.
Draw lines to connect all the ideas to the centre or to other words.
Write everything down as quickly as you can without pausing.
Use different colours if it makes things clearer.

Ｌ Descriptions often involve analysis:
The city consists of three different areas.
The exhibition comprises three separate periods.
*Each stanza is **made up/composed** of several verses.*

2 Ｌ The following are used in classifying ideas:

They can be	categorised classified grouped divided arranged	according to on the basis of depending on	size. whether there are side-effects or not.

3 Ｌ Difference and similarity are also elements of describing:
Identical: *This is **exactly/precisely/just** the same as that.*
Very similar: *This is **practically/more or less/almost/nearly** the same as that.*
Partly different: *This is not **quite/exactly/precisely** the same as that.*
Totally different: *This is **completely/totally/entirely** different from that.*
There's no similarity whatsoever.
They are strikingly similar.
*Let's list the **main/key** differences.*

Ｌ Notice the use of *distinguish* and *differentiate*:
*How can we **distinguish/differentiate** between the male and the female?*
*How can we **distinguish/differentiate** the male from the female?*
The male is distinguished by its red wing markings.

4 Ｌ In making a comparison, you can say:
If we compare these two events in detail, we'll see that ...
If we compare this figure with last year's, we'll find that ...
A detailed comparison of the two events shows that ...
***In comparison/compared** with New Zealand, Australia is huge.*
The films are similar in that they are both set in Russia.
*The countries are **different/dissimilar** in that Latvia has a much larger Russian-speaking population.*

This is not exactly the same

Defining and exemplifying

1 How would you define *identity*?
Who can define a botanist?
Please define the word 'zoology' for us.
*Can anyone **provide/give** me a **scientific/precise** definition of 'intelligence'?*

2 What is a good example of a pollutant?
Who can provide us with an example of a Celtic language?
What further examples of climate change are there?
How could this point be illustrated?
What (examples) do you have to illustrate what you are saying?

---

1 📖 Examples of typical defining structures include:
*A **nationalist** is a person who wants their country to become independent.*
Linguistics is the study of language.
Zoology can be defined as the scientific study of animals and their behaviour.
Anthropology is concerned with the origins and development of the human race.
Phonology deals with the sounds of a particular language.

2 📖 The following phrases are useful when presenting an example:
*For **example/instance**, ...*
*One example of this **is/would be** ...*
Examples of this include ...
*This is **an example/a good example** of recycling.*
*A good **example/illustration** of this **idea/phenomenon/ process** is ...*
Artists such as Manet and Renoir are examples of ...

Describing processes and effects

1 What happens first?
*What is the first **step/stage** in this process?*
What would be the next step?
How does this develop?
What steps follow on from this point?
What stages are involved in this process?
*In what order does this **happen/occur**?*
What is the chronological order for these changes?

2 What was the result of this?
What happened as a result?
What were the consequences of this?
What effect did this have?

---

1 📖 In describing processes, you may want to use some of the following phrases. These phrases also give students important signposts when they are following a more formal presentation.
*This process **involves/consists of** the following **steps/stages**:*
First(ly) ... second (ly) ...
Next ... then ... later (on) ... afterwards ... subsequently...
***Last(ly)/ Finally/In the end/To conclude** ...*
This leads on to the second stage.
Following this, we move on to stage three.
This is followed by the third and final stage.

📖 In academic discourse, the passive is typically used in describing processes:
The outer layer of bark was carefully removed.
It was then dried for several months.

⇒ Tasks which involve classifying and ordering information practise important learning skills:
See if you can arrange these facts in order of importance.
Try to arrange the stages of this process in the appropriate order.
Try to find a logical pattern in this list.
See if you can identify the irrelevant information.

---

2 📖 In talking about cause and effect, remember that there are several alternative forms. Some examples:

Verb:
Icy road conditions caused the accident.
The accident was caused by icy road conditions.
*Crop failure **resulted in/led to** widespread famine.*

Noun:
*The **cause of/reason for** the accident was icy road conditions.*
*The **result/effect/consequence** of crop failure was widespread famine.*

Connective:
*The road was icy, **therefore/so** there was an accident.*
*The crop failed; **as a result/for this reason/because of this** there was a famine.*
*There was a famine **because of/as a result of/owing to** crop failure.*
***Because/Since** the road was icy, there was an accident.*

⊗ Be careful with *affect* (verb) and *effect* (noun):
It affected ~~to/on~~ the result. ✗ *It affected the result.* ✓
It ~~effected~~ the result. ✗ *It had an effect on the result.* ✓

Using statistics

1 How many per cent?

*What **per cent/percentage/proportion** of the population
    agreed?*
What was the total amount?
Can you express that as a percentage?

2 What changes have taken place?

Has the number of cases risen or fallen?
Has there been a rise or fall in the number of cases?
Has there been a steady increase?
What trend can you see?

3 What can we conclude?

*What can we **infer/deduce** from the **table/figures/data/
    information**?*
What can you say on the basis of these results?

---

1 Be careful with *per cent*. Notice the singular and plural verb:
    65% of Finland is covered by forest.
    30% of the applicants were interviewed.

   ⊗ *Typical mistakes: twenty-five per cents ✗; twenty-five pro cent. ✗*

   If you can't remember the exact figures, you can always
    approximate:
    ***Approximately/Something like/Roughly/About** fifty thousand
        people were there.*
    ***Nearly/Almost/Close on/More than/Well over** half of them were
        Liverpool supporters.*
    ***Some five or six/Between five and six** hundred were arrested.*

   Notice the following patterns for expressing a total:
    *Money spent on cinema tickets **totalled/amounted to** €50
        million.*
    *Mobile phone exports **make up/account for** 45% of foreign trade.*

2 Remind yourself of how to say numbers and years:
    Decimals: *2.3 = two point three. 36.36= thirty-six point three six.*
    *19.06 = nineteen point **o/zero/nought** six.*
    Fractions: *5½ km = five and a half kilometres. ½ km = half a
        kilometre. ¾ km = three-quarters of a kilometre. 1½ years = one
        and a half years, a year and a half.*
    Years: *1968 = nineteen sixty-eight. 2006 = twenty o six, two
        thousand and six.*

   If you want to do calculations aloud, remember:
    *19 + 13 = 32 Nineteen **plus/and/added to** thirteen **equals/makes/is**
        thirty-two.*
    *96 − 64 Ninety-six **minus/take away/less** sixty-four.*
    *8 × 4 Eight **times/multiplied by** four.*
    *128 / 4 A hundred and twenty-eight **divided by/over** four.*

Notice the different patterns to express statistical change:

The number of road accidents has	risen increased gone up climbed fallen decreased gone down dropped	rapidly. sharply. steadily. steeply. slightly. by 10%. by over 2,000. from 6,000 to 4,000.

There has been a	rapid sharp steep steady slight sudden huge 5%	rise increase climb fall drop decline decrease reduction	in the number of accidents.

*Between 1995 and 2005 the number **doubled/trebled/quadrupled**.*
In 2005 there was a tenfold increase.

---

3 In presenting conclusions, you can say:
    ***According to/On the basis of** these figures, we can **conclude/infer/
        predict** that ...*
    *This **table/text/graph** seems to **suggest/indicate/prove** that ...*
    There appears to be (statistical) evidence that ...

In 2006 there was a tenfold increase

Explaining and hypothesizing

1 Why does this happen?

Can you explain the reason(s) for this?
How can this be explained?
What is the explanation for this?
What would be a reasonable explanation?

2 What's your hypothesis?

Have you got a theory to explain/about this reaction?
How can we test/prove/confirm this hypothesis?

3 What if ... ?

What if there is/was/were a pandemic? What then?
Consider this possibility/scenario/hypothetical case.
Suppose we look at the problem from another viewpoint.
Suppose the situation changed, how would you respond/react?
Let's suppose there is no cure. How will that affect things?

---

2 ⌐ In asking for and presenting possible explanations and hypotheses, you can say:
Try to come up with a suitable hypothesis to explain this sudden change.
Work out a theory to account for this trend.
One (possible) explanation might be that ...
One way of explaining it would be to say that ...
Another hypothesis that is worth considering is that ...

⌐ Notice that the word stress changes:
hy'pothesis, hypo'thetical, hy'pothesize

Consider a hypothetical situation..

 6

Thinking critically (1)

1 What does the text say?

What factual information are you given?
What are/appear to be the most important points?
What arguments are presented/put forward?

2 How did you react?

What surprised/shocked/confused you in the text/extract?
How did this extract present the issue in a new light?
How balanced/fair were the opinions presented here?
What new points were raised for you?

3 What does the writer think?

Where does the writer stand?
What is the writer's stance/position on this question?
What opinion is the writer presenting?
Is the writer impartial/biased?
How does the author try to persuade us that she is telling the truth?
What arguments is the author trying to make/answer?

4 Do you agree?

What is your opinion?
What do you agree and disagree with in this text?
Do you share the writer's views?
Can you defend/counter the views presented?
How does the problem affect you personally?
To what extent can you relate to this issue?
How does this relate to your own experience/background/observations?
In what ways can you relate to the opinions expressed here?

---

2 ⌐ The following phrases express personal experience:
I have personally found that ...
From my experience/observations I can say that ...
If I relate this to my own experience, then I would say ...
Based on my experience I can say that ...

4 ⌐ You may want your students to give a brief oral or written report on their discussion:
One of you can act as the secretary/chair/chairperson.
Afterwards I want you to report back to the class.
We'll finish with a debriefing session.
Each group can present its report to the rest of the class.
I'll ask you to come out to the front to present your report.
Which group will be reporting/presenting on topic 2?
Try to pick out/choose the most important points for your presentation.
Try and sum up what was said in your group.

⇨ Remember to comment on each report and acknowledge what was said:
Thank you for sharing your ideas/thoughts with us.

That was a very	interesting	
	fascinating	report.
	stimulating	presentation.
	provocative	summary.
	thorough /ˈθʌrə/	overview.
	exhaustive	

Thinking critically (2)

1 What other opinions are there?

*What **alternative/counter** opinions exist on this subject?*
What other ways are there of looking at this problem?
Can we look at the problem from another point of view?
What are the arguments for and against?
What are the pros and cons?

2 What is the solution to this problem?

How can we solve this problem?
What approaches are there to solving this problem?
What options do we have to solve this problem?
What kind of solution are we looking for?

3 What's wrong with this theory?

*What is the main problem with this **approach/theory/idea**?*
What problems can you see with this approach?
*Can anyone identify any **problems/difficulties** with this idea?*
*Where do the main **problems/difficulties** lie?*
What are the strengths and weaknesses of this idea?
What are the merits and shortcomings of this proposal?
*Is this a **sensible/reasonable** approach?*

4 How does this change your opinion?

*To what extent does this **affect/influence** your opinion?*
*Does this confirm or challenge your own thinking
on this topic?*
*Has this changed **the way you think/your thinking**
on this question?*
*Have you **seen/looked at** this issue in this light before?*

5 What more do you need to know?

*Do you have all the **necessary/relevant** facts?*
Do you need to find out more about this issue?
Are you taking all of the details into consideration?
Have you examined all the evidence?
Have you analysed all the available information?
*Have you **forgotten/omitted/overlooked** any important
facts?*
*Are you certain that you've taken all of the details
into account?*
Have you looked at both sides in a balanced and fair way?
Have you critically assessed all the alternatives?
What are the criteria for assessing this?
Is there conclusive evidence for this?
Can you make a reasoned judgement?

---

1 🔊 Useful phrases for presenting alternative points of view:
On the other hand …
Alternatively …
Another point of view could be …
The opposite might also be true.
To look at it another way …
Alternatively, we could look at it from another viewpoint.
*To look at this **from a different angle/in a different light** …*

---

3 🔊 For commenting on problems:
*The main **problems/difficulties/obstacles** I can see are **political/
economic/environmental**.*
*One problem **may/appears to** be that …*
*It might be **impossible/difficult/awkward/problematic** to …*

🔊 Sometimes a compromise can be reached:
*If we put these two **ideas/approaches/options** together, what will
be the result?*
*How can we **combine/reconcile** these two **views/opinions/
options**?*

---

4 🔊 To change one's opinion takes courage. The following phrases
might be useful for students to structure their thoughts and
comments:
I had understood that … but now I think that maybe …
Earlier I thought … but maybe …
*Maybe this issue isn't as **clear-cut/simple** as I thought.*
*I hadn't taken this point into **account/consideration** before.*
*I realize now that I **over/under**estimated the importance of this.*

⇨ Group work allows deeper discussion of a topic. Students can
use their own knowledge or experience of events and issues,
or they can respond to a listening or reading text, which
presents any relevant subject-specific vocabulary. It can be
less threatening to students if they start by analysing a given
opinion. They then can look at their own views. It is important
to create an open and non-judgemental environment where
students feel encouraged to examine different opinions and
even to change their mind.

---

5 ⇨ There are five tools of thinking which students need to develop:
1 background knowledge (getting the information about a
topic that they require for thoughtful reflection);
2 criteria for judgement (having a basis for deciding which
alternative is the most sensible or appropriate);
3 critical thinking vocabulary (having the concepts related to
presenting viewpoints and arguments);
4 thinking strategies (using decision-making procedures and
models); and
5 habits of mind (acquiring certain values and attitudes, such
as being open-minded and critical).

See Useful reading and resources, page 171.

Classroom essentials

ASKING QUESTIONS (3)

More about *Wh-* questions

In Unit 4 we looked at *Wh-* questions and focused mainly on problems with word order, especially in indirect questions, for example, *Can you tell me where he went?* In this unit we will be concerned with more precise *Wh-* questions, the types of questions you ask your students when dealing with a topic in detail.

else and *other*

- Notice how *else* and *other* are used to ask for additional information:

  What else have you found out? ✓ ~~*What have you found out, too?*~~ ✗
  What other reasons might there be? ✓
  ~~*What reasons might there be, too?*~~ ✗
  Which other preposition can you use? ✓
  ~~*Which preposition can you use, too?*~~ ✗

- If you have a precise number of possible answers in mind, you can ask, for example:

  What three reasons does he give?
  What other three reasons can we find in the text?
  Which four cities are mentioned?
  Which other four cities are given as examples?

- *What else?* and *anything else?* are also useful as ways of asking students to add to a list.

  OK, firstly they forgot that they had a meeting the following day. What else?
  So they had bread, butter, tomatoes. Anything else?

What ... like?

- For a general description it is useful to ask *How* and *What ... like* questions:

  What's Helsinki like? — *It's a busy modern city.*
  What was your holiday like? — *It was fantastic!*
  What's the weather like? — *Freezing!*
  How was your trip? — *Very exhausting.*

- In longer *What ... like?* questions (for example, containing a relative clause), *like* usually comes after the noun it is associated with, but it also often occurs in sentence final position:

  What was the film like you went to see last weekend?
  What was the film you went to see last weekend like?

- *What ... like* is also used with verbs of sensation. Notice the alternative form with *how*:

What did it	feel look smell sound taste	like?	How did it	feel? look? smell? sound? taste?

- Replies can use an adjective, *like* and a noun, or *as if* and a verb phrase:

It	felt	nice/like winter/as if I could fly.
	looked	new/like gold/as if it would rain.
	smelled	horrible/like fish/as if there had been a fire.
	sounded	strange/like Mozart/as if they were arguing.
	tasted	stale/like peach/as if it had gone off.

- A typical mistake is to use *how* and *like* together:
  ~~How did it look like?~~ ✗

much and *many*

- Remember to include an additional *of* when asking precise questions with *much* or *many*:
  What did they have too much of?—They had too much freedom.
  What haven't they got many of?—They haven't got many power stations.

- The same *of* is needed in all questions that use expressions of quantity and numbers (for example, *a lot of, some of, any of, enough of, ten of*):
  What did they buy three of?—They bought three books.
  What wasn't there enough of?—There wasn't enough water.

Time and place

- Many *Wh-* questions related to time and place are formed using prepositions, especially *at, in, on,* and *to*. Modern English usage tends to place the preposition at the end of the question, but in several cases no preposition is needed at all.
  In which year was Shakespeare born?
  Which year was Shakespeare born in?
  Which year was Shakespeare born?

- Check the following list of examples. If there are brackets around both prepositions, then use of the preposition is optional.

(In)	which month did war break out	(in)?
(On)	which day will you leave	(on)?
(On)	what date does it end	(on)?
(At)	what time does it start	(at)?
(For)	how long did it last	(for)?
(For)	how many years did they wait	(for)?
(At)	what age can you vote	at?
Since when	has Latvia been independent?	
	Where are you going	(to)?
(From)	where are you coming	from?
(From)	which part of Finland is he	from?
(In)	which direction are they going	(in)?
	Which way did he go?	

- Notice that in phrases like *in what way, in what sense, in what respect,* the preposition cannot be placed at the end of the sentence:
  In what way does this change the situation?
  In what respects is this case different?

Size and weight

- There are three ways of asking questions about size and dimensions:

How	big is the package? large is the park? tall is the building? high is Mount Everest? long is the Panama Canal?	What is	the size of the package? the *size/area* of the park? the height of the building? the height of Mount Everest? the length of the Panama Canal?

What	size size height height length	is it?

- Questions of the following type often cause problems:

How	big large tall high long	a package an area a building a mountain a canal	is it?	What size package What size area What height building What height mountain What length canal	is it?

- The other adjective and noun pairs are:

  deep–depth, thick–thickness, wide–width, broad–breadth.

- You can ask about weight in a number of ways:

  How heavy is the bridge?
  What weight is the bridge?
  ***What/How much** does the bridge weigh?*

- Notice the pronunciation: height /haɪt/, but weight /weɪt/.

- Replies to these questions also use nominal and adjectival forms:

  It is two metres long.   *Its length is 2 metres.*
  It has a length of 2 metres.   *It is 2 metres in length.*
  It is 10 cm wide.   *Its width is 10 cm.*
  It has a width of 10 cm.   *It is 10 cm in width.*

Shape, colour, and age

- Questions about shape and colour are:

  What shape is the box?   What colour are her eyes?   What shape box is it?
  What colour eyes does she have?   It's round in shape.   They're blue in colour.

- In connection with questions about age, notice:

	She is 29 (years old).
How old is Maya?	She is 29 years of age.
What age is Maya?	She is aged 29
	Maya is a 29-year-old woman.

⊗ **Not**: a 29-years-old woman. ✗

Make and type

- When asking about types and makes, notice the use of *of*:

  What make of car do you drive?
  Not: *What ~~mark~~ of car ...?* ✗
  What brand of washing powder do you use?
  What kind of books do you read?
  What sort of man is he?
  What type of films do you like?

Miscellaneous

- The following sentences are examples of other useful question types:

  What time train did they catch?
  What price holidays are you interested in?
  What number bus should I take?
  What percentage of the students passed?
  How many euros' worth of bananas did you buy?
  Whereabouts in London does he live?
  What temperature is it?

Prompting

You probably like to prompt your students, in other words help
them to answer by giving them the frame for the correct answer, or
by saying the first few words. With *Wh-* questions this kind of prompting
takes two forms.

1 A change in word order, with the *Wh-* question word or phrase at the end:

   And this city here is called ... what? Does anybody know?
   The library closes at ... what time? Anyone?

2 A normal *Wh-* question, followed by the beginning of the answer:

   Which year did he leave? He left in ... ? Anybody?
   What is this tool called? Yes, it's called a ... ? Marco, please.
   Notice that very often the last word of the prompt phrase is lengthened
   and a rising intonation is used.

⊗ See 🎧 6.1

Practice

1 Ask *Wh-* questions that will produce the complete answers given below.
   Ask about the words in italics.

   EXAMPLE:
   Mr Evans left at three o'clock.—What time did Mr Evans leave?
   1 Mrs Jones started her new job *in June*.
   2 The first settlers landed *in 1730*.
   3 Our friends came on the *4 o'clock train*.
   4 The tsunami disaster happened *two years ago*.
   5 We were hoping we wouldn't be late *for the concert*.
   6 They decided to spend the evening *with some friends*.
   7 To get into town you'll have to take a *number 8 bus*.
   8 David is interested in *Mercedes and Aston Martin cars*.
   9 Julie is fond of *fashion* magazines.
   10 Jamie prefers *White-Out* toothpaste to all the others.
   11 The room should have been *6 metres in length*.
   12 The sculpture *had a height of 12 metres*.
   13 He was looking for a *blue pullover*.
   14 These new student buildings are *round in shape*.
   15 It was *wonderful*, just lying in the sun.

16 The village *resembled something straight out of a tourist brochure.*
17 His voice sounded *like a creaking door.*
18 The car was heading *north.*
19 She works *in Fleet Street, to be precise.*
20 He bought *as much petrol as he could for the $20 he had on him.*

2 In the following situations, you are thinking aloud. Find an appropriate question beginning with the word given in brackets that you might ask next.

EXAMPLE:
The tourists visited three cities. The students have found two of them.
(*Where*)
Where else did the tourists visit?

1 The text refers to five reasons for climate change. They've only mentioned three so far. (What)
2 Good! They at least remembered the name of the painter. But is that all they know about this painting? (What)
3 Let's see if they noticed that almost 25% of the people interviewed were under the age of 18 (What)
4 I know that quite a few of them went to a rock concert. I wonder how it was? (What)
5 OK. The war affected his health. Good answer, but did it change him in any other way? (How)
6 The brothers in the story had only £25, but it wasn't enough. They were short of £50. (What)
7 Finland has more than 60,000 ... what? Aah, lakes. Let's see if they know that. (What)
8 Did they notice in the text that wearing a cycle helmet became compulsory in 1999? (Since)
9 The incident had a huge effect on the peace talks, but do they see how? (In)
10 Right, they've told me it was a French car the woman was driving, but can't they be more precise? (What)

Exercises and activities

1 Prepositions, articles, and vocabulary

See the OUP website http://www.oup.com/elt/teacher/pce.

2 Reading aloud

RECORD Choose a passage of some 25–30 lines and duplicate enough copies for the rest of the group. Prepare the passage carefully; for example, think about pauses, intonation, problem words, any possible voice characterizations. Your task is then to have the members of the group read the text aloud. You will use it to practise pronunciation, especially problem sounds, word stress, rhythm, and intonation, by repeating and imitating. You will have to act as the model. Be prepared to deal with any pronunciation problems the group may have suddenly developed!

3 Using a recording

RECORD Work in small groups. For this task you will need a short recorded dialogue suitable for the age group that you teach. It could be from an authentic radio programme or a recording accompanying a textbook. Listen to the dialogue together and then discuss:
1   how to prepare your students for the listening task;
2   what the aim of listening to this particular text is;
3   any possible difficulties;
4   how to break up the text into sections;
5   any possible follow-up tasks.

When the group has come up with a good lesson plan, take turns introducing the task to the other groups.

4 Detailed working with a text

RECORD Find a passage of some 15–20 lines from a newspaper or magazine. The idea is to take a close look at some of the structural and lexical features of the text. The phrases in section 6, B1 will help you get ideas. Then:
1   Go through the text and pick out five structures that you would like to bring to the attention of your students, either by explaining or through question-and-answer.
2   Pick out five words that are used in a special way or which have useful related forms, synonyms, or antonyms.
3   Think of two questions that ask the students to explain a reference in the text or to give their own understanding of the text.
4   Try out your text and questions on your fellow students. If several groups work on the same text, you can compare your choice of words and questions.

5 Spelling and punctuation

For this exercise, work with a partner. Student A should look at the questions on this page, while Student B should look at page 158. Take it in turns to read out your sequences of letters and punctuation. Without looking, your partner should try to write down the sequence as quickly and as accurately as possible. Notice that the letter sequences are all anagrams of English words. Once you have solved the anagram together, try to explain its meaning. Alternatively, you can choose your own words to spell out as anagrams.

Student A	
1 gajuar	5 *+'!,-\?
2 leooygg	6 aeresehr
3 wnshiadc	7 oihhyopspl
4 !?.;/:(),	

6 Running a discussion

RECORD Prepare and run a five-minute teacher-led discussion session with fellow students on one of the following topics. Make sure you involve everybody and bring the discussion to a conclusion.

1 Buying presents is a waste of time and money.
2 Everyone should have a three-day weekend.
3 Family reunions do more harm than good.
4 Mobile phones — a curse or a blessing?
5 Do we have healthier lives than our parents?
7 There is nothing we can do to reverse global warming.

7 Correcting errors

Comment on and correct any errors in the following sentences. Your comments and questions should help to guide students to seeing their own mistakes. Sentences 1–5 contain spelling and punctuation errors, sentences 6–15 grammatical and lexical errors, and sentences 16–20 pronunciation errors.

1 The boy droped the beerpottle on the flor.
2 Do you think swedish is a useful langauge.
3 Hello he said. This foot ball is for You my freind.
4 Santa claus is also calld fathre chrismas
5 I know, that the childrens' parents speak japanese.
6 The sun raises in every morning.
7 I am going often with the bus.
8 I become interested about fishing for ten years ago.
9 Shakespeare is born year 1564 in Stratford-upon-Avon.
10 Many peoples are liking about the pancakes.
11 There is one question that we need to think.
12 Look the record's name from the etiquette.
13 He has made all his homeworks on Wednesday.
14 Everyone of the boys was wearing white skirt and tie.
15 Listen my three first sentences before you will decide.
16 Do you want /vɒnt/ some chewing /tʃuːvɪŋ/ gum?
17 There is /deərɪs/ ice cream /griːm/ for dessert /desət/.
18 Roger /rəʊɡə/ stayed in a hotel /həʊtəl/ in Edinburgh /edɪnbɜːɡ/.
19 The scissors /skɪsɔːs/ were hidden under the junk /də dʒʌŋk/.
20 They did an analysis /ænəˈlaɪsɪs/ of six fruit juices /fruɪt juːsɪz/.

8 Critical thinking

In groups, work out five good questions that would make your students think critically about the following questions. Suggest strategies for finding answers to the questions. Then try your questions out on your fellow students.

1 How good were the 'good old days'?
2 How difficult is it to learn English?
3 What do national heroes have in common?

Audio practice

1 Classroom intonation

🎧 **6.1** Practise asking prompting questions based on the underlined words in the sentences below. Remember to lengthen the final word of the question and use a rising intonation. Add *Anybody?* or *Any suggestions?* or *Does anybody know?* at the end.

EXAMPLE

The same day she bought <u>a new computer</u>.
And the same day she bought ... what? Any suggestions?

1 They arrived home <u>at half-past nine</u>.
2 After calling in at her office she went <u>home</u>.
3 The French for *town* is <u>ville</u>.
4 One coat was red and the other was <u>green</u>.
5 There are <u>three</u> official languages in Switzerland.

🎧 **6.2** Now use the other form of prompting with the following sentences.

EXAMPLE

The same day she bought <u>a new computer</u>.
What did she buy the same day? She bought a ... ? Anybody?

1 She left on <u>Wednesday</u>.
2 This building was designed by <u>Alvar Aalto</u>.
3 This area is called the <u>Lake District</u>.
4 The earthquake happened in <u>1994</u>.
5 The Finnish word for *strawberry* is <u>mansikka</u>.

2 Key sounds

🔑🎧 **6.3** In the following sentences identify examples of the sounds /r/, /l/, and /h/. Then read the sentences aloud. Notice that there are some examples of a linking /r/ sound and missing /h/.

1 You have half an hour to hand in your homework.
2 Listen carefully and then write a summary of the lecture.
3 Familiarize yourselves with the correct version.
4 Perhaps you can try to behave properly.
5 I'm very sorry. I'll try and remember it for Friday.
6 Please read the rest of the lesson at home.
7 I asked him how he had heard about it
8 If I'm honest, the whole exhibition was rather boring.
9 You need a little oral practice. Just relax and round your lips.
10 Please collect in the labels or any original diagrams.

🎧 **6.4** The following words are often mispronounced. Try reading the list aloud. If necessary, use a dictionary to check the meaning. Then listen and repeat.

1 biscuit broad bruise
2 busy chaos choir
3 doubt height irony
4 recipe sword yacht
5 queue salmon receipt
6 chemistry humour miniature
7 stomach scheme nuisance
8 soup flour tough
9 muscle spiral brochure
10 opera ache exaggerate

3 Word stress

6.5 This exercise can be done individually or in pairs. The following table contains 72 words in English that are often stressed incorrectly. Choose a column or a row at random and practise reading it aloud in both directions until you are fluent. Then move on to a new row or column. It may be easier to listen to the correct version first or to begin with the table written in phonetic transcription on page 165.

	A	B	C	D	E	F
1	academy	adjective	adverb	alternative	analyse	analysis
2	apostrophe	balloon	biology	canal	canary	canoe
3	cassette	catastrophe	cathedral	Catholic	character	commerce
4	compete	concerto	criticism	crooked	cucumber	democracy
5	develop	development	diameter	economy	effort	event
6	executive	geography	guitar	horizon	hotel	idea
7	injury	laboratory	machine	medicine	motive	museum
8	naked	opponent	orchestra	ordinary	origin	original
9	personnel	philosophy	photograph	photographer	photography	piano
10	prejudice	process	product	pronoun	psychology	racism
11	recipe	referee	refugee	salad	technique	technology
12	theology	vehicle	violin	violinist	voluntary	wicked

4 Live lessons

You will hear some short extracts from different classroom situations. Listen to each extract and then answer the questions.

Live lesson transcripts can be found on page 166.

6.6 Asking for an opinion

1. What language problem does the teacher deal with at the beginning of the extract?
2. What was probably the original question that the teacher asked the student?
3. Who are told to be quiet?
4. The teacher corrects a small prepositional slip. What is it?
5. The student tries to explain why the programme is special. Write down exactly what he says:
   'Because he _____ difficult case.'
   What do you think the student is trying to say? Does the teacher understand the student's reply? Why doesn't he correct it?
6. What grammatical slip does the teacher himself make and then correct?

Vocabulary list for exercise 6, page 100:

> **Student B**
> Nouns: belt, stamp, wallet, eraser, coward, hospital, woodpecker, lens, economy, honesty.
> Adjectives: narrow, fascinating, boring, violent.
> Verbs: to ache, to employ, to snore.

6.7 Running a discussion

1 The students have been working in groups and discussing the pros and cons of cosmetic surgery for teenagers. Which of the following arguments are NOT put forward by the students?
   a There are always medical risks.
   b Cosmetic surgery is expensive.
   c Plastic surgery will not change your basic personality.
   d The long-term effects on a growing body aren't clear.
   e You cannot reverse cosmetic surgery.
   f It is a sign that you have a weak self-image.

2 What does the teacher write on the board while the students are presenting their ideas? Why?

3 The teacher says *'That's it for you?'* What does she mean?

6.8 Interpreting a political cartoon. The teacher is using the cartoon below, which appeared in a newpaper in 1945.

1 What event in European history is this group studying?

2 The activity involving the cartoon has two parts. What are they?

3 Why does the teacher introduce the word *swastika* right at the beginning of the activity?

4 How many of the people in the statue does the student identify correctly?

5 Do the students seem to understand the idea expressed in the cartoon?

6 How does Anna solve the problem of not knowing the English for the German word *machtlos* (= powerless)? How does the teacher react? What does the student then do?

THE ROCK

From the *Daily Herald*, 13 February 1945

Anagrams for exercise 5, page 154:

Student B	
8 eiyurivstn	12 [],:'*\?;
9 teayedomlr	13 eohyopxln
10 iouotqatn	14 utqiearoenisn
11 /\',;='!	

Answer key

Unit 1

Exercises and activities

2 Classroom scenario

1. Good morning, Simon. How are you today?
2. Put your tennis racket in your locker.
3. Maya, hang your anorak up on the coat rack.
4. Let's go in, shall we? / Go in and take your seats.
5. Come on in, Will.
6. Close the door behind you.
7. Good morning, everybody.
8. I hope you all had a good weekend and are feeling fit.
9. How are you today, Sonya?
10. And how are you getting on, Mike?
11. Let me introduce myself. My name is Mr/Mrs/Miss ...
12. I've got three lessons a week with you: on Mondays, Tuesdays and Thursdays.
13. I'm looking forward to working with you.
14. Let's see if everyone is here.
15. Has anybody seen Lena this morning?
16. Who wasn't here last time?
17. It's nice to see you again, Marie.
18. Ask your friends to tell you what we've been doing.
19. All right. It's time to start.
20. I'm waiting for you to be quiet.
21. Close your desk, Maya.
22. Put your chemistry books away, Joe.
23. Why are you late, Tom?
24. I see. Well, sit down and we can start.
25. I'll have to report you if you're late again.

Audio practice

🎧 1.2 The tonic syllables are underlined

1. How <u>are</u> you today, Paolo?
2. Have you all under<u>stood</u>?
3. Who hasn't <u>fin</u>ished?
4. Does anybody know where <u>Mi</u>a is?
5. Who was a<u>way</u> last Friday?
6. And how are <u>you</u>, Birgit?
7. And have you <u>all</u> understood the idea?
8. Who <u>has</u>n't done number 3?
9. Does <u>any</u>body know why Tim's late?
10. Who <u>was</u>n't here last time?

🎧 1.6 Notice that *with* can be pronounced with either /ð/ or /θ/:

1. That's the third time this week.
   /ð/   /ð/ /θ/   /ð/
2. That will do for this time, thank you.
   /ð/   /ð/   /θ/
3. I'll go through this with you next Thursday.
     /θ/   /ð/ /θ///ð/   /θ/
4. I think you need more than three minutes on this exercise.
    /θ/   /ð/ /θ/   /ð/
5. Do you think there is something the matter with Kathy?
          /θ/ /ð/   /θ/ /ð/   /θ/or/ð/ /θ/

🎧 1.7 1st syllable: register, corridor, excellent, dialogue, difficulty, history, substitute, project
2nd syllable: alarm, vocabulary, apologies, success, museum, trainee, biology, report, geography, apologize
3rd syllable: introduce, oversleep

🎧 1.8 1. The class is held in the middle of the spring vacation.
2. February 9th, one month earlier.
3. OK, right.
4. To help the students 'tune in' to English again.

🎧 1.9 1. They reply very unenthusiastically the first time.
2. A Chinese test that seems to worry the students.
3. Yes. The teacher is going to ask some 'review questions'.
4. *Let me ask/see*, and *Let's*.

🎧 1.10 1. She doesn't want to repeat the instructions.
2. Returning a test and making Halloween decorations.
3. She asks a student to tell her the order of the two activities.
4. How does that sound?

🎧 1.11 1. Social studies and history.
2. A3, B1, C2
3. She was herself confused about the dates and is now improvising a solution. She has to make sure the students have understood the new arrangements.
4. whereas, parallel.

🎧 1.12 1. The students will get their test results. If she gave them at the beginning, it would probably disrupt the class.
2. Yes.
3. A student gives the page number in Spanish. The teacher carries on as if the reply had been in English.
4. She gives them a prompt phrase or word. Notice the intonation. 'We have to do ... what?' 'To ...?'
5. Can I have your attention, please?

🎧 1.13 1. c, d, g, e, b, f, h, i, a.

Unit 2

Classroom essentials

1 Suggested answers

1. Have you all understood?
2. Don't you have a pencil?
3. Are you having problems?
4. Have you finished?
5. Has anybody done question 7?
6. Is there anybody who hasn't finished?
7. Do you have any questions?
8. Is there anybody who doesn't know the answer?
9. Would you do the next one, Anders?
10. Haven't you got a book?
11. Is this difficult?
12. Aren't you listening?

2 Suggested answers.

1 Does anybody know whether Aleksi speaks Spanish?
2 Have you any idea whether she's leaving next Saturday?
3 Do you remember whether we've done this exercise already?
4 Can anyone tell me whether Anne will be away next time?
5 Does anyone happen to remember whether we stopped on page 45 last time?
6 Do you know if this had ever happened before?
7 Have you any idea if he did well in the test?
8 Do any of you know if Riga is the capital of Latvia?
9 Can anybody tell me if Laura has a driving licence?
10 Do you remember if Tim will be playing in next Saturday's match?

3 1 Aleksi speaks Spanish, doesn't he?
2 She's leaving next Saturday, isn't she?
3 We've done this exercise already, haven't we?
4 Anne will be away next time, won't she?
5 We stopped on page 45 last time, didn't we?
6 This hadn't ever happened before, had it?
7 He did well in the test, didn't he?
8 Riga is the capital of Latvia, isn't it?
9 Laura has a driving licence, doesn't she?
10 Tim will be playing in next Saturday's match, won't he?

Exercises and activities

2 Rephrasing. Suggested answers

1 We have plenty of time.
2 I'd like you to divide yourselves into two teams.
3 I must have overlooked it.
4 In your own time, Laura.
5 It makes no difference which group you join.
6 You didn't make a single mistake.
7 Is there anybody who hasn't had a turn?
8 Could I just squeeze past, please?
9 Keep it up!
10 That's more like it!
11 This one gave you a lot of trouble.
12 Come and sit at the front if you can't hear.
13 You, by yourself, Mats.
14 Let's take it in turns to read, starting with Lena.
15 You made a good job of that.
16 Carry on with your work while I'm away.
17 Today's date is May 7th.
18 You'll have to spend some more time practising this.
19 No damage done.
20 Any volunteers to clean the board?

3 Classroom scenario. Suggested answers

1 I'm afraid I'm not feeling too well today. I have a headache.
2 Bless you!
3 I hope you're not catching the flu.
4 Best of luck. I hope you win.
5 Many happy returns, Norbert.
6 First of all, we shall watch a video.
7 I'm so sorry, Margarete.
8 Can you all see?
9 Can you hear all right?
10 Come and sit at the front if you can't see.
11 Not all together, please. One at a time.
12 I want you to work in pairs for five minutes.
13 Tell me something about your winter hobbies, Susanna.
14 Sorry, I didn't catch what you said, Minna.
15 You have already had a turn, Piia. Someone else.
16 Is there anybody who didn't have a turn?

17 Any volunteers to clean the board?
18 Thank you for your help.
19 I want you to work in groups of four, please.
20 I'll leave it up to you to decide.
21 One of you is the customer, the other is the salesperson.
22 Now you can change round.
23 Your pronunciation is very good, Uwe.
24 Don't give up. You can do it!
24 I was very pleased with your work today.
26 Enjoy your winter holiday!

Audio practice

🎧 **2.1** Sentences 2, 4, 5, 6 and 10 had a rising intonation.

🎧 **2.2** The main stress is shown in **bold**. There may be alternative answers.

1 Could I get **past**?
2 Do you mind **mov**ing?
3 Can you all **see**?
4 Am I speaking **loud** enough for you?
5 Do you want to try it a**gain**?
6 Are you **sure** about that?
7 Would you ex**cuse** me for a moment?
8 Could you step **aside**, please?
9 Is that the **best** you can do?
10 Could you re**peat** what you said?

🎧 **2.4** The tags in questions 1, 3, and 4 have rising intonation.

🎧 **2.8**
1 sheet /ʃ/
2 cassette /s/
3 enjoy /dʒ/
4 much /tʃ/
5 easy /z/
6 projector /dʒ/
7 choose /tʃ/ /z/
8 mention /ʃ/
9 television /ʒ/
10 catch /tʃ/
11 noise /z/
12 join /dʒ/
13 excuse (verb) /z/
14 sure /ʃ/
15 close (adj.) /s/
16 version /ʃ/ (AE /ʒ/)
17 manage /dʒ/
18 question /s/ /tʃ/
19 use (noun) /s/
20 damage /dʒ/

🎧 **2.9**
1 Make sure you use as much English as possible.
   /ʃ/   /z/ /z/ /tʃ/   /ʃ/ /z/ /s/
2 Did you manage to finish the job?
   /dʒ/   /ʃ/   /dʒ/
3 Ask each other some questions and then change over.
   /tʃ/   /s/   /s/ /tʃ/ /z/   /tʃ/ /dʒ/
4 Arrange the chairs in a circle.
   /dʒ/   /tʃ/ /z/   /s/
5 Now you have a chance to choose which exercise you do.
   /tʃ/ /s/   /tʃ/ /z/   /tʃ/ /s/ /s//z/
6 Then you should show your answer sheet to your partner.
   /ʃ/   /ʃ/   /s/ /ʃ/

🎧 **2.10** 1st syllable: misprint, damage, volume, handout, progress, secretary, overhead
2nd syllable: transparency, cassette, arrange, cooperate, mistake, divide, CD, terrific, appreciate
3rd syllable: interrupt, individually, volunteer, independently

🎧 **2.11** 1 No.
2 Into groups of four.
3 By joining one group herself and asking the teaching assistant to be the fourth member.
4 a works b move c join.

🎧 **2.12** 1 a F b F c T d F e T f F g F.

🎧 **2.13** 1 Great! Fantastic! Marvellous!
2 At a table at the front of the class.

1 The two forms of the indefinite article, *a* and *an*.
2 The student has to put it away or the teacher will take it away.
3 Confiscate.
4 She allows the students to answer in Finnish because they are probably not able to express the same ideas in English.

2.15 1 outlandish (= strange, unusual)
2 Because they have the approval of the native speaker.
3 No, because she suggests the punishment should be to buy Brett lunch.
4 They are all in fact questions and said on a rising intonation.

2.16 1 To construct their own words, using typical suffixes.
2 No.
3 After the incorrect word, *communismize*, she reminds the students of *socialize* and then the correct word *sovietize*. She then uses the nominalization (*sovietization*) in context and explains it.

Unit 3

Classroom essentials

1 Suggested answers
1 a Would you like to come and sit at the front, Emilia?
   b Could you come and sit at the front, Emilia, please?
2 a Mari, I wonder if you would like to start.
   b Mari, would you mind starting?
3 a I want everybody to read three lines each.
   b I'd like everybody to read three lines each, please.
4 a Suzanne, could you come out to the front, please?
   b Suzanne, do you mind coming out to the front?
5 a Do you think you could help me with the CD player, Arminda?
   b Would you so kind as to help me with the CD player, Arminda?
6 a Emil, clean the blackboard for me, if you don't mind.
   b Emil, would you be kind enough to clean the blackboard for me, please?
7 a I'd like you to work in pairs for today.
   b Do you think you could work in pairs for today?
8 a Toni, do you mind not shouting?
   b Stop shouting, could you, please, Toni?
9 a Would you be so kind as to pass me that dictionary off the shelf, Alex?
   b Do you think you could pass me that dictionary off the shelf, Alex?
10 a Rubén, would you like to change places with Miriam?
   b Rubén, would you mind changing places with Miriam?
11 a Would you like to work with this group?
   b I want you to work with this group.
12 a I wonder if you could collect in the test papers, Natalia.
   b Could you collect in the test papers, Natalia, please?

Exercises and activities

2 Rephrasing
1 Go and sit down again.
2 Could I have a bit of quiet?
3 Turn round and face the front.
4 Bring your work out here for me to look at.
5 Hurry up. We haven't got all day.
6 How many points did you get altogether?
7 Mind you don't trip over the cable.
8 Return your seats to where they belong.

9 This time we need to move tables round.
10 It is important that I have your full attention.
11 Keep your voices down. You're a bit too noisy.
12 Add your name at the top of the page.
13 Who would like to play the part of Watson?
14 Put your hands up if you need any help.
15 Please pick all the rubbish up off the floor.

3 Situations. Suggested answers
1 How about opening the window?
2 Can I have you attention, please?
3 Perhaps you could just step outside for a moment.
4 Please arrange the chairs in a horseshoe shape.
5 Make sure you pick up any rubbish near to you and put it in the bin.
6 Could someone give me a hand?
7 Don't disturb your neighbour, please.
8 Let's check to see if the radiator is on.
9 Please put the desks in groups of four.
10 Return to your work please.
11 Remember to straighten the desks and chairs before you go.
12 What's happening on that side of the class?
13 OK, calm down everyone.
14 Please raise your hand if you have something to say.
15 No copying, thank you.
16 Were the instructions clear for everyone?
17 I'll come round during the lesson and mark your work.
18 Please come to the front of the class.
19 Go back to your own seats, please.
20 Keep your attention on your work, please.
21 We'll use the recording as an accompaniment today.
22 Let's pull the blinds down.
23 I'm very pleased with the way you've worked today.
24 Shall we turn that light off?
25 Don't keep tapping the desk, please.
26 Return your desks to their original places, please.
27 Quieten down now.
28 Make sure your phones are switched off!
29 Mind the bag!
30 Everyone sit down and stop talking now.

Audio practice

3.5 1st syllable: radiator, melody, circulate, reference, furniture, problem, comfortable, mobile
2nd syllable: narrator, display, applause, accompaniment, original, certificate, equipment, applause, distract, guitar, piano
3rd syllable: definition

3.6 1 b, c, e.
2 b.
3 The boys are probably sitting somewhere near the back of the class. If they cannot concentrate, they will have to move to the front.
4 She is giving the boys responsibility for how they behave.

3.7 1 Living Memory.
2 She asks one of the students with a watch to tell her when it is 8.35.
3 To match two lists of words in German and English.
4 Yes, because it is quite simple and revises material from earlier lessons.

🎧 **3.8** 1 She wants to revise the past tense, which the students will study next. The students had a holiday the previous week so it will natural for them to talk about what happened.

2 The students throw the ball to one another. When they catch it, they have to say one thing they did during the holiday.

3 The students shouldn't throw the ball all over the classroom.

4 The students cannot hold the ball long. They will have to think about what they are going to say in advance.

5 If they catch the ball a second time, they have to say something else. Everybody should get a chance to answer.

🎧 **3.9** 1 A circle.

2 c, e.

3 *it might be, it must be*.

4 He gives the English translation (for example, *earth*, *orange*) as a natural part of the classroom dialogue.

5 Probably a second circle inside the first.

🎧 **3.10** 1 The students get a slip of paper with a statement on it. They must decide whether the statement represents communist or capitalist ideology and then sit on the appropriate side of the class.

2 To introduce them in a simple way to some basic principles of capitalism and communism.

3 She tries to dramatize the situation by asking the students to imagine an Iron Curtain dividing the classroom as it once divided Europe.

4 The students will probably read out their statements and the teacher will check they are sitting in the right part of the class.

Unit 4

Classroom essentials

1 Suggested answers

1 Is Mrs Jones a secretary or a researcher?

2 What is this, a book or a pencil?

3 Is the correct answer A or is the correct answer B?

4 Would Mia like to answer the next one, or would Sally?

5 Which is the correct preposition, at, in, or on?

6 Was Shakespeare born in the 16th or 17th century?

7 Is the capital of Peru La Paz, Lima, or Santiago?

8 How does Mari spend her summer holidays, travelling round Europe or relaxing at her summer cottage?

9 Did Crick and Watson win the Nobel prize for their work on DNA or did Best and Banting?

10 Is Michael 11, 12, or 13?

2 1 Who knows the student? Who does the teacher know?

2 Who handed out the textbooks? What did the teacher hand out?

3 Who beat the student in the race? Who did the teacher beat in the race?

4 Who wanted to see the teacher after class? Who did the student want to see after class?

5 Who helped the student check her homework? Who did the teacher help check her homework?

6 Who saw the teacher arriving late? Who did the student see arriving late?

7 Who marked the student's test? What did the teacher mark?

8 Who stared at the student in amazement? Who did the teacher stare at in amazement?

9 What depended on hard work? What did her success depend on?

10 What led to several accidents? What did the dangerous road conditions lead to?

3 Suggested answers

1 What is the capital of Canada? Do you know what the capital of Canada is? What do you think (is) the capital of Canada (is)?

2 Why can you leave it out? Have you any idea why you can leave it out? Why do you think you can leave it out?

3 What does the word mean in Finnish? Can you tell me what the word means in Finnish? What do you suppose the word means in Finnish?

4 When can you say *Bless you!*? Do you remember when you can say *Bless you!*? When do you imagine you can say *Bless you!*?

5 Where does the adverb of time usually come? Does anybody know where the adverb of time usually comes? Where did I tell you the adverb of time usually comes?

6 Who was insulin discovered by? Has anybody any idea who insulin was discovered by? Who do you think insulin was discovered by?

7 How is the word pronounced? Do you remember how the word is pronounced? How do you suppose the word is pronounced?

8 Where must you put the stress? Do you know where you must put the stress? Where would you say you must put the stress?

9 What did the student spend the whole night thinking about? Do you know what the student spent the whole night thinking about? What do you think the student spent the whole night thinking about?

10 What happened last night? Have you heard what happened last night? What do you reckon happened last night?

Exercises and activities

2 Prepositions

1 at	6 in	11 on	16 in	21 in	26 on
2 on	7 in	12 to	17 to	22 on	27 to
3 at	8 in	13 at	18 in	23 at	28 on
4 in	9 in	14 on	19 to	24 to	29 on
5 to	10 in	15 at	20 in	25 in	30 to

7 Suggested answers

1 Take out your textbooks, please, and open them at page 65.

2 Is there anybody who didn't remember their textbook?

3 Don't forget it next time.

4 Håkan, you will have to share with Stine this time.

5 Today's text is about British pop music in the 1990s.

6 Would you read through the text on your own, please?

7 Was everything clear?

8 Can you give me the gist of the passage?

9 Let's start by looking at some difficult parts of the text.

10 Have you all found the place?

11 It's the third paragraph from the top.

12 The fourth line, and the second to last word.

13 This means the same as new or full of new ideas.

14 How would you translate *innovative*?

15 Let's read the text aloud, in turns, please.

16 Copy this down in your notebooks, please.

17 Henning, could you collect the notebooks in, please, and put them on my desk?

18 For the next thing, take out your workbooks and turn to page 76.

19 Before you begin, let me tell you what I want you to do.
20 I want you to do the first half of exercise 10B.
21 You can leave number 3 out.
22 I think you have had long enough on this.
23 All right, everybody stop what you're doing, please.
24 Let's go through the exercise together.
25 Stig, what have you put for the first one?
26 Does anybody have any alternative suggestions for number 1?
27 Good idea! I hadn't thought of that.
28 There was just one little slip in what you said.
29 What's a better way of saying it?
30 Let's try the exercise orally before you write it down.
31 I'd like you write your answers out at home in your notebooks.

8 Suggested answers
1 Of course, the photographer will be here. I had forgotten all about that.
2 That's a good point. They wanted to throw them out and get rid of them.
3 Yes, you're right. Nobody knew how many died in the crash and how many survived.
4 Yes, even nowadays raising sheep and cattle is an important part of Highland life.
5 Glasgow was very important, and ships really could sail up the river as far as the city.
6 Yes, it's in the west of Scotland where the language still survives.
7 Well, in some ways it's the same as the first one, but maybe not so much.
8 Of course he did. He wanted his friends to come and celebrate with him.

Audio practice

🎧 **4.3** The normal *Wh-* questions were sentences 1, 3, 4, and 6 The rest were echo questions.

🎧 **4.5** 1st syllable: effort, dictionary, diagram, reference, detail, error.
2nd syllable: appendix, equivalent, illegible, predict, describe, omit, alternative, refer, familiar, variety.
3rd syllable: academic, scientific, correspond, satisfactory.

🎧 **4.6** 1 She lends her own copy to the student Atsuko.
2 She mustn't write in the book at all.
3 They must cover the text but they can look at the pictures.
4 She wants her students to concentrate on listening.

🎧 **4.7** 1 'To be treated', 'the League of Nations', and 'to feel threatened'.
2 Deliberate(ly), 'to take the brunt'. She demonstrates 'deliberately' and explains it. She uses the phrase 'take the brunt' in an everyday and memorable context.
3 To make sure that all the students have understood.
4 One of her students offers a very good German translation for the phrase 'to take the brunt'.

🎧 **4.8** 1 It *might be*, it *must be*, it *can't be*.
2 Forget (this) for a moment. 'This' probably means the basic text in the textbook.
3 He uses an everyday situation (waiting at home when the door bell rings) that the students can relate to.
4 The dialogue between the teacher and his students is, of course, not normal conversation, but it is very natural. His prompts and questions lead the students to the correct answers in a motivating way.

🎧 **4.9** 1 Fill in *a*, *an*, or *the* where necessary. Fill in the missing articles.

2 The students can explain their choices. In this way the teacher can make sure the students have really understood the rules for using the definite and indefinite articles.
3 It illustrates when to use the definite article.
4 Four.

🎧 **4.10** 1 *I was*/*you were -ing*.
2 The 't' in *listen* is silent.
3 He asks the student to direct the question to another student in the class.
4 What *was* you doing?
5 He draws the student's attention to the verb and asks which form, 'was' or 'were', follows 'you'. The student successfully corrects the mistake.
6 7 o'clock becomes 4 o'clock.

Unit 5

Classroom essentials

1 I suggest turning this way and facing the screen.
2 What if we try to speed things up a bit?
3 You might as well copy these words down in your notebooks.
4 I'd rather you didn't spend more than five minutes on this.
5 Take my advice and organize your files.
6 It wouldn't be a bad idea to check this in the dictionary.
7 You had better not waste any more time on this.
8 What about coming out to the front and showing the others?
9 My suggestion is that you work in groups of three or four.
10 If I were you, I'd use capital letters for this.

Exercises and activities

2 Suggested answers
1 Come out and point to Los Angeles on the map, Heidi.
2 OK, Kim. You've already been out to the board twice. Let's give someone else a turn.
3 Kris, could you step aside so that everyone else can see?
4 Can anyone correct the spelling mistake in sentence 4?
5 I'd like someone to clean the board for me, please.
6 You don't need to wipe that exercise off.
7 Could you go next door and fetch me a marker pen?
8 I'll adjust the focus. Is that better?
9 We need an extension lead. Could someone go next door and fetch one?
10 Who'd like to operate the projector today?
11 I'm sorry. I seem to have put the picture in upside down.
12 Oh dear, I seem to have brought the wrong video.
13 This next part of the DVD shows some typically Scottish scenery.
14 I'll pass this book round for you all to see.
15 Sorry! I'll just plug the CD player in.
16 Just wait a moment while I try to find the place.
17 Before we begin, we'll just do a test run to check that everything's working.
18 That's a relief. We can carry on now.
19 Don't forget to use the spellchecker. It will really help.
20 Let's see what you can find about butterflies on the Internet.
21 Don't forget to save your work regularly and make a back-up.
22 This has got me beaten. I'm afraid we need an expert to help us.
23 Could you please send me your work as an email attachment?

Audio exercises

1 a *video* camera
2 a *fax* machine
3 a DVD player
4 a *data* projector
5 a digital *camera*
6 a *satellite* dish
7 a *key*board
8 a USB connection
9 a plastic *bag*
10 a *mouse* button
11 a remote con*trol*
12 an ex*ten*sion cable
13 a *head*set
14 a *web* browser
15 an overhead trans*par*ency
16 a CD player
17 an *ink* cartridge
18 an *op*erating system

🎧 **5.5 The stressed syllables are in italics.**

1 You'll find the command in one of the *pull*-down menus
2 This *on*line dictionary is really handy.
3 Don't forget to make a *back*-up.
4 Have you installed the latest *up*dates?
5 Don't forget to log *off* when you've finished.
6 It has two *built*-in speakers.
7 Let's go on*line* and link up with the other class.
8 This is a phrase that you'll have to look *up*.
9 We should buy the *up*grade as soon as possible.
10 I've forgotten my *log*-on name.

🎧 **5.6** 1 No.
2 She wants the students to concentrate on listening and understanding.
3 Here goes.

🎧 **5.7** 1 NATO. He uses the German pronunciation.
2 Albania.
3 Word order: 'Why they didn't take part ….?'
4 The difference between the noun 'socialism' and the adjective 'socialist'. This is an important difference that the students should know in order to be able to discuss history and international relations. The other mistakes do not interfere with intelligibility.

🎧 **5.8** 1 It may be the first time the students have worked in this way and the teacher wants to make the method absolutely clear.
2 She repeats with them, trying to maintain rhythm and fluency.
3 It isn't always clear which part of the sentence is to be substituted. In this example some students say 'He's looking at his girlfriend' and others say 'His girlfriend's looking at the poster'.

🎧 **5.9** 1 The statues express the main message of capitalism and communism.
2 The students who are on the 'capitalist' side of the class will work with one statue (The Statue of Liberty) and the 'communists' with the other one.
3 She says it is to avoid boring them with superfluous information, but her real reason is to involve them in the discussion.

4 Whether Ellis Island is part of New York.
5 University.
6 She is now going to deal with the other picture representing communist ideology.

Unit 6

Classroom essentials

1 Suggested answers

1 Which month did Mrs Jones start her new job (in)?
2 (In) which year did the first settlers land?
3 What time train did our friends come on?
4 How long ago did the tsunami disaster happen?
5 What were we hoping we wouldn't be late for?
6 Who did they decide to spend the evening with?
7 What number bus will I have to take to get into town?
8 What makes of car is David interested in?
9 What kind of magazines is Julie fond of?
10 What brand of toothpaste does Jamie prefer to all the others?
11 How (many metres) long/What length should the room have been?
12 What height was the sculpture?
13 What colour pullover was he looking for?
14 What shape are these new student buildings?
15 What was it like, just lying in the sun?
16 What did the village look like?
17 What did his voice sound like?
18 Which direction was the car heading (in)?
19 Whereabouts in London does she work?
20 How many dollars worth of petrol did he buy?

2 Suggested answers

1 What other two reasons for climate change are mentioned in the text?
2 What else do you know about this painting?
3 What percentage of the people interviewed were under the age of 18?
4 What was the rock concert like?
5 How else did the war affect him?
6 What didn't the brothers in the story have enough of?
7 What does Finland have more than 60,000 of?
8 Since when has wearing a cycle helmet been compulsory?
9 In what way did the incident have a huge effect on the peace talks?
10 What make of French car was the woman driving?

Exercises and activities

5 The anagrams:

1 jaguar (= a member of the cat family)
2 geology (= the study of rocks)
3 sandwich (= a snack)
6 rehearse (= to practise a play)
7 philosophy (= the meaning of life)
8 university (= place of learning)
9 moderately (= not in excess)
10 quotation (= 'To be or not to be')
13 xylophone (= a musical instrument)
14 questionnaire (= a paper used for carrying out research)

7 Errors are in **bold** print.

1 The boy dropped the **beer bottle** on the floor.
2 Do you think **S**wedish is a useful lang**u**age**?**
3 **'Hello,'** he said. 'This **football** is for **y**ou, my friend.'
4 Santa **C**laus is also called Father **C**hristma**s.**
5 **I** **know that** the children**'s** parents speak Japanese.
6 The sun **rises** ~~in~~ every morning.
7 I **often go on** the bus.
8 I **became** interested **in** fishing ~~for~~ ten years ago.
9 Shakespeare **was born in Stratford-upon-Avon in** 1564
10 Many **people like** ~~about the~~ pancakes.
11 There is one question (that) we need to think **about.**
12 Look **for the name of the record on** the label.
13 He **did** all **his homework** on Wednesday.
14 **Every boy** was wearing **a** white **shirt** and tie.
15 Listen **to** my **first three** sentences before you ~~will~~ decide.
16 Do you want /wɒnt/ some chewing /tʃuːɪŋ/ gum?
17 There is /ðeərɪz/ ice cream /kriːm/ for dessert /dɪˈzɜːt/.
18 Roger /rˈɒdʒə/ stayed in a hotel /həʊˈtel/ in Edinburgh /edɪnbərə/.
19 The scissors /sɪzəs/ were hidden under the junk /ðə dʒʌŋk/.
20 They did an analysis /əˈnæləsɪs/ of six fruit juices /fruːt dʒuːsɪz/.

Audio exercises

🎧 **6.3** Cases of silent 'h' and linking 'r' are marked.

1 You have half an <u>hour</u> to hand in your homework.
5 I'm very sorry. I'll try and remem<u>ber it</u> for Friday.
8 If I'm <u>honest</u>, the whole exhibition was rather boring.
10 Please collect in the labels <u>or any</u> original diagrams.

🎧 **6.6** 1 The student has trouble saying *It depends.*
2 What time do you usually go to bed?
3 Eugenio and the group of people around him (*Eugenio and company*).
4 The student says *In Channel 4.* The teacher corrects it to *on.*
5 *makes difficult, he resolved difficult case.* The student probably means *he solves difficult cases.* The teacher understands what is meant but makes no correction since he is encouraging the student to communicate.
6 He says *people who* is *ill,* but corrects it immediately to *'are'.*

🎧 **6.7** 1 B, F.
2 She probably writes key words from the students' arguments. She will be able to use these to check whether an argument has already been given and later for summarizing the discussion.
3 She means *Has your group presented all its arguments?*

🎧 **6.8** 1 The Yalta conference at the end of World War II.
2 First to describe it and then to discuss the cartoonist's attitude to the Yalta conference.
3 There is a swastika in the cartoon, so the students will need the word when describing it.
4 Two. Stalin and Churchill. She is not sure about Roosevelt.
5 Yes.
6 She uses the German word in her sentence. She knows that her teacher speaks German and will understand. The teacher then provides the correct English word, which the student then uses in her next sentence.

🎧 **6.5**

	A	B	C	D	E	F
1	əˈkædəmi	ˈædʒɪktɪv	ˈædvɜːb	ɔːlˈtɜːnətɪv	ˈænəlaɪz	əˈnæləsɪs
2	əˈpɒstrəfi	bəˈluːn	baɪˈɒlədʒi	kəˈnæl	kəˈneəri	kəˈnuː
3	kəˈset	kəˈtæstrəfi	kəˈθiːdrəl	ˈkæθlɪk	ˈkærəktə	ˈkɒmɜːs
4	kəmˈpiːt	kənˈtʃɜːtəʊ	ˈkrɪtɪsɪzəm	ˈkrʊkɪd	ˈkjuːkʌmbə	dɪˈmɒkrəsi
5	dɪˈveləp	dɪˈveləpmənt	daɪˈæmɪtə	ɪˈkɒnəmi	ˈefət	ɪˈvent
6	ɪgˈzekjətɪv	dʒiˈɒgrəfi	gɪˈtɑː	həˈraɪzn	həʊˈtel	aɪˈdɪə
7	ˈɪndʒəri	ləˈbɒrətri	məˈʃiːn	ˈmedɪsn	ˈməʊtɪv	mjuˈziəm
8	ˈneɪkɪd	əˈpəʊnənt	ˈɔːkɪstrə	ɔːdnri	ˈɒrɪdʒɪn	əˈrɪdʒənl
9	pɜːsəˈnel	fəˈlɒsəfi	fəʊtəgrɑːf	fəˈtɒgrəfə	fəˈtɒgrəfi	piˈænəʊ
10	ˈpredʒudɪs	ˈprəʊses	ˈprɒdʌkt	ˈprəʊnaʊn	saɪˈkɒlədʒi	ˈreɪsɪzem
11	ˈresəpi	refəˈriː	refjuˈdʒiː	ˈsæləd	tekˈniːk	tekˈnɒlədʒi
12	θiˈɒlədʒi	ˈviːəkl	vaɪəˈlɪn	vaɪəˈlɪnɪst	ˈvɒləntri	ˈwɪkɪd

Live lesson transcripts

Unit 1

🎧 **1.8**

T: OK then, let's get started. We finished our last lesson on say February 9th, right, so you haven't been studying English for a whole month. Or maybe you have been studying at home, very eagerly, right? OK, anyway, and we will have the next lesson on April 13th, so we are in the middle of spring vacation. I think it's good to have a lecture special lecture today so that you will not forget your English, right? OK. I think I you need to warm up your English a little bit, right, because you know, I haven't seen you for a whole month. So let me tell you about my trip to Vietnam and Cambodia, OK, and I will ask you some questions after that. OK?

🎧 **1.9**

T: Right, good morning. Stand up. Let's stand up. OK, good. Good morning, boys. Good morning, girls.

Ss: Morning.

T: Let's try it again. Good morning, boys. Good morning, girls.

Ss: Good morning, teacher.

T: Yes. How are you today?

S: Terrible.

T: Terrible? Why?

S: I don't know.

T: Why do you feel terrible?

S: I don't know.

T: Do you have a test today?

S: Yes.

T: Do you? What's your test?

S: Chinese test.

T: What, a Chinese test, is it?

S: No.

T: That's an easy test. Do you only have the Chinese test or do you have another test as well? Chinese? Just the Chinese, OK. Right. OK, boys and girls, let's sit down and take out our *Get Together* books. Let me ask you a few, let me ask you a few review questions. Let me see how you do. Let's open our books at page 11, page 11. OK? I want you to do this now. Page 11

🎧 **1.10**

T: I'm telling you all at once, I don't want to say things, I don't want to say things fifteen times. I want to speak when you all are ready to start. Ola, are you ready to start?

S: Yes.

T: OK. Good morning, everyone.

Ss: Good morning.

T: How are you today?

S: Fine, thanks.

T: OK. OK, today we do two things. One, we talk about the test that we had last, err, this week on Monday. I'm going to give you back your tests, yes, today. Not at the very beginning but in the middle of the lesson, OK? And number 2, we are going to talk about Halloween a little bit.

Ss: Yeah!

T: OK, and as you noticed your friends already made some decorations and we are going to help the Cafeteria Amanda ladies and we are going to make some big decorations for the cafeteria. OK? How does that sound? So let's try to work hard and be quick with the test then we have more time for doing the crafts. OK? So, well what did I say, when are we going to do, which one is number 1 and which one is number 2? Petro?

🎧 **1.11**

T: OK, good morning.

Ss: Good morning.

T: Erm, OK. First of all I've got some announcements to make concerning the next, the following lessons. I really want to use the lesson on Monday for history. Because we've done lots and lots of social studies lately and I would really need this lesson because I'd like to write a test about this on the 30th of September, which is Friday. And – No wait a minute, wait a minute. No I don't, I don't. I want to write on Thursday and because you've got another lesson on Friday whereas the others don't and I want you to be parallel. I'll ask Mr Springer to give me a lesson as a present next Wednesday. So just to make sure you're all right. So on the 28th of September we will have a double lesson, history, and then we will have a test on the 29th and then on the 30th we can do something more relaxed. OK. Because we've got an additional lesson here.

🎧 **1.12**

T: At the end of the class I'll give you your results, OK? I'll give you your test results, but only at the very, very end of the class, yeah?, only at the very end of the class. Not before, not before. What is 'before'?

Ss: *Antes.*

T: Yes, because you need the word for the next exercise afterwards. Yes, not before. Now we have, we have to do what?

Ss: Homework.

T: To ...?

Ss: Check homework

T: To check homework, and that's it. We need to check our homework first as usual, and then we'll go on to do other exercises and other things. OK, then, so. Do we have any volunteers? All right, yes, I'll do it at the end at the end of the class. OK. Alenay, at the end of the class. No. Volunteers for homework? This is ... what page was that, what page was that?

S: *Treinta y seis.*

T: That was page 36, OK. Listen, Julia. Can I have your attention, please? Page 36, OK. Thanks.

🎧 **1.13**

T: OK. (*rings bell*) I'm sorry to stop your game. You were doing a good job, most of you. Some of you could concentrate on the game instead of doing other things in the classroom. Niko, I want to have a word with you after the lesson, please. Please bring me back the dice and mark your homework. You can see it on the blackboard, exercises 7 and 8a. On page 50 in your workbook. All right? Thank you. And as soon as you have marked your homework you can go, that's all for today. Bye-bye.

Ss: Bye-bye.

Unit 2

🎧 **2.11**
T: OK. For the next seven minutes about, we are going to play a little game. In groups of four. So you need to find a group of four. We are missing some people, so we are going to have one group of ... No, we're going to have two groups ... of five...No...Err, no it works better if we have... You have a group of four here, you have a group of four there. Neija, you move over here so it's a group of four, and I'm going to join you and we're going to play in a group of three. Is that OK? Well, maybe we ask the young teacher to come here as well to play with us. All right.

🎧 **2.12**
T: Cosmetic surgery and teenagers. Is it responsible to subject teenagers to cosmetic surgery? There are probably pros, advantages, and there are probably cons, counter arguments, so I would you like you to work in pairs or in groups of three if – you two and you – there is one person who writes down whatever you are saying to each other and later we will agree on aspects together and we'll have a nice list of pros and cons and then I think we can talk about the situation because there's also a text that we have that gives some quotations about plastic surgeons or cosmetic surgeons and about teenagers, parents, too, and maybe they come down to the same results as you do. OK, so preparation of let's say 5 to 10 minutes. I'll see when you are more or less finished. You work in pairs. You try to note down what are your pros and cons towards the subject of cosmetic surgery on teens or in teens. OK? The three of you are working together here? I need one writer per group. Are you four working together? Have you started? We want to concentrate on your discussion, first in little groups and then the whole class.
S: We can work in threes?
T: Yes, that's the idea. Exactly. If it is possible, try to talk in English to each other.

🎧 **2.13**
T: Have you finished? Have you – have you all finished your work?
Ss: Yes.
T: Niina, we are doing this box now, OK? So, Hugo? Hugo wants to start.
S1: Colin's grandmother was old and rich.
T: Exactly. So Colin's grandmother was old and rich. Perfect. Alan, the second one.
S2: She lived in a house called the Grange.
T: She lived in a house called the Grange. Perfect. Super. Next one.
S3: She only had three relatives.
T: Yes, super, she only had three relatives. Fiona, Peter and Colin. And the last one, who wants to do the last one? Not always this table in front of me.

🎧 **2.14**
T: Well done! That's good! Exactly. This is a red apple. Just like you said. Why? Why? It's an apple anyway. Why? Why? Tuukka? Tuukka, why? Why **a** red apple? Although it's the same apple. Sshh! Hey, put your mobile away **now** or I will have to confiscate it. I don't want to see it here in the lesson at all. Roosa?
S1: *Se 'red' alkaa konsonantilla. (Finnish: 'red' begins with a consonant).*
T: Yes, it's the next word that tells you.
S: *Mä sanoin jo. (Finnish: I said that already).*
T: Hm. Good job, yep, but that's what Roosa said as well. Excellent job.

🎧 **2.15**
T: OK, good. Well. OK.
S: This custom is very outlandish for me.
T: Lan, outlandish
S: Outlandish for me.
T: Outlandish for me. Good, perfect. Good. OK, good. I'm very happy because your sentences are passed, OK, by a native speaker. Your sentences are so natural. OK, so. Next. No more? You've done it? That means you didn't do your homework? OK, who didn't raise your hand? OK. Hey, who didn't say your sentences? Ah, yes, we have to

punish you. OK. OK. The punishment is you should treat Brett for lunch. Nice treat. OK. So who, who else? No more? OK. Then the word that we didn't mention is 'non-conforming'. Non-conforming hasn't come up. Who will write a sentence with it? Or with conforming? No idea? OK. Then let's go to E, E. OK. Why don't we read together?

🎧 **2.16**
T: Daniel, have you got something for us, some opinion?
S: I think the general aim was to communismize Europe.
T: Wow! Good word! I mean, this is a good attempt actually at building your own word. Which is good, OK. I'll say this explicitly. Do that, build your own words. Actually, the word is, the technical term which the historians use is not to communismize, it's also not to socialize, which is a lot different, but it's they use the word to sovietize, and they speak of the sovietization actually of Eastern Europe. Making it, make the Soviet system, yes, spread in the whole of Eastern Europe.

Unit 3

🎧 **3.6**
T: OK. Are we ready to start? Are you guys ready to start?
S: Yes.
T: Have we got everyone in the class? No? Hey, boys, I would like you to sit in the rows. Why don't you, Mattias, please move your desk, Alu you as well. Alu, Alu, move your desk so that you're sitting behind Henka, and Mattias move your desk so that you're sitting behind Samuel. And I warn you boys: if you cannot concentrate when you are sitting over there, there are nice empty seats here in front. So I will ask you to move up front if you cannot work well there where you are. Is that clear? That's fair, isn't it? Now I have warned you.

🎧 **3.7**
T: OK, alright. So let's look at our schedule today. I promised to play a game with you – 'Living Memory' – we will do that at the end of the lesson. Now, you can – who has got a watch? Then you can tell me at 35, 8:35.
S: OK.
T: Then you can tell me when it is time, time for our game. Good. We will also start with a short game, with a vocab game, a word game. There are a few words we had yesterday, and there are a few new words, OK? Jakob? There are a few new words. And there are the words in German. Now look at the words, at the English words, and see whether you can find a pair. OK. These are the English words and these are the German. *Nervous, ill, maid, poison, relative, office, business, grandson,* and *worried.* Who can find a pair here? Here are the German words.

🎧 **3.8**
T: OK, since we had a holiday last week, let's play a little game, it's a holiday game, and next unit we are heading towards, after the test, we are bringing back into our heads how to talk in the past tense, that's what happen*ed*, for example, during the holiday. What happened last week? What did you do? Last year we practised that a little and I just want to wake it up in your heads so that it's ready there when we need it. OK? And I would like you to toss the ball, nice catches, don't throw it all over the class, and say one thing that you did on your holiday, and this is a very hot ball, so you cannot mmmm hold it for a long time. You have to be quick so think ready already in advance. Put down your pencil because you cannot catch the ball if you have a pencil in your hand, Toni. You as well. OK? So be ready to catch the ball. If you catch it twice, then you say another thing, so it's OK. Just make sure you all get the ball at least once. And we try to play as quickly as we can, OK, so that everybody can say something about their holiday. OK?

🎧 **3.9**

T: Let's see. (*draws a circle*). OK. David? What is it?
S1: It might –
T: You have to imagine it.
S1: It might be a ball.
T: It might be a ball. OK. It might be a ball. All right. Javier?
S2: It might be a cycle.
T: A cycle. OK. Yes, it is a cycle.
S3: *Tierra.* It might be *tierra.* It might be –
T: It might be –
S3: *Tierra.*
T: *Tierra.* You mean the planet?
S3: Yes.
T: The planet. And in English?
S3: Earth?
T: Earth.
S3: Earth.
T: It might be the Earth, the planet Earth. OK. Yes, it might be. But can you say it must be? No, because we are not sure. It might be, right. Alfonso?
S4: It might be a ball.
T: A ball, yes. He has already said a ball. So, another? Think about, well let's – Hector?
S5: It can be an orange.
T: *Qué?*
S: An orange, orange.
T: An orange, yes. A fruit. An orange. Yes, it might be. Right. But if I do something like (*draws*). Look. Now, it might be …
S1: It must be a wheel.
T: OK, very good, it must be a wheel, a car wheel. Right? A car wheel. OK?

🎧 **3.10**

T: I'd like us to do a little experiment. I will hand out little sheets of paper like this and every single one contains a statement. It is either the statement of a capitalist or a communist. And I'd like – it's a very simple, simple, yes, a very simple statement, so don't worry, it's just to give you first of all a rough idea of what communism and capitalism is about. OK? It's not scientific, but it's rough. OK, I'll just hand them out and then what I'd like you to do is those of you who sit in this part of the class and have a communist statement to sit, stay, keep your seat but those who sit in this part of the class and have a capitalist statement, please get up and move to the other side of the class. And the same for you. You're the capitalists, all of you, and if you have a communist statement, if you get a communist statement, please move to the other side of the class. OK. Has everybody got a sheet of paper? All right now, I'll say. If you are on the wrong side of the class, please move. If you belong to the communists, you have to move. Because you're on the capitalist side. Very clearly. This is the Iron Curtain running through this class, dividing Europe.

Unit 4

🎧 **4.6**

T: Shall we go on to Unit 25? OK. Now would you please take a look at Unit 25? Does everybody have a textbook? I have one extra. So Atsuko, you don't have a textbook, right? I have my copy so, here you are. OK. But don't don't write down anything at all, OK?
S: Thank you.
T: You're welcome. Now, let's see. OK, as usual, don't take a look at the dialogue part, OK. I want you to cover up the dialogue part like this and just look at the pictures only. OK. Cover up the dialogue part, don't don't look at the dialogue part, very good. OK. And first let's listen to the tape. Now, ready? OK.

🎧 **4.7**

T: OK, the text is page 85 but first of all I'd like to have your attention. I'm quite sure that you know most of these words. I just want to check. 'To be treated' in German. Ulrike?

S1: *Behandelt werden.*
T: 'The League of Nations.' Nils?
S2: *Völkerbund.*
T: Mm, and 'to feel threatened'. Martin?
S3: *Sich bedroht fühlen.*
T: OK. You know all of these words. 'Deliberate'. To do something deliberately. OK, if I push that over (*crash*), I've done that deliberately, for a purpose, for a purpose, I wanted to do it.
S4: *Absichtlich.*
T: Yeh. Mm, to 'take the brunt', mm. Somewhat strange. If, it's if you take the biggest burden, or the biggest share. Let's say you've got five suitcases, you carry four of them, your friend carries one. You take the brunt. How would you translate that? I had my difficulties translating that. Anne?
S5: *Die Hauptlast tragen.*
T: Mmm?
S5: *Die Hauptlast tragen.*
T: That's nice. That's much nicer than what I've got actually.

🎧 **4.8**

T: Do you remember? Why does Lars say 'They might not be stones.' Because he knows they are not stones or he thinks they aren't. Is he sure?
S1: No. Er, he think, he thinks …
T: He thinks they are, but he's not sure. So, he thinks maybe they are stones, maybe not. OK. And the other example? The next one. Hector?
S2: They might be metal.
T: They might be metal. So. Is Lars sure that they are metal or not?
S2: No.
T: No. All right. OK, let's say. Imagine – forget this for a moment – imagine that you are waiting for a friend. You are at home and you are waiting for someone who told you that he is coming at 6 o'clock. Right. And then the doorbell rings, ding-dong, what do you think? It might be, it must be?
S1: It must be. It must be Peter.
T: It must be Peter. Why?
S1: Because I know. He said me …
T: He told me.
S1: He told me.
T: He's coming.
S1: He's coming.
T: He's coming at six o'clock. It is six o'clock, so you say: It must be Peter. OK. Imagine that your friend Peter now is in France.
S1: It can't be Peter.
T: It can't be Peter. Why?
S1: Because he's in France.
T: If he's, if he is in France, he can't be –
S1: Here.
T: By the door, that's for sure. Right. OK. Perfect.

🎧 **4.9**

T: OK. Tuukka, are you finished? Good. I think everybody is about ready. (*rings bell*) Let's check this, please. Read the whole sentence and then we can discuss it in Finnish as well why you chose the article you did. OK? So please read number 1. Err, Linda, please.
S1: I have a rucksack with me.
T: Good.
T: Hey, Juhana take number 3, please.
S2: The rucksack is very old. It's my father's.
T: Yes, why did you choose 'the'?
S2: *Äsken sanottiin 'a'. Nyt puhutaan siitä toista kertaa. (Finnish: We just said 'a'. Now we're talking about it a second time.)*
T: Right, we already know which rucksack it is, exactly. And 4. Anyone? Come on, any volunteers? Neija?
S3: Guess what I have in my bag. There is a big sandwich.
T: Yes. I didn't quite hear. Did you have an article here? We have the little word 'my' so if you had the article there, just take it out.

🎧 **4.10**

T: Can you repeat, please?

S1: Listen to music, listening to music.

T: Listening. Remember, you don't pronounce 't' in listening. Listening?

S1: To music.

T: I was listening to music. All right. Javier, what were you doing at five o'clock?

S2: I was playing basketball.

T: You were playing basketball. All right. OK. Do you understand? OK, Badel? You make a question. Ask someone what he, he or she was doing.

S2: What was Ariel ...

T: No, no, ask her directly. What were you doing?

S2: Ariel, what was you doing at seven o'clock?

T: OK, Badel. What ... can you repeat the verb? What ...

S2: What was you doing ...

T: You. Think about the verb, you. If it is you, you need was or were?

S2: Aah, what were you doing at four o'clock?

T: Ariel, what were you doing at four o'clock?

S3: I was doing my homework.

T: OK.

Unit 5

🎧 **5.6**

T: Hey, you can discuss this after the lesson, OK? Well, last time we talked about the new story. And I would like to listen to that story one more time. Keep your books closed, so just listen carefully. Alright? 'It's all free'. That's the name of the story. Niko, close your book please. Just listen and try and remember what happened in the story. Ready? Here goes.

Tape: Surprise.

🎧 **5.7**

T: So, but there's more information in this overlay now. Yes, what can you say about, what additional information do we get when we put this on top, this transparency? Yes, please, Phillip?

S: You see how this changed after the Warsaw Pact and formation of the NATO.

T: Mm-mm.

S: And so the socialism countries, like the DDR, the Soviet Union, and Poland and so on, and on the other hand you see the non-socialism ...

T: Wait a minute. It's socialist ...

S: Non-socialist.

T: Socialism is the noun and socialist is the adjective.

S: And the socialist countries of the Western Europe.

T: Mm-mm, yes.

S2: And I can see Yugoslavia and Albania are Communist countries. Why they didn't take part in the Warsaw Pact?

T: Good question. Does anybody know? It's a very special story.

🎧 **5.8**

T: Now, how about substitution drill, substitution drill, OK. I will give you a sentence, then I will say a word or words, and you are supposed to substitute the words with a part of the original sentence. Let me tell you in Japanese. (*Japanese*).

T: OK. Now. Then repeat after me at first. Victor's standing outside the movie theatre.

Ss: Victor's standing outside the movie theatre.

T: The library.

Ss: Victor's standing outside the library.

T: Repeat after me. Victor's standing outside the library.

Ss: Victor's standing outside the library.

T: My sister.

Ss: My sister's standing outside the library.

T: The supermarket ...

T: Now, please, the next one. Let's go to the next one. Repeat after me. He's looking at his watch.

Ss: He's looking at his watch.

T: OK, how about the clock on the wall.

Ss: He's looking at the clock on the wall.

T: OK, the poster.

Ss: He's looking at the poster.

T: Er, his girlfriend.

Ss: His girlfriend ... /He's looking ...

T: Oh, sorry. He's looking at his girlfriend. Oh, sorry. Confusing. Sorry, sorry. (*laughs*). Sorry, sorry, sorry. OK, he's looking at his, he's looking at his girlfriend. Or his girlfriend is looking at the poster. OK, sorry about that. Confusing, huh? I'm sorry about that. All right, and the next, let's go to the next one. OK. Repeat after me: An old man's coming out of the theatre.

Ss: An old man's coming out of the theatre.

T: The school.

🎧 **5.9**

T: Now I'd like to go into more depth. And we'll do that by having a look at two pieces of art which were built in order to express the message, the main message, of the respective ideologies. No, please stay seated because I'd like the communists to do this statue and deal with that statue, and then I'd like the capitalists on the other side of the class to deal with this one. Now first of all, do you know any of these statues, and do you know anything about them already? So that I don't bore you with superfluous information. Yes, please, HaNam?

S1: The first one is the Statue of Liberty.

T: Yes.

S1: It is in New York and was a present for the US government from the Paris government.

T: Yes, correct. Do you know what the occasion was of the present?

S1: I think it was in the *Bürgerkrieg*.

T: The Civil War.

S1: Or in the independence war –

T: Or in the War of Independence. OK, we have to be more precise. Can you make that a bit more precise, Sabrina?

S2: I think it was in the French Revolution because the Americans helped the French and so –

T: Yes, it has something to do with the French Revolution.

S3: It's a present from the French to the Americans at the fourth of July 1776 after the War of Independence and it's not in New York.

T: Oh well. I'd like to correct you.

S4: I would say it is in New York.

T: Thank you. It is in New York. It's on Liberty Island, just outside New York.

S3: So it's not *in* New York.

T: (laughter) Yes, good. OK, it's on an island outside or off the shore of New York, it's Liberty Island, that's where it stands. It's 93.5 metres high. It was in fact a present by the French government, but not in 1776 but in 1883. Now 1883 was the hundredth univers..., anniversary of the United States. But the date which is written down here is the 4th of July 1776, so it does in fact refer back to the independence, and because it was a present from France it definitely makes up a connection between the French Revolution, which was later than that but of course the United States was seen as the first country to put these revolutionary ideas into practice back then, and that's what why the French gave the United States a present because they helped to put through these ideals of the French Revolution. OK?

Unit 6

🎧 **6.6**

S: Its depends.

T: It depends.

S: Its depend.

T: No, it depends.

S: It depends. If there is a programme that I want I want to watch, I stay, I stay until ten o'clock, half past ten.

T: OK, if there is an interesting programme on TV, then you normally watch it. Yes? All right. Can you tell me what is an interesting programme for you? Can you tell me one?

S: House, House.

T: House. Sshh! Shut up Eugenio and company, please.

S: In channel four.

T: Channel, on channel 4. House. And what is the programme. It is about buildings?

S: No, it's about –

T: Because the name is House.

S: No.

T: Is it a house or –

S: It's a man.

T: It's a house who is a man, a man who is a house?

S: House is a doctor. And –

T: It's the name.

S: Yes.

T: Of the doctor. Ahaa.

S: Is the name of the doctor.

T: Is it funny, is it sad?

S: Special, special.

T: Special. Yes. Why?

S: Because he makes difficult, he resolved difficult case, difficult.

T: People who is ill.

S: Ill.

T: People who are, sorry, people who are ill, and then? They go – Pardon. He works, where does he work, the doctor?

S: Where?

T: Where.

S: Hospital.

T: So, it's not a private doctor, but in hospital.

S: Yes, it's a hospital but they are a group and they are in a special room, in a special part of the built, the building, and they finish difficulties.

T: OK. And Javier, what is your favourite TV programme?

🎧 **6.7**

T: Can we put everything together? OK, who's starting? At the back. Cosmetic surgery and teenagers. So, Anja?

S: Yes. When people are like seventeen years old or something, then they are not fully grown so when they do cosmetic surgery and you get older, you don't know what the changes will be to –

T: What the implications –

S: – your body. With your body.

T: Good. Good argument. So, the body is not fully grown. You don't know the implications in the long term. OK. Are there more negative arguments?

S3: If you are under the eighteen, you can make a mistake and you have to grow a little bit, so if you make a mistake, it's for your whole life, and you can't change.

T: So if you make a mistake in your decision in selecting cosmetic surgery, it can't be undone. I think we already had that. It can't be undone. Do you have?

S3: Yes.

T: Anything else?

S4: Er, what if the operation fails when there, when there goes something wrong with the operation?

T: On a medical basis or just as far as the results go?

S4: No, when the operation, when there's something wrong.

T: It's still a medical operation. I mean, it is not without risks. Is that what you mean?

S4: Yes.

T: Yes. So (writes on board) it's still a medical operation. There are risks. It can fail. People can die. That's it for you? Antonia, your group?

S5: We had what about your personality? What happens to it?

T: So, if it can be covered by plastic?

S5: Yes.

T: Good. OK.

🎧 **6.8**

T: Now I've got a cartoon here which was published two days after the Yalta conference finished. Let's have a look at it. And yes. First of all we probably need a description and then I'd like to know something about the attitude of the cartoonist, what the cartoonist thought of the outcome of this conference. You might need this word here, swastika, that's *Hakenkreuz*, OK, who can describe the picture? Are these human beings, are these human beings in the cartoon? What are they represented as? I mean, these are –

S: Stones.

T: Yes, yes. Like statues, made from a rock, it's like a huge rock. OK.

S: And on the stones there reads 'Complete agreement' and in front of them there is a swastika.

T: OK. Now, who are these people? Who'd guess?

S2: Stalin.

T: Yep.

S2: Truman and Roosevelt.

T: OK. Truman is Roosevelt's vice-president, so and this is still Mr Roosevelt there and so he's the American, Stalin is the Soviet leader. Now, who's the person in the middle, the little round guy, usually smoking a cigar?

S2: Churchill.

T: Yes, it is Churchill. OK, now let's say something about the attitude of the cartoonist concerning this, the Yalta agreement because it was published two days after the Yalta conference had finished or had closed, and it's called 'The Rock'. So, can you explain what the cartoonist wanted to express? What did he think of the conference outcome?

S3: I think it shows because it's still the war and they are still fighting and maybe it should show that the Germans could do whatever they want they wouldn't get past these nations because –

T: Very good.

S3: Yes.

T: Mm-mm. Yes? Yes, it shows that the three, the big three, Churchill, Stalin, Roosevelt, stand together in complete agreement against the Nazi flood. OK, that's – and they are a grand alliance and nothing can come between them, especially not the Nazis. OK, so did the cartoonist think Yalta was a success or not? The conference? Anna?

S4: I think he thinks it's a success.

T: Yes.

S4: Because as you see the water is *machtlos*.

T: Yes, it's powerless, uh-uh.

S4: It's powerless. Nobody can do something against the complete agreement.

Useful reading and resources

Books

Language learning

Cook, V. 1996. *Second Language Learning and Language Teaching.* London: Arnold.

Cummins, J. 1979. 'Cognitive/academic language proficiency, linguistic interdependence, the optimum age question and some other matters.' *Working papers on Bilingualism.* 19, 121–129

Ellis, R. 1985. *Understanding Second Language Acquisition.* Oxford: OUP.

Johnson, K. 2000. *An Introduction to Foreign Language Learning and Teaching.* Harlow: Longman.

Lightbown, P.M. and **N. Spada** 2006. *How Languages are Learned.* (3rd edition) Oxford: OUP.

Teaching English

Brewster, J. and **G. Ellis** 2002. *The Primary English Teacher's Guide.* London: Penguin.

Davies, P. and **E. Pearse** 2000. *Success in English Teaching.* Oxford: OUP.

Halliwell, S. 1992. *Teaching English in the Primary Classroom.* Harlow: Longman.

Harmer, J. 2001. *The Practice of English Language Teaching.* (3rd edition) Harlow: Longman.

Hedge, T. 2000. *Teaching and Learning in the Language Classroom.* Oxford: OUP.

Larsen-Freeman, D. 2000. *Techniques and Principles in Language Teaching.* (2nd edition) Oxford: OUP.

Lindsay, Cora and **P. Knight** 2006. *Learning and Teaching English.* Oxford: OUP.

Ur, P. 1996. *A Course in Language Teaching: Practice and Theory.* Cambridge: CUP.

Widdowson, H.G. 1978. *Teaching Language as Communication.* Oxford: OUP.

Using English in the classroom

Deller, S. and **C. Price** 2006. *Teaching Other Subjects through English.* Oxford: Oxford University Press.

Lynch, T. 1996. *Communication in the Language Classroom.* Oxford: OUP.

Salaberri, S. 1995. *Classroom Language.* Oxford: Macmillan Heinemann.

Slattery, M. and **J. Willis** 2001. *English for Primary Teachers.* Oxford: OUP.

Voss, B. 1995. *A Coursebook in Classroom English.* Frankfurt: Peter Lang.

Willis, J. 1981. *Teaching English through English.* Harlow: Longman.

Language skills

Hedge, T. 2005. *Writing.* Oxford: OUP.

Laroy, C. 1995. *Pronunciation.* Oxford: OUP.

Morgan, J. and **M. Rinvolucri** 2004. *Vocabulary.* Oxford: OUP.

Nolasco, R. and **L. Arthur** 1987. *Conversation.* Oxford: OUP.

White, G. 1998. *Listening.* Oxford: OUP.

Thornbury, S. 2006. *Grammar.* Oxford: OUP.

Music and songs

Graham, C. 2006. *Creating Chants and Songs.* Oxford: OUP.

Murphey, T. 1992. *Music and Song.* Oxford: OUP.

Drama

Porter Ladousse, G. 1987. *Role Play.* Oxford: OUP.

Phillips, S. 1999. *Drama with Children.* Oxford: OUP.

Wessels, C. 1987. *Drama.* Oxford: OUP.

Games and activities

Hadfield, J. 1999a. *Communication Games.* Harlow: Longman.

Hadfield, J. 1999b. *Grammar Games.* Harlow: Longman.

Hadfield, J. 1999c. *Vocabulary Games.* Harlow: Longman.

Hancock, M. 1995. *Pronunciation Games.* Cambridge: CUP.

Lewis, G. 1999. *Primary Resource Books for Teachers: Games for Children.* Oxford: OUP.

Lindstromberg, S. (ed.) 1990. *The Recipe Book: Practical Ideas for the Language Classroom.* London: Pilgrims Longman.

Lindstromberg, S. (ed.) 1997. *The Standby Book: Activities for the Language Classroom.* Cambridge: CUP.

Marsland, B. 1999. *Lessons from Nothing.* Cambridge: CUP.

Medgyes, P. 2002. *Laughing Matters: Humour in the Language Classroom.* Cambridge: CUP.

Rinvolucri, M. 1984. *Grammar Games.* Cambridge: CUP.

Rinvolucri, M. and **P. Davis** 1995. *More Grammar Games.* Cambridge: CUP.

Ur, P. and **A. Wright** 1992. *Five-Minute Activities.* Cambridge: CUP.

Watcyn-Jones, P. 1995. *Grammar Games and Activities for Teachers.* London: Penguin Books.

Watcyn-Jones, P. (ed.) 1981. *Pair Work 1, 2 & 3* London: Penguin Books.

Wright, A., **D. Betteridge** and **M. Buckby** 1984. *Games for Language Learning.* Cambridge: CUP.

Using visual media

Dobbs, J. 2001. *Using the Board in the Language Classroom.* Cambridge: CUP.

Sanderson, P. 1999. *Using Newspapers in the Classroom.* Cambridge: CUP.

Stempleski, S. and **B. Tomalin** 2001. *Film.* Oxford: OUP.

Wright, A. 1984. *1000+ Pictures for Teachers to Copy.* Harlow: Longman.

The Longman Photo Dictionary 2002. Harlow: Longman.

The Oxford Picture Dictionary 1999. Oxford: OUP.

The Oxford Visual Five-Language Dictionary 2006. Oxford: OUP.

Computers and the Internet

Dudeney, G. 2000. *The Internet and the Language Classroom.* Cambridge: CUP.

Lewis, G. 2004. *The Internet and Young Learners.* Oxford: OUP.

Teeler, D. 2000. *How to Use the Internet in ELT.* Harlow: Longman.

Windeatt, S., **D. Hardisty** and **D. Eastment** 2000. *The Internet.* Oxford: OUP.

Classroom management

Bennett, B. and P. Smilanich 1994. *Classroom Management: A Thinking and Caring Approach*. Toronto: Bookstation, Inc.
Langness, T. (eds.) 2000. *First-Class Teacher: Success Strategies for New Teachers* (new edn.). Los Angeles: Canter and Associates.
Kyriacou, C. 1998 *Essential Teaching Skills* (2nd edition). Cheltenham: Stanley Thomas.

Learning strategies

Davis, P. 1999. *Ways of Doing: Students Explore Their Everyday and Classroom Processes*. Cambridge: CUP.
Oxford, R. L. 1989. *Strategy Inventory for Language Learning (SILL)*.
Oxford, R. L. 1990. *Language Learning Strategies: What Every Teacher Should Know*. Rowley, MA., Newbury House.

Study skills

K-W-L-Plus (Know-Want-Learn-Map-Summarize)
Carr, E. and D. Ogle 1987. 'K-W-L Plus: A Strategy for Comprehension and Summarization'. *Journal of Reading*, 30(7), 626-631.
MURDER (Mood-Understand-Recall-Detail-Expand-Review)
O'Donnell, A. M. and D.F. Dansereau 1992. 'Scripted cooperation in student dyads: A method for analyzing and enhancing academic learning and performance' in R. Hertz-Lazarowitz and N. Miller (eds.) *Interactions in Cooperative Groups. The Theoretical Anatomy of Group Learning* (pp. 120-141). New York, NY: Cambridge University Press.
Caverly, D. C., T.P. Mandeville and S.A. Nicholson 1995. 'PLAN: A study-reading strategy for informational text'. *Journal of Adolescent and Adult Literacy*, 39 (3), 190-199.
PLAN (Plan-Locate-Add-Note)
Simpson, M. L., N. Stahl and C. Hayes 1988. 'PORPE: A comprehensive study strategy utilizing self-assigned writing'. *Journal of College Reading and Learning*, 20, 51-57.
PORPE (Predict-Organize-Rehearse-Practise-Evaluate)
SQR3, SQR4 (Survey-Question-Read-(Reflect)-Recite-Review)
Robinson, F. P. 1961, 1970. *Effective Study* (4th edition). New York, NY: Harper & Row

Critical thinking

Case, R., L. Daniels and P. Schwartz (eds.). 1996. *Critical Challenges in Social Studies for Junior High Students*. Richmond: The Critical Thinking Consortium.

Internet resources

These web links were correct at the time of going to press. Please visit our website at www.oup.com/elt/teacher/pce for updates, or to report problems or suggestions.
Inclusion in this list does not imply that these pages or their content are endorsed by the authors or publisher.

Learner types and learning styles

http://www.engr.ncsu.edu/learningstyles/ilsweb.html
http://www.vark-learn.com/english/page.asp?p=questionnaire
http://www.ncsu.edu/felder-public/ILSpage.html
http://www.metamath.com/lsweb/dvclearn.htm
http://www.bbc.co.uk/keyskills/extra/module1/1shtml

Study skills and strategies

http://www.bbc.co.uk/learning/returning/betterlearner
  /studyskills/index.shtml
http://www.studygs.net/
http://www.eduplace.com/graphicorganizer/
http://www.coun.uvic.ca/learn/hndouts.html
http://www.creax.net
http://www.inspiration.com
http://www.ucc.vt.edu/lynch/TextbookReading.htm

Teaching software

Hot Potatoes authoring program: **http://hotpot.uvic.ca/**
Clipart: **http://web.uvic.ca/hcmc/clipart/**
Creative Technology: **http://www.cict.co.uk/**
Commercial authoring programs: **http://www.wida.co.uk**

Online dictionaries and reference works

British National Corpus: **http://www.natcorp.ox.ac.uk/index.xml**
Oxford Advanced Learner's Dictionary: **http://www.oup.com/elt/ catalogue/teachersites/oald7/lookup?cc=global**
Bilingual dictionaries: **http://www.alphadictionary.com/langdir.html**
Wikipedia: **http://en.wikipedia.org/wiki/Main_Page**

Online newspapers

World's Newspapers: **http://www.all-links.com/newscentral/**
BBC News: **http://news.bbc.co.uk**
CNN Interactive: **http://www.cnn.com**
Electronic Telegraph: **http://www.telegraph.co.uk**
Guardian Unlimited: **http://www.guardian.co.uk**
The Washington Post: **http://www.washingtonpost.com**
Toronto Globe and Mail: **http://www.globeandmail.com**
Sydney Morning Herald: **http://smh.com.au**

Teaching ideas and material

Dave Sperling's ESL Café: **http://www.eslcafe.com/**
Language Funland: **http://www.linguistic-funland.com/tesl.html**
Aardvark's English Forum: **http://www.english-forum.com/oo/ interactive/**
Puzzles, games, anagrams: **http://www.manythings.org/**

Language magazines

http://www.maryglasgowmagazines.com/
http://www.speakeasy-mag.com/